D1758616

000000489169

❧ ILLUSTRATED ❧
HISTORY OF
FURNITURE

Frederick Litchfield

ARCTURUS

Frontispiece: SECRÉTAIRE.
Marquetry, with Sèvres Plaques,
& Ormoulu Mounts
French. Period of Louis XV.
Jones Bequest. South Kensington Museum.

DUDLEY PUBLIC
LIBRARIES

000000489169	
Bertrams	23/08/2011
749.09	£19.99
	DU

ARCTURUS

This edition published in 2011 by
Arcturus Publishing Limited
26/27 Bickels Yard, 151–153
Bermondsey Street,
London SE1 3HA

Copyright © 2011
Arcturus Publishing Limited

All rights reserved. No part of this
publication may be reproduced, stored
in a retrieval system, or transmitted, in
any form or by any means, electronic,
mechanical, photocopying, recording or
otherwise, without written permission
in accordance with the provisions of
the Copyright Act 1956 (as amended).
Any person or persons who do any
unauthorised act in relation to this
publication may be liable to criminal
prosecution and civil claims for
damages.

ISBN: 978-1-84837-803-2
AD001734EN

Printed in China

CONTENTS

PREFACE

In the following pages the author has placed before the reader an account of the changes in the design of Decorative Furniture and Woodwork, from the earliest period of which we have any reliable or certain record until the present time.

There is history writ in Furniture; and the social and political changes which gave rise to and influenced successive styles and their modifications are here traced and exemplified. Renaissances and Decadences, Revolutions and Restorations, have their Monuments in Mahogany and Marqueterie, no less than in Literature and Laws.

A careful selection of illustrations has been made from examples of established authenticity, the majority of which are to be seen, either in the Museums to which reference is made, or by permission of the owners; and the representations of the different 'interiors' will convey an idea of the character and disposition of the Furniture of the periods to which they refer. These illustrations are arranged, as far as is possible, in chronological order, and the descriptions which accompany them are explanatory of the historical and social changes which have influenced the manners and customs, and directly or indirectly affected the Furniture of different nations. An endeavour is made to produce a 'panorama' which may prove acceptable to many, who, without wishing to study the subject deeply, may desire to gain some information with reference to it generally, or with regard to some part of it, in which they may feel a particular interest.

It will be obvious that within the limits of a single volume of moderate dimensions it is impossible to give more than an outline sketch of many periods of design and taste which deserve far more consideration than is here bestowed upon them; the reader is, therefore, asked to accept the first chapter, which refers to 'Ancient Furniture' and covers a period of several centuries, as introductory to that which follows, rather than a serious attempt to examine the history of the Furniture during that space of time. The fourth chapter, which deals with a period of some hundred and fifty years, from the time of King James the First until that of Chippendale and his contemporaries, and the later chapters, are more fully descriptive than some others, partly because trustworthy information as to these times is more accessible, and partly because it is probable that English readers will feel greater interest in the Furniture of which they are the subject. The French *meubles de luxe*, from the latter half of the seventeenth century until the Revolution, are also treated more fully than the Furniture of other periods and countries, on account of the interest which has been manifested during the past ten or fifteen years in this description of the cabinet-maker's and metal-mounter's work. There is evidence of this appreciation in the enormous prices realised at notable auction sales, when such furniture has been offered for competition to wealth connoisseurs.

In order to gain a more correct idea of the design of Furniture of different periods, it has been necessary to notice the alterations in architectural styles which influenced, and were accompanied by, corresponding changes in the fashion of interior woodwork. Such comments are made with some diffidence, as it is felt that this branch of the subject would have received more fitting treatment by an architect, who was also an antiquary, than by an antiquary with only a limited knowledge of architecture.

Some works on 'Furniture' have taken the word in its French interpretation, to include everything that is 'movable' in a house; other writers have combined with historical notes, critical remarks and suggestions as to the selection of Furniture. The author has not presumed to offer any such advice, and has confined his attention to a description of that which, in its more restricted sense, is understood as 'Decorative Furniture and Woodwork'. For his own information, and in the pursuit of his business, he has been led to investigate the causes and the approximate dates of the several changes in taste which have taken place, and has recorded them in as simple and readable a story as the difficulties of the subject permit.

Numerous acts of kindness and co-operation, shown while the work was preparing for the press, have rendered the task very pleasant; and while the author has endeavoured to acknowledge, in a great many instances, the courtesies received, when noticing the particular occasion on which such assistance was rendered, he would desire generally to record his thanks to the owners of historic mansions, the officials of our Museums, the Clerks of City Companies, Librarians, and others, to whom he is indebted. The views of many able writers who have trodden the same field of enquiry have been adopted where they have been confirmed by the writer's experience or research, and in these cases he hopes he has not omitted to express his acknowledgments for the use he has made of them.

The large number of copies subscribed for, accompanied, as many of the applications have been, by expressions of goodwill and confidence beforehand, have been very gratifying, and have afforded great encouragement during the preparation of the work.

If the present venture is received in such a way as to encourage a larger effort, the writer hopes both to multiply examples and extend the area of his observations.

F.L.

Many new works on the subject have appeared since the First Edition of this *Illustrated History of Furniture* was published, and numerous magazine articles have dealt with particular styles and periods of Furniture. None of these however have attempted a comprehensive sketch of the history of Furniture of all countries from the earliest periods to the present time, and as the publishers report an increased demand for the book within the past year, it is evident that it still retains favour with those who are interested in the subject, and that a new and up-to-date Edition is justified.

I have endeavoured to profit by the fresh information which has become available since the Sixth Edition was published, and the new issue will be found to contain many details concerning designers and makers of Furniture, particularly those of the seventeenth and eighteenth century English work, a period which is now of increased interest to collectors; additional information is also added about some of the famous French *ébenistes* of the eighteenth century, and a chapter on Colonial Furniture is included.

Many new illustrations are given and several unsatisfactory ones omitted: these illustrations, which now number four hundred, are chiefly from photographs of examples in our Museums, or from books of designs by such artists as Robert Adam, Thomas Chippendale, A. Heppelwhite, T. Sheraton and others, so that there can be no doubt as to attribution.

With these few words of introduction I venture to hope for a favourable reception of my new Edition.

FREDERICK LITCHFIELD
Exton House, Hove, Sussex
May, 1922

CHAPTER I

Ancient Furniture

BIBLICAL REFERENCES : Solomon's House and Temple—Palace of Ahasuerus. ASSYRIAN FURNITURE : Nimrod's Palace—Mr. George Smith quoted. EGYPTIAN FURNITURE : Specimens in the British Museum—The Workman's Stool—Various Articles of Domestic Furniture—Dr. Birch quoted. GREEK FURNITURE : The Bas-reliefs in the British Museum—The Chest of Cypselus—Laws and Customs of the Greeks—House of Alcibiades—Plutarch quoted. ROMAN FURNITURE : Position of Rome—The Roman House—Cicero's Table—Thyine Wood—Customs of wealthy Romans—Downfall of the Empire.

BIBLICAL REFERENCES

T HE first well-known reference to woodwork is to be found in the Book of Genesis, in the instructions given to Noah to make an Ark of gopher* wood, "to make a window," to "pitch it within and without with pitch," and to observe definite measurements. From the specific directions thus handed down to us, we may gather that mankind had acquired at a very early period of the world's history a knowledge of the different kinds of wood, and of the use of tools.

We know, too, from the bas-reliefs and papyri in the British Museum, how advanced were the Ancient Egyptians in the arts of civilisation, and that the manufacture of comfortable and even luxurious furniture was not neglected. In them, the Hebrews must have had excellent workmen for teachers and taskmasters, to have enabled them to acquire sufficient skill and experience to carry out such precise instructions as were given for the erection of the Tabernacle, some 1,500 years before Christ—as to the kinds of wood, measurements, ornaments, fastenings ("loops and

* Gopher is supposed to mean cypress wood. See Notes on Woods (Appendix).

taches "), curtains of linen and coverings of dried skins.   We have only
to turn for a moment to the 25th chapter of Exodus to be convinced
that all the directions there mentioned were given to a people who had
considerable experience in the methods of carrying out work, which must
have resulted from some generations of carpenters, joiners, weavers, dyers,
goldsmiths and other craftsmen.

A thousand years before Christ, we have those descriptions of the
building and fitting by Solomon of the glorious work of his reign, the
great Temple, and of his own, "the King's house," which gathered from
different countries the most skilful artificers of the time, an event which
marks an era of advance in the knowledge and skill of those who were
thus brought together to do their best work towards carrying out the grand
scheme.   It is worth while, too, when we are referring to Old Testament
information bearing upon the subject, to notice some details of furniture
which are given, with their approximate dates as generally accepted,
not because there is any particular importance attached to the precise
chronology of the events concerned, but because, speaking generally, they
form landmarks in the history of furniture.   One of these is the verse
(2 Kings chap. iv.) which tells us the contents of the " little chamber
in the wall," when Elisha visited the Shunammite, about B.C. 895 ; and
we are told of the preparations for the reception of the prophet : " And
let us set for him there a bed and a table and a stool and a
candlestick."   Another incident is some 420 years later, when, in the
allusion to the grandeur of the Palace of Ahasuerus, we catch a glimpse
of Eastern magnificence in the description of the drapery which furnished
the apartment ; " Where were white, green and blue hangings, fastened
with cords of fine linen and purple, to silver rings and pillars of marble ;
the beds were of gold and silver, upon a pavement of red and blue and
white and black marble."   (Esther i. 6.)

There are, unfortunately, no trustworthy descriptions of ancient
Hebrew furniture.   The illustrations in Kitto's Bible, Mr. Henry Soltau's
" The Tabernacle, the Priesthood, and the Offerings," and other similar
books, are apparently drawn from imagination, founded on descriptions in
the Old Testament.   In these, the " table for shew-bread " is generally
represented as having legs partly turned, with the upper portions square,
to which rings were attached for the poles by which it was carried.   As a
nomadic people, their furniture would be but primitive, and we may take it
that as the Jews and Assyrians came from the same stock, and spoke the
same language, such ornamental furniture as there was would, with the
exception of the representations of figures of men or of animals, be of
a similar character.

ASSYRIAN FURNITURE

The discoveries which have been made in the oldest seat of monarchical government in the world, by such enterprising travellers as Sir Austin Layard, Mr. George Smith, and others who have thrown so much light upon domestic life in Nineveh, are full of interest in connection with this branch of the subject. We learn from these authorities that the furniture was ornamented with the heads of lions, bulls and rams; tables,

PART OF ASSYRIAN BRONZE THRONE AND FOOTSTOOL, ABOUT B.C. 888,
REIGN OF ASSHURNAZIRPAL.
(*From a Photo by Mansell & Co. of the Original in the British Museum.*)

thrones and couches were made of metal and wood, and probably inlaid with ivory; the earliest chair, according to Sir Austin Layard, having been made without a back, and the legs terminating in lions' feet or bulls' hoofs. Some were of gold, others of silver and bronze. On the monuments of Khorsabad, representations have been discovered of chairs supported by animals, and by human figures, probably those of prisoners.

In the British Museum is a bronze throne, found by Sir A. Layard amidst the ruins of Nimrod's Palace, which shows ability of high order for skilled metal work.

Mr. Smith, the famous Assyrian excavator and translator of cuniform inscriptions, has told us in his "Assyrian Antiquities" of his finding close to the site of Nineveh, portions of a crystal throne somewhat similar in design to the bronze one mentioned above, and in another part of this interesting book we have a description of an interior that is useful in assisting us to form an idea of the condition of houses of a date which can be correctly assigned to B.C. 860:—"Altogether in this place I opened six chambers, all of the same character, the entrances ornamented by clusters of square pilasters, and recesses in the rooms in the same style; the walls were coloured in horizontal bands of red, green and

ASSYRIAN CHAIR FROM   ASSYRIAN CHAIR FROM   ASSYRIAN THRONE.
        KHORSABAD.   XANTHUS.
(*In the British Museum.*)   (*In the British Museum.*)   (*In the British Museum.*)

yellow, and where the lower parts of the chambers were panelled with small stone slabs, the plaster and colours were continued over these." Then follows a description of the drainage arrangements, and finally we have Mr. Smith's conclusion that this was a private dwelling for the wives and families of kings, together with the fact that on the other side of the bricks he found the legend of Shalmeneser II. (B.C. 860), who probably built this palace.

In the British Museum is an elaborate piece of carved ivory, with depressions to hold coloured glass, etc., from Nineveh, which once formed part of the inlaid ornament of a throne, showing how richly such objects were ornamented. This carving is said by the authorities to be of

Egyptian origin. The treatment of figures by the Assyrians was more clumsy and more rigid, and their furniture generally was more massive than that of the Egyptians.

An ornament often introduced into the designs of thrones and chairs is a conventional treatment of the tree sacred to Asshur, the Assyrian Jupiter; the pine cone, another sacred emblem, is also found, sometimes as in the illustration of the Khorsabad chair on page 4, forming an ornamental foot, and sometimes being part of the merely decorative design.

The bronze throne, illustration on page 3, appears to have been of sufficient height to require a footstool, and in " Nineveh and its Remains " these footstools are specially alluded to. " The feet were ornamented, like those of the chair, with the feet of lions or the hoofs of bulls."

The furniture represented in the following illustration, from a bas-relief in the British Museum, is said to be of a period some two hundred years later than the bronze throne and footstool.

REPOSE OF KING ASSHURBANIPAL.
(From a Bas-relief in the British Museum.)

EGYPTIAN FURNITURE

In the consideration of ancient Egyptian furniture we find valuable assistance in the examples carefully preserved to us, and accessible to every one in the British Museum, and one or two of these deserve passing

STOOL.　　STAND FOR A VASE.　WORKMAN'S STOOL.　VASE ON A STAND.
HEAD REST OR PILLOW.

FOLDING STOOL.　　　　EBONY SEAT INLAID WITH IVORY.
(From Photos by Mansell & Co. of the Originals in the British Museum.)

notice.   Nothing can be more suitable for its purpose than the " Workman's Stool ": the seat is precisely like that of a modern kitchen chair (all wood), slightly concaved to promote the sitter's comfort, and supported by three legs curving outwards.   This is simple, convenient and admirably adapted for long service.   For a specimen of more ornamental work, the folding stool in the same glass case should be examined; the supports

AN EGYPTIAN OF HIGH RANK SEATED.
(From a Photo by Mansell & Co. of the Original Wall Painting in the British Museum.)
Period: B.C. 1500-1400.

are crossed in a similar way to those of a modern camp-stool and the lower parts of the legs carved as heads of geese, with inlayings of ivory to assist the design and give richness to its execution.

Portions of legs and rails, turned as if by a modern lathe, mortice holes and tenons, fill us with wonder as we look upon work which, at the most modern computation, must be 3,000 years old, and may be of a date still more remote.

In the same room, arranged in cases round the wall, is a collection of several objects which, if scarcely to be classed under the head of

AN EGYPTIAN BANQUET.
(From a Wall Painting at Thebes.)

furniture, are articles of luxury and comfort, and demonstrate the extraordinary state of civilisation enjoyed by the old Egyptians, and help us to form a picture of their domestic habits.

Amongst these are boxes, some inlaid with various woods, and also with little squares of bright turquoise blue pottery let in as a relief; others veneered with ivory; wooden spoons carved in most intricate designs, of which one, representing a girl amongst lotus flowers, is a work of great artistic skill; boats of wood, head rests and models of parts of houses and granaries, together with writing materials, different kinds of tools and implements, and a quantity of personal ornaments and requisites.

"For furniture, various woods were employed, ebony, acacia, or sont, cedar, sycamore and others of species not determined. Ivory, both of the hippopotamus and elephant, were used for inlaying, as also were glass pastes; and specimens of marquetry are not uncommon. In the paintings in the tombs, gorgeous pictures and gilded furniture are depicted. For cushions and mattresses, linen cloth and coloured stuffs, filled with feathers of the waterfowl, appear to have been used, while seats have plaited bottoms of linen cord or tanned and dyed leather thrown over them, and sometimes the skins of panthers served this purpose. For carpets they used mats of palm fibre, on which they often sat. On the whole an Egyptian house was lightly furnished, and not encumbered with so many articles as are in use at the present day."

The above paragraph forms part of the notice with which the late Dr. Birch, the eminent antiquary, formerly at the head of this department of the British Museum, has prefaced a catalogue of the antiquities alluded to. The visitor to the Museum should be careful to procure one of these useful and inexpensive guides to this portion of its contents.

Some illustrations taken from the ancient statues and bas-reliefs in the British Museum, from copies of wall paintings at Thebes and other sources, give us a good idea of the furniture of this ancient people. Amongst the group of illustrations on page 6 will be seen a representation of a wooden head-rest, which prevented the disarrangement of the coiffure of an Egyptian lady of rank. A very similar head-rest, with a cushion attached for comfort to the neck, is still in common use by the Japanese of the present day.

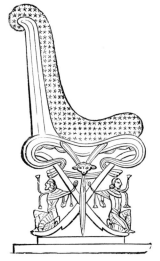

CHAIR WITH CAPTIVES AS SUPPORTS.
(From Papyrus in British Museum.)

BACCHUS AND ATTENDANTS VISITING ICARUS.

(Reproduced from a Bas-relief in the British Museum.)

PERIOD: ABOUT A.D. 100.

GREEK FURNITURE

An early reference to Greek furniture is made by Homer, who describes coverlets of dyed wool, tapestries, carpets and other accessories, which must therefore have formed part of the contents of a great man's residence centuries before the period which we recognise as the " meridian " of Greek Art.

In the second Vase room of the British Museum the painting on one of these vases represents two persons sitting on a couch, upon which is a cushion of rich material, while for the comfort of the sitters there is a footstool, probably of ivory. Facing this page there is an illustration of a bas-relief in stone, " Bacchus received as a guest by Icarus," in

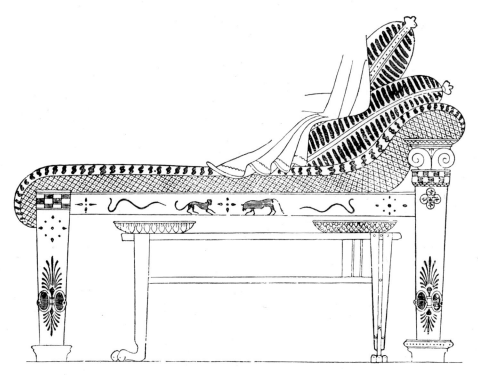

GREEK BEDSTEAD WITH A TABLE.
(From an old Wall Painting.)

which the couch has turned legs and the feet are ornamented with carved leaf work. Illustrations of tripods used for sacred or other purposes, and as supports for braziers, lead us to the conclusion that tables were made of wood, of marble and of metal ; also folding chairs, and couches for sleeping and resting, but not for reclining at meals, as was the fashion at a later period. In most of the designs for these various articles of furniture there is a similarity of treatment of the head, legs and feet of

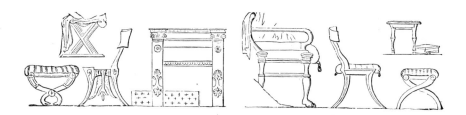

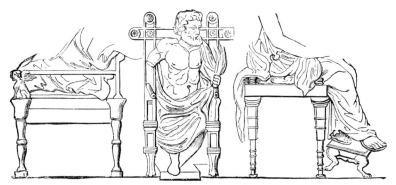

GREEK FURNITURE.

(From Antique Bas-relief.)

lions, leopards and sphinxes to that which we have noticed in the Assyrian patterns.

The description of an interesting piece of furniture may be noticed here, because its date is verified by its historical associations, and it was seen and described by Pausanias about 800 years afterwards. This is the famous chest of Cypselus of Corinth, the story of which runs that when his mother's relations, having been warned by the Oracle of Delphi that her son would prove formidable to the ruling party, sought to murder him, his life was saved by his concealment in this chest, and he became ruler of Corinth for some thirty years (B.C. 655-625). It is said to have been made of cedar, carved and decorated with figures and bas-reliefs, some in ivory, some in gold or ivory part gilt, and inlaid on all four sides and on the top.

The peculiar laws and customs of the Greeks at the time of their greatest prosperity were not calculated to encourage display or luxury in private life, or the collection of sumptuous furniture. Their manners were simple and their discipline was very severe. Statuary, sculpture of the best kind, painting of the highest merit—in a word, the best that Art could produce—were all dedicated to the national service in the enrichment of Temples and other public buildings, the State having indefinite and almost unlimited power over the property of all wealthy citizens. The public surroundings of an influential Athenian were therefore in direct contrast to the simplicity of his home, which contained the most meagre supply of chairs and tables, while the *chefs d'œuvre* of Phidias, Apelles and Praxiteles adorned the Senate House, the Theatre and the Temple.

There were some exceptions to this rule, and we have records that during the later years of Greek prosperity such simplicity was not observed. Alcibiades is said to have been the first to have his house painted and decorated, and Plutarch tells us that he kept the painter Agatharcus a prisoner until his task was done, and then dismissed him with an appropriate reward. Another ancient writer relates that " The guest of a private house was enjoined to praise the decorations of the ceilings and the beauty of the curtains suspended from between the columns." This occurs, according to Mr. Perkins, the American translator of Dr. Falke's German book " Kunst im Hause," in the " Wasps of Aristophanes," written B.C. 422.

The illustrations, taken from the best authorities in the British Museum, the National Library of Paris and other sources, show the severe style adopted by the Greeks in their furniture.

ROMAN FURNITURE

As we are accustomed to look to Greece in the time of Pericles for purity of style and perfection of taste in Art, so do we naturally expect its gradual demoralisation in its transfer to the great Roman Empire. From that little village on the Palatine Hill, founded some 750 years B.C., Rome had spread and conquered in every direction, until in the time of Augustus she was mistress of the whole civilised world, herself the centre of wealth, civilisation, luxury and power. Antioch in the East, and Alexandria in the South, ranked next to her as great cities of the world.

From the excavations of Herculaneum and Pompeii we have learned enough to conceive some general idea of the social life of a wealthy Roman in the time of Rome's highest prosperity. The houses had no upper storey, but enclosed two or more quadrangles, or courts, with arcades into which the rooms opened, receiving air and ventilation from the centre open court. The illustration on opposite page will give an idea of this arrangement.

In Mr. Hungerford Pollen's useful handbook there is a description of each room in a Roman house, with its proper Latin title and purpose; and we know from other descriptions of Ancient Rome that the residences in the Imperial City were divided into two distinct classes—that of *domus* and *insula*, the former being the dwellings of the Roman nobles, and corresponding to the modern *Palazzi*, while the latter were the habitations of the middle and lower classes. Each *insula* consisted of several sets of apartments, generally let out to different families, and was frequently surrounded by shops. The houses described by Mr. Pollen appear to have had no upper storey, but as ground became more valuable in Rome, houses were built to such a height as to be a source of danger, and in the time of Augustus there were not only strict regulations as to building, but the height was limited to 70 feet. The Roman furniture of the time was of the most costly kind. Tables were made of marble, gold, silver and bronze, and were engraved, damascened, plated and enriched with precious stones. The chief woods used were cedar, pine, elm, olive, ash, ilex, beech and maple. Ivory was much used, and not only were the arms and legs of couches and chairs carved to represent the limbs of animals, as has been noted in the Assyrian, Egyptian and Greek designs, but other parts of furniture were ornamented by carvings in bas-relief of subjects taken from Greek mythology and legend. Veneers were cut and applied, not as some have supposed for the purpose of economy, but because by this means the

INTERIOR OF AN ANCIENT ROMAN HOUSE.

Said to have been that of Sallust.

PERIOD: B.C. 20 to A.D. 20.

most beautifully marked or figured specimens of the woods could be chosen, and a much richer and more decorative effect produced than would be possible when only solid timber was used. As a prominent instance of the extent to which the Romans carried the costliness of some special pieces of furniture, we have it recorded on good authority (Mr. Pollen) that the table made for Cicero cost a million sesterces, a sum equal to about £9,000, and that one belonging to King Juba was sold by auction for the equivalent of £10,000.

A ROMAN STUDY.

Showing Scrolls or Books in a "Scrinium"; also Lamp, Writing Tables, etc.

Cicero's table was made of a wood called Thyine—wood which was brought from Africa and held in the highest esteem. It was valued not only on account of its beauty but also from superstitious or religious reasons. The possession of thyine wood was supposed to bring good luck, and its sacredness arose from the fact that from it was produced the incense used by the priests. Dr. Edward Clapton, of St. Thomas' Hospital, who made a collection of woods named in the Scriptures, managed to secure a specimen of thyine, which a friend of his obtained on the Atlas Mountains. It resembles the woods which we know as tuyere and amboyna.*

* See also Notes on Woods (Appendix).

Roman like Greek houses were divided into two portions — the front for the reception of guests and the duties of society, with the back for household purposes and the occupation of the wife and family; for although the position of the Roman wife was superior to that of her Greek contemporary, which was little better than that of a slave, still it was very different to its later development.

The illustration following page 18, of a repast in the house of Sallust, represents the host and his eight male guests reclining on the seats of the period, each of which held three persons, and was called a triclinium, making up the favourite number of a Roman dinner party, and possibly giving us the proverbial saying—" Not less than the Graces nor more than the Muses "—which is still held to be a popular regulation number for a dinner party.

This relic of Ancient Rome was seen by the writer in 1911, parts of the house including the dining room still extant, but the ruins are now

ROMAN SCAMNUM OR BENCH.

ROMAN BISELLIUM, OR SEAT FOR TWO PERSONS.
But generally occupied by one, on occasions of festivals, etc.

some 30 to 40 feet below the surface of the present city, and another house has been built above it.

From discoveries at Herculaneum and Pompeii a great deal of information has been gained of the domestic life of the wealthier Roman citizens, and there is a useful illustration on the preceding page of the furniture of a library or study in which the designs are very similar to the Greek ones we have noticed; it is not improbable they were made and executed by Greek workmen.

It will be seen that the books, such as were then used, instead of being placed on shelves or in a bookcase, were kept in round boxes called *Scrinia*, which were generally of beech wood, and could be locked or sealed when required. The books in rolls or sewn together were thus easily carried about by the owner on his journeys.

Mr. Hungerford Pollen mentions that wearing apparel was kept in *vestiaria*, or wardrobe rooms, and he quotes Plutarch's anecdote of the purple cloaks of Lucullus, which were so numerous that they must have been stored in capacious hanging closets rather than in chests.

In the *atrium,* or public reception room, was probably the best furniture in the house. According to Moule's "Essay on Roman Villas," "it was here that numbers assembled daily to pay their respects to their patron, to consult the legislator, to attract the notice of the statesman, or to derive importance in the eyes of the public from the apparent intimacy with a man in power."

The growth of the Roman Empire eastward, the colonisation of Oriental countries, and subsequently the establishment of an Eastern Empire, produced gradually an alteration in Greek design, and though, if we were discussing the merits of design and the canons of taste, this might be considered a decline, still its influence on furniture was doubtless to produce more ease and luxury, more warmth and comfort, than would be possible if the outline of every article of useful furniture were

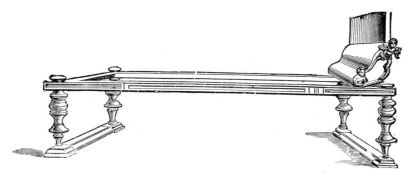

ROMAN COUCH, GENERALLY OF BRONZE.
(*From an Antique Bas-relief.*)

decided by a rigid adherence to classical principles. We have seen that this was more consonant with the public life of an Athenian; but the Romans, in the later period of the Empire, with their wealth, their extravagance, their slaves, their immorality and gross sensuality, lived in a splendour and with a prodigality that well accorded with the gorgeous colouring of Eastern hangings and embroideries, of rich carpets and comfortable cushions, of the lavish use of gold and silver, and meretricious and redundant ornament.

This slight sketch, brief and inadequate as it is, of a history of furniture from the earliest time of which we have any record, until from the extraordinary growth of the vast Roman Empire, the arts and manufactures of every country became as it were centralised and focussed in the palaces of the wealthy Romans, brings us down to the commencement of what has been deservedly called "the greatest event in history"—the

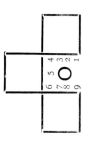

Plan of Triclinium

THE ROMAN TRICLINIUM, OR DINING ROOM.

The plan in the margin shows the position of the guests; the place of honour was that which is indicated by "No. 1," and that of the host by "No. 9."

(*The Illustration is taken from Dr. Jacob von Falke's "Kunst im Hause."*)

decline and fall of this enormous empire. For fifteen generations, for some five hundred years, did this decay, this vast revolution, proceed to its conclusion. Barbarian hosts settled down in provinces they had overrun and conquered, the old Pagan world died as it were, and the new Christian era dawned. From the latter end of the second century until the last of the Western Cæsars, in A.D. 476, it is, with the exception of a short interval when the strong hand of the great Theodosius stayed the avalanche of Rome's invaders, one long story of the defeat and humiliation of the citizens of the greatest power the world has ever known. It is a vast drama that the genius and patience of a Gibbon has alone been able to deal with, defying almost by its gigantic catastrophes and ever raging turbulence the pen of history to chronicle and arrange. When the curtain rises on a new order of things, the age of Paganism has passed away, and the period of the Middle Ages will have commenced.

ROMAN BRONZE LAMP AND STAND.
(*Found in Pompeii.*)

CHAPTER II

The Middle Ages

Period of 1,000 years from fall of Rome, A.D. 476, to Capture of Constantinople, 1453—The Crusades—Influence of Christianity—Chairs of St. Peter and Maximian at Rome, Ravenna and Venice—Edict of Leo III. prohibiting Image worship—The Rise of Venice—Charlemagne and his successors—The Chair of Dagobert—Byzantine character of Furniture—Norwegian carving—Russian and Scandinavian—The Anglo-Saxons—Sir Walter Scott quoted—Descriptions of Anglo-Saxon Houses and Customs—Norman influence—Art in Flemish Cities—Gothic Architecture—The Coronation Chair at Westminster Abbey—Furniture at York Minster—Penshurst—French Furniture in the Fourteenth Century—Description of rooms—Development of the chair—Transition from Gothic to Renaissance—German carved work; the Credence, the Buffet and Dressoir.

 HE history of furniture is so thoroughly a part of the history of the manners and customs of different peoples, that one can only understand and appreciate the several changes in style, sometimes gradual and sometimes rapid, by reference to certain historical events and influences by which such changes were effected.

Thus, we have during the space of time known as the Middle Ages, a stretch of some thousand years, dating from the fall of Rome itself, in A.D. 476 to the capture of Constantinople by the Turks under Mahomet II. in 1453, an historical panorama of striking incidents and great social changes bearing upon our subject. It was a turbulent and violent period, which saw the completion of Rome's downfall, the rise of the Carlovingian family, the subjection of Britain by the Saxons, the Danes and the Normans; the extraordinary career and fortunes of Mahomet; the conquest of Spain and a great part of Africa by the Moors; and the Crusades, which united in a common cause the swords and spears of friend and foe.

It was the age of monasteries and convents, of religious persecutions and of heroic struggles of the Christian Church. It was the age of feudalism, chivalry and war, but towards its close a time of comparative civilisation and progress, of darkness giving way to the light which followed; the night of the Middle Ages preceding the dawn of the Renaissance.

With the growing importance of Constantinople, the capital of the Eastern Empire, families of well-to-do citizens flocked thither from other parts, bringing with them all their most valuable possessions: and the houses of the great became rich in ornamental furniture, the style of which was a mixture of Eastern and Roman,—that is, a corruption of the early Classic Greek developing into the style known as Byzantine. The influence of Christianity upon the position of women materially affected the customs and habits of the people. Ladies were allowed to be seen in chariots and open carriages, the designs of which therefore improved and became more varied; the old custom of reclining at meals ceased, and guests sat on benches; and though we have, with certain exceptions, such as the chair of St. Peter at Rome, and that of Maximian in the Cathedral at Ravenna, no specimens of furniture of this time, we have in the old Byzantine ivory bas-reliefs such representations of circular throne chairs and of ecclesiastical furniture as suffice to show the class of woodwork then in vogue.

The chair of St. Peter is one of the most interesting relics of the Middle Ages. The woodcut will show the design, which is, like other work of the period, Byzantine, and the following description is taken from Mr. Hungerford Pollen's introduction to the Victoria and Albert Museum catalogue:—" The chair is constructed of wood, overlaid with carved ivory work and gold. The back is bound together with iron. It is a square with solid front and arms. The width in front is 39 inches; the height in front 30 inches, showing that a scabellum or footstool must have belonged to it. . . . . . In the front are 18 groups or compositions from the Gospels, carved in ivory with exquisite fineness, and worked with inlay of the purest gold. On the outer sides are several little figures carved in ivory. It formed, according to tradition, part of the furniture of the house of the Senator Pudens, an early convert to the Christian faith. It is he who gave to the Church his house in Rome, of which much that remains is covered by the Church of St. Pudenziana. Pudens gave this chair to St. Peter, and it became the throne of the See. It was kept in the old Basilica of St. Peter's." Since then it has been transferred from place to place, until now it remains in the present Church of St. Peter, but is completely hidden from view by the seat or covering made in 1667, by Bernini, out of bronze taken from the Pantheon.

Much has been written about this famous chair. Cardinal Wiseman and the Cavaliere de Rossi have defended its reputation and its history, and Mr. Nesbitt, some years ago, read a paper on the subject before the Society of Antiquaries.

CHAIR OF ST. PETER, ROME.

Formerly there was in Venice another "chair of St. Peter," of which there is a description and illustration in Mrs. Oliphant's "Makers of Venice." It is said to have been a present from the Emperor Michael, son of Theophilus (824-864), to the Venetian Republic in recognition of services rendered, by either the Doge Gradonico, who died in 864, or his predecessor, against the Mohammedan incursions. Fragments only now remain, and these are preserved in the Church of St. Pietro at Castello.

There is also a chair of historic fame preserved in Venice, and now kept in the treasury of St. Mark's. Originally in Alexandria it was sent to Constantinople and formed part of the spoils taken by the Venetians in 1204. Like both the other chairs, this was also ornamented with ivory plaques, but these have been replaced by ornamental marble.

The earlier of the before-mentioned chairs, namely, the one at Ravenna, was made for the Archbishop about 546 to 556, and is thus described in Mr. Maskell's "Handbook on Ivories," in the Science and Art series:— "The chair has a high back, round in shape, and is entirely covered with plaques of ivory arranged in panels carved in high relief with scenes from the Gospels and with figures of saints. The plaques have borders with foliated ornaments, birds and animals; flowers and fruits filling the intermediate spaces. Du Sommerard names amongst the most remarkable subjects, the Annunciation, the Adoration of the Wise Men, the Flight into Egypt, and the Baptism of our Lord." The chair has also been described by Passeri, the famous Italian antiquary, and a paper upon it was read by Sir Digby Wyatt, before the Arundel Society, in which he remarked that as it had been fortunately preserved as a holy relic, it wore almost the same appearance as when used by the prelate for whom it was made, save for the beautiful tint with which time had invested it.

Long before the general break up of the vast Roman Empire influences had been at work to decentralise Art, and cause the migration of trained and skilful artisans to countries where their work would build up fresh industries, and give an impetus to progress where hitherto there had been stagnation. One of these influences was the decree issued in A.D. 726 by Leo III., Emperor of the Eastern Empire, prohibiting all image worship. The consequences to Art of such a decree were doubtless similar to the fanatical proceedings of the English Puritans of the seventeenth century; and artists, driven from their homes, were scattered to the different European capitals, where they were gladly received and found employment and patronage.

It should be borne in mind that at this time Venice was gradually rising to that marvellous position of wealth and power which she afterwards held.

> "A ruler of the waters and their powers:
> And such she was;—her daughters had their dowers
> From spoils of nations, and the exhaustless East
> Pour'd in her lap all gems in sparkling showers;
> In purple was she robed and of her feasts
> Monarchs partook, and deemed their dignity increased."

Her wealthy merchants were well acquainted with the arts and manufactures of other countries, and Venice would be just one of those cities to attract the artist refugee. It is indeed here that wood carving as an Art may be said to have specially developed itself, and though, from its destructible nature, there are very few specimens extant dating from this early time, yet we shall see that two or three hundred years later, ornamental woodwork flourished in a state of perfection which must have required a long probationary period.

Turning from Venice. During the latter end of the eighth century the star of Charlemagne was in the ascendant, and though we have no authentic specimen, and scarcely a picture of any wooden furniture of this reign, we know that, in appropriating the property of the Gallo-Romans, the Frank Emperor-King and his chiefs were in some degree educating themselves to higher notions of luxury and civilisation. Paul Lacroix, in

DAGOBERT CHAIR.
Chair of Dagobert, of gilt bronze, now in the Museé de Souverains, Paris. Originally as a folding chair
said to be the work of St. Eloi, seventh century; back and arms added by the Abbé Suger in twelfth century.
There is an electrotype reproduction in the Victoria and Albert Museum.

"Manners, Customs, and Dress of the Middle Ages," tells us that the *trichorum*, or dining room, was generally the largest hall in the palace: two rows of columns divided it into three parts, one for the royal family, one for the officers of the household, and the third for the guests who were generally numerous. No person of rank who visited the King could leave without sitting at his table or at least draining a cup to his health.

The King's hospitality was magnificent, especially on great religious festivals, such as Christmas and Easter.

In other portions of this work of reference we read of "boxes" to hold articles of value, and of rich hangings, but beyond such allusions little can be gleaned of any furniture besides. The celebrated chair of Dagobert (illustration on page 25), now in the Louvre and of which there is a cast in the Victoria and Albert Museum, dates from some 150 years before Charlemagne and is probably the only specimen of furniture belonging to this period which has been handed down to us. It is made of gilt bronze and it is said to be the work of a monk.

For the designs of furniture of the tenth to the fourteenth centuries we are in a great measure dependent upon old illuminated manuscripts and missals of these remote times. There are some illustrations of the seats of State used by sovereigns on the occasions of grand banquets or of some ecclesiastical function, to be found in the valuable collections of old documents in the British Museum and the National Libraries of Paris and Brussels. It is evident from these authorities that the designs of State furniture in France and other countries dominated by the Carlovingian monarchs were of Byzantine character, that pseudo-classic style which was the prototype of furniture of about a thousand years later, when the Cæsarism of Napoleon I. during the early years of the nineteenth century produced so many designs which we now recognise as "Empire."

No history of mediæval woodwork would be complete without noticing the Scandinavian furniture and ornamental wood carving of the tenth to the fifteenth centuries. There are in the Victoria and Albert Museum plaster casts of some three or four carved doorways of Norwegian workmanship, of the tenth, eleventh and twelfth centuries, in which scrolls are entwined with contorted monsters, or to quote Mr. Lovett's description " dragons of hideous aspect and serpents of more than usually tortuous proclivities." The woodcut of a carved lintel conveys a fair idea of this work, and represents one of the old juniper wood tankards of a much later time.

There are also at Kensington other casts of curious Scandinavian woodwork of more Byzantine treatment, the originals of which are in the Museums of Stockholm and Copenhagen where the collection of antique woodwork of native production is very large and interesting, and proves how wood carving as an industrial Art has flourished in Scandinavia from the early Viking times. One can still see in the old churches of Borgund and Hitterdal much of the carved woodwork of the seventh and eighth centuries; and lintels and porches full of national character are to be found in Thelemarken.

A CARVED NORWEGIAN DOORWAY.
Period: X. to XI. Century.

Under the heading of "Scandinavian" may be included the very early Russian school of ornamental woodwork. Before the accession of the Romanoff dynasty in the sixteenth century the Ruric race of kings came originally from Finland, then a province of Sweden, and so far as one can see from old illuminated manuscripts, there was a similarity of design to those of the early Norwegian and Swedish carved lintels which have been noticed above.

CARVED WOOD CHAIR, SCANDINAVIAN WORK.
Twelfth and Thirteenth Century.

The coffers and caskets of early mediæval times were no inconsiderable items in the valuable furniture of a period when the list of articles coming under that definition was so limited. These were made in oak for general use, and some were of good workmanship, but of the earliest few remain. In the fine old city of York there are many charming relics in stone and wood which remind us of a remote past, and by no means the least interesting of these is the ancient hall of the Merchant Adventurers or Trinity Hall as it is sometimes called. There is to be seen in this old building a plain oak chest bound with iron and which still boasts of one of the original three locks which protected the documents of the Company. These documents bore the date of 1100, and the chest has every appearance of being of that period or even earlier. There were however others smaller and of a special character, made in ivory of the walrus and elephant, of horn and whalebone, besides those of metal, which from their more valuable and ornamental character have been preserved. In the British Museum is one of these, of which the cover is illustrated on this page. The carving represents a man defending his house against an attack by enemies armed with spears and shields. Other parts of the casket are carved with subjects and runic inscriptions which have enabled Mr. Stephens an authority on this period of archæology to assign its date to the eighth century and its manufacture to that of Northumbria. It most probably represents a local incident, and part of the inscription refers to a word signifying "treachery." It was purchased by the late Sir A. W. Franks, F.S.A., and is one of the many valuable specimens given to the British Museum by its generous curator.

COVER OF A CASKET CARVED IN WHALEBONE.
(*Northumbrian. Eighth Century. British Museum.*)

Of the furniture of our own country previous to the eleventh or twelfth centuries we know but little. The habits of the Anglo-Saxons were rude and simple, and they advanced but slowly in civilisation until after the Norman invasion. To convey however to our minds some idea of the interior of a Saxon thane's castle, we may avail ourselves of Sir Walter Scott's antiquarian research, and borrow his description of the chief apartment in Rotherwood the hospitable hall of Cedric the Saxon. Though the time treated of in "Ivanhoe" is quite at the end of the twelfth century, yet we have in Cedric a type of man who would have gloried in retaining the customs of his ancestors, who detested and despised the new-fashioned manners of his conquerors, and who came of a race that had probably done very little in the way of "refurnishing" for some generations. If, therefore, we have the reader's pardon for relying upon the *mise en scène* of a novel for an authority, we shall imagine the more easily what kind of furniture our Anglo-Saxon forefathers indulged in.

"In a hall, the height of which was greatly disproportioned to its extreme length and width, a long oaken table—formed of planks rough hewn from the forest, and which had scarcely received any polish— stood ready prepared for the evening meal. . . . . On the sides of the apartment hung implements of war and of the chase, and there were at each corner folding doors which gave access to the other parts of the extensive building.

SAXON HOUSE OF NINTH OR TENTH CENTURY.
(*From the Harleian MSS. in the British Museum.*)

" The other appointments of the mansion partook of the rude simplicity of the Saxon period, which Cedric piqued himself upon maintaining. The floor was composed of earth mixed with lime, trodden into a hard substance, such as is often employed in flooring our modern barns. For about one quarter of the length of the apartment, the floor was raised by a step, and this space, which was called the daïs, was occupied only by the principal members of the family and visitors of distinction. For this purpose a table richly covered with scarlet cloth was placed transversely across the platform, from the middle of which ran the longer and lower board, at which the domestic and inferior persons fed, down towards the bottom of the hall. The whole resembled the form of the letter T or some of those ancient dinner tables which, arranged on the same principles, may still be seen in the ancient colleges of Oxford and Cambridge. Massive chairs and settles of carved oak were placed on the daïs, and over these seats and the elevated tables was fastened a canopy of cloth, which served in some degree to protect the dignitaries who occupied that distinguished station from the weather, and especially from the rain which in some places found its way through the ill-constructed roof. The walls of this upper end of the hall, as far as the daïs extended, were covered with hangings or curtains which were adorned with some attempt at tapestry or embroidery, executed with brilliant or rather gaudy colouring; upon the floor there was a carpet. Over the lower range of table the roof had no covering, the rough plastered walls were left bare, the rude earthen floor was uncarpeted, the board was uncovered by a cloth and rude massive benches supplied the place of chairs. In the centre of the upper table were placed two chairs more elevated than the rest, for the master and mistress of the family. To each of these was added a footstool curiously carved and inlaid with ivory, which mark of distinction was peculiar to them."

A drawing in the Harleian MSS. in the British Museum is shown on opposite page, illustrating a Saxon mansion in the ninth or tenth century. There is a hall in the centre, with "chamber" and "bower" on either side, there being only a ground floor as in the earlier Roman houses. According to Mr. Wright, F.S.A., who has written on the subject of Anglo-Saxon manners and customs, there was only one instance recorded of an upper floor at this period, and that was in an account of an accident which happened to the house in which the Witan or Council of St. Dunstan met when according to the ancient chronicle which he quotes, the Council fell from an upper floor and St. Dunstan saved himself from a similar fate by supporting his weight on a beam.

The illustration here given shows the Anglo-Saxon chieftain standing at the door of his hall with his lady, distributing food to the needy poor. Other woodcuts represent Anglo-Saxon bedsteads, which were little better than raised wooden boxes with sacks of straw placed therein, and these were generally in recesses. There are old inventories and wills in existence which show that some value and importance was attached to these primitive contrivances, which at this early period in our history were the luxuries of only a few persons of high rank. A certain will recites that the "bedclothes (bed-reafs) with a curtain (hyrfte) and sheet (hepp-scrytan), and all that thereto belongs," should be given to the testator's son.

ANGLO-SAXON FURNITURE OF ABOUT THE TENTH CENTURY.
(*From old MSS. in the British Museum.*)

1. A Drinking Party.
2. A Dinner Party, in which the attendants are serving the meal on
    the spits on which it has been cooked.
3. Anglo-Saxon Beds.

In the account of the murder of King Athelbert by the Queen of King Offa, as told by Roger of Wendover, we read of the Queen ordering a chamber to be made ready for the Royal guest which was adorned for the occasion with what was then considered sumptuous furniture. "Near the King's bed she caused a seat to be prepared, magnificently decked and surrounded with curtains, and underneath it the wicked woman caused a deep pit to be dug." The author from whom the above translation is quoted adds with grim humour, "It is clear that this room was on the ground floor."

THE SEAT ON THE DAÏS.   SAXON STATE BED.

There are in the British Museum other old manuscripts whose illustrations have been laid under contribution, representing more innocent occupations of our Anglo-Saxon forefathers. "The seat on the daïs," "an Anglo-Saxon drinking party," and other illustrations which are in existence, prove generally that, when the meal had finished the table was removed and drinking vessels were handed round from guest to guest; the story-tellers, the minstrels and the gleemen (conjurers) or jesters beguiling the festive hour with their different performances.

Some of these Anglo-Saxon houses had formerly been the villas of the Romans during their occupation, which were altered and modified

to suit the habits and tastes of their later possessors. Lord Lytton
has given us, in the first chapter of his novel "Harold," the description
of one of such Saxonized Roman houses, in his reference to Hilda's
abode.

The gradual influence of Norman civilisation, however, had its effect,
though the unsettled state of the country prevented any rapid development of industrial arts. The feudal system, by which every powerful
baron became a petty sovereign, often at war with his neighbour,
rendered it necessary that household treasures should be few and easily
transported or hidden, and the earliest oak chests which are still preserved
date from about this time. Bedsteads were not usual except for kings,
queens and great ladies, tapestry covered the walls and the floors were
generally sanded. As the country became more calm, and security for

ENGLISH FOLDING CHAIR.
Fourteenth Century.

CRADLE OF HENRY V.

property more assured, this comfortless state of living disappeared; the
dress of the ladies was richer and the general habits of the upper classes
became more refined. Stairs were introduced into houses, the "parloir" or
"talking room" was added and fire-places of brick or stonework were
made in some of the rooms, where previously the smoke was allowed to
escape through an aperture in the roof. Bedsteads were carved and draped
with rich hangings. Armoires made of oak and enriched with carvings,
and "Presses" date from about the end of the eleventh century.

It was during the reign of Henry III., 1216-1272, that wood-
panelling was first used for rooms, and considerable progress generally
appears to have been made about this period. Eleanor of Provence,
whom the King married in 1236, encouraged more luxury in the homes
of the barons and courtiers. Mr. Hungerford Pollen has quoted a royal

precept which was promulgated in this year, and it plainly shows that our ancestors were becoming more refined in their tastes. The terms of this precept were as follows, viz., "The King's great Chamber at Westminster to be painted a green colour like a curtain, that in the great gable or frontispiece of the said chamber a French inscription should be painted, and that the King's little wardrobe should be painted of a green colour to imitate a curtain."

In another 100 or 150 years we find mediæval Art approaching its best period, not only in England, but in the great Flemish cities, such as Bruges and Ghent, which in the thirteenth and fourteenth centuries played so important a part in the history of that time. The taste for Gothic architecture had now well set in, and we find that in this, as in every change of style, the fashion in woodwork naturally followed that of ornament in stone; indeed in many cases it is more than probable that the same hands which planned the cathedral or monastery also drew the designs for furniture, especially as the finest specimens of wood carving were devoted to the service of the church.

The examples therefore of the woodwork of this period to which we have access are found to be mostly of Gothic pattern, with quaint distorted conceptions of animals and reptiles, adapted to ornament the structural part of the furniture, or for the enrichment of the panels.

To the end of the thirteenth century belongs the Coronation Chair made for King Edward I., 1296-1300, and now in Westminster Abbey. This historic relic is of oak, and the woodcut on the following page gives an idea of the design and decorative carving. It is said that the pinnacles on each side of the gabled back were formerly surmounted by two leopards, of which only small portions remain. The famous Coronation Stone, which according to ancient legend is the identical one on which the patriarch Jacob rested his head at Bethel, when "he tarried there all night because the sun was set, and he took of the stones of that place and put them up for his pillows" (Gen. xxviii.), can be seen through the quatrefoil openings under the seat.*

The carved lions which support the chair are not original, but modern work; and were re-gilt in honour of the coronation of King George V. in 1910, when the chair was last used. The rest of the chair now shows the natural colour of the oak, except the arms which have a slight padding on them. The wood was however formerly covered with a coating of plaster gilded over, and it is probably due to this protection that it is now in such excellent preservation.

* Those who would read a very interesting account of the history of this stone are referred to the late Dean Stanley's "Historical Memorials of Westminster Abbey."

Standing by its side in Henry III.'s Chapel in Westminster Abbey is another chair, similar, but lacking the trefoil Gothic arches, which are carved on the sides of the original chair; this was made for and used by Mary, daughter of James II. and wife of William III. on the occasion of their double coronation. Mr. Hungerford Pollen has given us a long description of this chair, with quotations from the different historical

CORONATION CHAIR, WESTMINSTER ABBEY.

notices which have appeared concerning it. The following is an extract which he has taken from an old writer :—

"It appears that the King intended, in the first instance, to make the chair in bronze and that Eldam, the King's workman, had actually begun it. Indeed, some parts were even finished, and tools bought for the clearing up of the casting. However the King changed his mind and we have accordingly 100s. paid for a chair in wood, made after the same pattern as the one which was to be cast in copper; also 13s. 4d. for carving, painting and gilding two small leopards in wood, which were delivered to Master Walter, the King's painter, to be placed upon and on either side of the chair made by him. The wardrobe account of 29th Ed. I. shows that Master Walter was paid £1 19s. 7d. 'for making a step at the foot of the new chair in which the Scottish stone is placed; and for the wages of the carpenters and of the painters, and for colours and gold employed, and for the making a covering to cover the said chair.'"

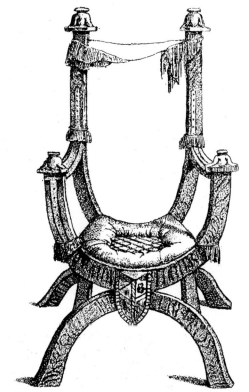

CHAIR IN THE VESTRY OF YORK MINSTER.
Late Fourteenth Century.

In 1328, June 1, there was a royal writ ordering the abbot to deliver up the stone to the Sheriff of London, to be carried to the Queen-Mother: however it was not sent. The chair has been used upon the occasion of every coronation since that time, except in the case of Tudor Mary, who is said to have used a chair specially sent by the Pope for the occasion.

The above drawing of a chair, which can still be seen in the Vestry of York Minster, and the two more throne-like seats on a full-page illustration, will serve to show the best kind of ornamental ecclesiastical furniture of the fourteenth century. According to the local guide books of York City, and the story of the Verger who conducts tourists over the

CHAIR.

From an Old English Monastery.

PERIOD : XV. CENTURY.

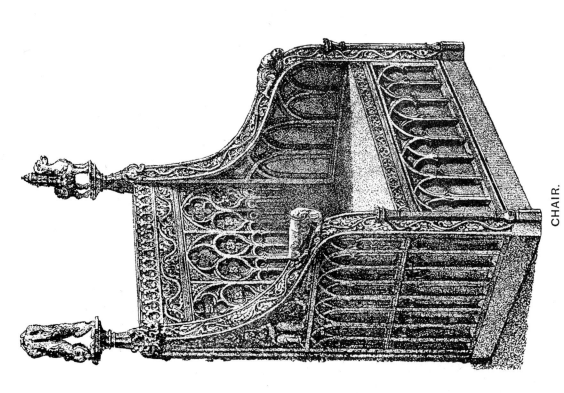

CHAIR.

In St. Mary's Hall, Coventry.

OAK CHEST IN THE VESTRY OF YORK MINSTER.

PERIOD: LATE XIV. CENTURY.

(Reproduced from Waddington's "Guide to York," by permission.)

Minster, this famous old chair was used for the coronation of some of the Saxon Kings, and also for the coronation of King Edward IV., Richard III. and James I. The tradition as to the Saxon Kings is doubtful, but the chair was almost certainly used for the three last named English monarchs. It was also the chair used for the enthronisation of the Archbishops of York until the time of Dr. Magee, when its frail condition rendered the preparation of the present Archbishop's chair necessary. In the choir of Canterbury Cathedral there is a chair which has played its part in history, and, although earlier than the above, it may be conveniently mentioned here. This is the Archbishop's throne, and it is also called the chair of St. Augustine. According to legend, the Saxon Kings were crowned thereon, but it is probably not earlier than the thirteenth century. It is an excellent piece of stonework, with a shaped back and arms, relieved from being quite plain by the back and sides being panelled with a carved moulding.

In the Vestry at York Minster there are besides the chair already described some ecclesiastical relics of great antiquity and historical interest stored in an oak cupboard, which has been composed of some old iron-bound doors and a cornice of fifteenth century carving. There is also a famous oak chest of fourteenth century work, elaborately carved with a representation of the legend of St. George and the dragon. This chest is in a wonderful state of preservation and deserves minute examination. The Gothic treatment of the castle and the archaic drawing of the figures enable us to confirm the guide-book description as to it being a specimen of fourteenth century woodwork. We are able to give an illustration of this very rare and interesting piece. The Vestry also contains the only two carved oak choir stalls rescued from the disastrous fire which occurred in 1829, when a madman, named Jonathan Martin, having dreamed that he was Divinely appointed to destroy the Cathedral, set fire to the building after the service which he attended, and succeeded alas in destroying the beautiful fifteenth century carving of the choir and chancel.

Penshurst Place, near Tonbridge, the residence of Lord de l'Isle and Dudley, the historic home of the Sydneys, is almost an unique example of what a wealthy English gentleman's country house was about the time of which we are writing, say the middle of the fourteenth century, or during the reign of Edward III. By the courtesy of the late Lord de l'Isle, the writer was allowed to examine many objects of great interest there, and from the careful preservation of many original fittings and articles of furniture, one may still gain some idea of the " hall " as it appeared when that part of the house was the scene of the chief events in the daily life of the family—the raised daïs for host and honoured guests, the better table which was placed there (as illustrated on

"Standing" Table at Penshurst, still on the Daïs in the Hall.

this page), and the commoner ones for the body of the hall; and though the ancient buffet which displayed the gold and silver cups is gone, one can see where it would have stood. Penshurst is said to possess the only hearth of that period now remaining in England, an octagonal space edged with stone in the centre of the hall, over which was once the simple opening for the outlet of smoke through the roof, and the old andirons or firedogs are still there.

An idea of the furniture of an apartment in France during the fourteenth century is conveyed by the illustration on this page, and it is

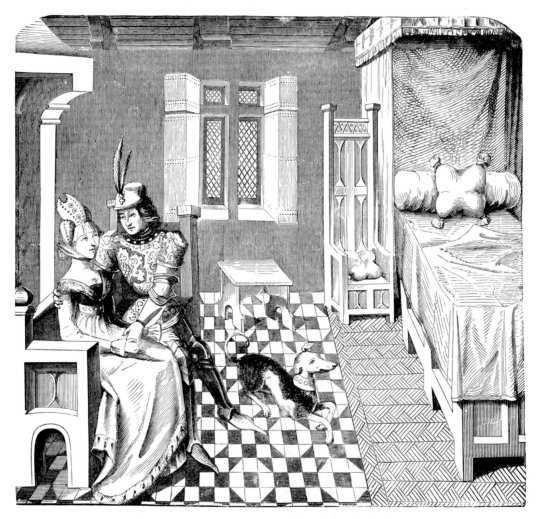

BEDROOM IN WHICH A KNIGHT AND HIS LADY ARE SEATED.
(*From a Miniature in "Othea," a Poem by Christine de Pisan. XIV. Century. French.*)

very useful, because, although we have on record many descriptions of the appearance of the furniture of state apartments, we have very few authenticated accounts of the way in which such domestic chambers as the one occupied by "a knight and his lady" were arranged. The prie-dieu chair was generally at the bedside, and had a seat which lifted up, the lower part forming a box-like receptacle

for devotional books then so regularly used by a lady of the time.
Towards the end of the fourteenth century a taste for bright and
rich colouring came into fashion; we have the testimony of an

BEDSTEAD AND CHAIR IN CARVED OAK.
(From Miniatures in the Royal Library, Brussels.)
PERIOD: XIV. CENTURY.

old writer who describes the interior of the Hotel de Bohême, which,
after having been the residence of several great personages, was given
by Charles VI. of France in 1388 to his brother, the Duke of Orleans.

"In this palace was a room used by the duke hung with cloth of gold bordered with vermilion velvet embroidered with roses; the Duchess had a room hung with vermilion satin embroidered with crossbows which were on her coat of arms; that of the Duke of Burgundy was hung with cloth of gold embroidered with windmills. There was besides eight carpets of glossy texture with gold flowers, one representing 'the seven virtues and seven vices,' another the history of Charlemagne, another that of Saint Louis. There were also cushions of cloth of gold, twenty-four pieces of vermilion leather of Aragon, and four carpets of Aragon leather, 'to be placed on the floor of rooms in summer.' The favourite arm-chair of the Princess is thus described in an inventory—'a chamber chair with four supports, painted in fine vermilion, the seat and arms of which are covered in vermilion morocco or cordovan, worked and stamped with designs representing the sun, birds and other devices bordered with fringes of silk and studded with nails.'"

The thirteenth and fourteenth centuries had been remarkable for a general development of commerce; merchants of Venice, Genoa, Florence, Milan, Ghent, Bruges, Antwerp and many other famous cities had traded extensively with the East and had grown opulent, and their homes naturally showed signs of wealth and comfort that in former times had been impossible to any but princes and rich nobles. Laws had been made in compliance with the complaints of the aristocracy, to place some curb on the growing ambition of the "bourgeoise"; thus we find an old edict in the reign of Philippe the Fair (1285-1314)—"No bourgeois shall have a chariot nor wear gold, precious stones nor crowns of gold and silver. Bourgeois not being prelates or dignitaries of state shall not have tapers of wax. A bourgeois possessing 2,000 pounds (tournois) or more, may order for himself a dress of 12 sous* 6 deniers, and for his wife one worth 16 sous at the most," etc., etc.

This and many other similar regulations were made in vain: the trading classes became more and more powerful, and we quote the description of a furnished apartment from P. Lacroix's "Manners and Customs of the Middle Ages":—

"The walls were hung with precious tapestry of Cyprus, on which the initials and motto of the lady were embroidered, the sheets were of fine linen of Rheims, and had cost more than 300 pounds, the quilt was

---

* The sous, which was but nominal money, may be reckoned as representing 20 francs, the denier 1 franc, but allowance must be made for the enormous difference in the value of silver which would make 20 francs in the thirteenth century represent upwards of 200 francs in the nineteenth century.

a new invention of silk and silver tissue, the carpet was like gold. The lady wore an elegant dress of crimson silk, and rested her head and arms on pillows ornamented with buttons of oriental pearls. It should be remarked that this lady was not the wife of a great merchant, such as those of Venice and Genoa, but of a simple retail dealer who was not above selling articles for 4 sous; such being the case, we cannot wonder that Christine de Pisan should have considered the anecdote 'worthy of being immortalized in a book.'"

"THE NEW BORN INFANT."
Showing the interior of an Apartment at the end of the fourteenth or commencement of the fifteenth century.
(*From a Miniature in "Histoire de la Belle Hélaine," National Library of Paris.*)

As we approach the end of the fourteenth century, we find canopies added to the "chaires" or "chayers á dorseret," which were carved in oak or chestnut, and sometimes elaborately gilded and picked out in colour. The canopied seats were very bulky and throne-like constructions, and were abandoned towards the end of the fifteenth century; and it is worthy of notice that though we have retained our word "chair," adopted from the Norman French, the French people discarded their synonym in favour of its diminutive "chaise" to describe the somewhat smaller and less massive seat which came into use in the sixteenth century.

The skilled artisans of Paris had arrived at a very high degree of excellence in the fourteenth century, and in old documents describing

PORTRAIT OF CHRISTINE DE PISAN.
Seated on a Canopied Chair of carved wood, the back lined with tapestry.
(*From Miniature on MS. in the Burgundy Library, Brussels.*)
PERIOD: XV. CENTURY.

valuable articles of furniture, care is taken to note that they are of Parisian workmanship. According to Lacroix, there is an account of the court silversmith, Etienne La Fontaine, which gives us an idea of the amount of extravagance sometimes committed in the manufacture and decorations of a chair, into which it was then the fashion to introduce the incrustations of precious stones; thus for making a silver arm chair and ornamenting it with pearls, crystals and other stones, he charged the King of France, in 1352, no less a sum than 774 louis.

The use of rich embroideries at state banquets and on grand occasions appears to have commenced during the reign of Louis IX.—Saint Louis, as he is called—and these were richly emblazoned with arms and devices. Indeed, it was probably due to the fashion for rich stuffs and coverings of tables, and of velvet embroidered cushions for the chairs, that the practice of making furniture of the precious metals died out, and carved wood came into favour.

STATE BANQUET, WITH ATTENDANT MUSICIANS.
(From Miniatures in the National Library, Paris.)
PERIOD: XV. CENTURY.

Chairs of this period appear only to have been used on very special occasions; indeed they were too cumbersome to be easily moved from place to place, and in a miniature from some MSS. of the early part of the fifteenth century, which represents a state banquet, the guests are seated on a long bench with the back carved in Gothic ornament of the time. In Skeat's Dictionary our modern word "banquet" is said to be derived from the "bancs" or benches used on these occasions.

MEDIÆVAL BED AND BEDROOM.

(From Viollet le Duc.)

PERIOD: XIV. TO XV. CENTURY. FRENCH.

The great hall of the King's Palace, where such an entertainment as that given by Charles V. to the Emperor Charles of Luxemburg would have taken place, was also furnished with three "dressoirs" for the display of the gold and silver drinking cups, and vases of the time; the repast

A HIGH BACKED CHAIR IN CARVED OAK (GOTHIC STYLE).
PERIOD: XV. CENTURY. FRENCH.

itself was served upon a marble table, and above the seat of each of the Princes present was a separate canopy of gold cloth embroidered with *fleur de lis.*

The furniture of ordinary houses of this period was very simple. Chests, more or less carved, and ornamented with iron work, settles of oak or of chestnut, stools or benches with carved supports, a bedstead and a prie-dieu chair, a table with plain slab supported on shaped standards would nearly complete the inventory of the furniture of the chief room in a house of a well-to-do merchant in France, until the fourteenth century had turned. The table was narrow, apparently not more than some 30 inches wide, and guests sat on one side only, the service taking

SCRIBE OR COPYIST
Working at his desk in a room in which are a reading desk and a chest with manuscript.
(From an Old Miniature.)
PERIOD: XV. CENTURY.

place from the unoccupied side of the table. In palaces and baronial halls, the servants with dishes were followed by musicians, as shown in an old miniature of the time, reproduced on page 47.

Turning to German work of the fifteenth century, there is, in the Victoria and Albert Museum, a cast of the famous choir stalls in the Cathedral of Ulm, which are considered to be the finest work of the Swabian school of German wood carving. The magnificent panel of foliage on the front, the Gothic triple canopy with the busts of Isaiah, David and Daniel, are thoroughly characteristic specimens of design; the signature of the artist, Jörg Syrlin, with date 1468, is carved on the work. There were originally eighty-nine choir stalls, and the work occupied the master from the date mentioned, 1468, until 1474.

The illustrations of the two chairs of German Gothic furniture, formerly in some of the old castles, are good examples of their time, and are from drawings made on the spot by Prof. Heideloff.

There are in the Victoria and Albert Museum some full sized plaster casts of important specimens of woodwork of the fifteenth and two previous centuries, and being of authenticated dates, we can compare them with the work of the same countries after the Renaissance had been adopted and had completely altered the style. Thus in Italy there was, until the latter part of the fifteenth century, a mixture of Byzantine and Gothic of which we can see a capital example in the casts of the celebrated Pulpit in the Baptistry of Pisa the date of which is 1260.

TWO GERMAN CHAIRS. LATE FIFTEENTH CENTURY.
(From Drawings made in Old German Castles by Prof. Heideloff.)

The pillars are supported by lions, which, instead of being introduced heraldically into the design, as would be the case some two hundred years later, are bearing the whole weight of the pillars and an enormous superstructure on the hollow of their backs in a most impossible manner. The spandrel of each arch is filled with a saint in a grotesque position amongst Gothic foliage, and there is in many respects a marked contrast to the casts of examples of the Renaissance period which are in the Museum.

This transition from Mediæval and Gothic to Renaissance is clearly noticeable in the woodwork of many cathedrals and churches in England and in Continental cities. It is evident that the chairs, stalls and pulpits in many of these buildings have been executed at different times,

and the change from one style to another is more or less marked. The
Flemish buffet illustrated (on opposite page) is an example of this transition,

CARVED OAK BUFFET IN GOTHIC STYLE (VIOLLET LE DUC).
PERIOD: XV. CENTURY. FRENCH.

and may be contrasted with the French Gothic buffet illustrated above,
and referred to on page 54. There is also in the central hall of the Victoria

FLEMISH BUFFET

Of Carved Oak; open below, with panelled cupboards above. The back evidently of later
work, after the Renaissance had set in.

(*From a Photo by Messrs. R. Sutton & Co. from the Original in the
Victoria and Albert Museum.*)

Transition Period: Gothic to Renaissance. XV. Century.

and Albert Museum a plaster cast of a carved wood altar stal. in the Abbey of St. Denis, France: the pilasters at the sides have the familiar Gothic pinnacles, while the panels are ornamented with arabesques, scrolls and an interior in the Renaissance style; the date of this is late in the fifteenth century.

English examples of this period are very scarce, and the buffet illustrated here is a favourable specimen of our national work late in the fifteenth century. While the crocketed enrichment in the brackets shows the Gothic taste, there are mouldings and some details in the upper part which mark the tendency to adopt classic ornament which came

OLD ENGLISH OAK BUFFET. FIFTEENTH CENTURY.
(*Drawn from the original in the possession of Seymour Lucas, Esq., R.A.*)

in at the end of the fifteenth century. It was probably made for one of our old abbeys, but Mr. Seymour Lucas, R.A., to whom it belongs and from whose drawing the illustration is made, says it was for a long time at Freenes Court, Sutton, the ancient seat of Sir Henry Linger.

The buffet on page 52 is an excellent example of the best fifteenth century French Gothic oak work, and the woodcut shows the arrangement of gold and silver plate on the white linen cloth with embroidered ends, in use at this time.

We have now arrived at a period in the history of furniture which is confused and difficult to arrange and classify. From the end of the fourteenth century to the Renaissance is a time of transition, and specimens may be easily mistaken as being of an earlier or later date than they really are. M. Jacquemart notices this "gap," though he fixes its duration from the thirteenth to the fifteenth century, and he quotes as an instance of the indecision which characterised this interval, that workers in furniture were described in different terms; the words coffer maker, carpenter and huchier (trunk-maker) frequently occurring to describe the same class of artisan.

It is only later that the word "menuisier," or joiner, appears, and we must enter upon the period of the Renaissance before we find the term "cabinet maker," and later still, after the end of the seventeenth century, we have such masters of their craft as Riesener described as "ébenistes," the word being derived from ebony, which with other eastern woods, came into use after the Dutch settlement in Ceylon. Jacquemart also notices the fact that as early as 1360 we have record of a specialist, "Jehan Petrot," as a "chessboard maker."

INTERIOR OF AN APOTHECARY'S SHOP.
Late XIV or Early XV. Century. Flemish
(*From an Old Painting.*)

CARVED OAK SEAT.

With movable Backrest, in front of Fireplace.

A TAPESTRIED ROOM IN A FRENCH CHATEAU.

With Oak Chests as Seats.

PERIOD: LATE XV. CENTURY. FRENCH.

INTERIOR OF A FRENCH CHATEAU SHOWING FURNITURE OF THE TIME.

PERIOD: LATE XIV. OR EARLY XV. CENTURY.

(From Viollet le Duc.)

LADIES OF THE COURT OF QUEEN ANNE OF BRITTANY.

(*From a Miniature in the Library of St. Petersburg.*)

Representing the Queen weeping on account of her Husband's absence during the
Italian War.

PERIOD: XV. CENTURY.

CHAPTER III

The Renaissance

IT IS impossible to write about the period of the Renaissance without grave misgivings as to one's ability to render justice to a period which has employed the pens of so many cultivated writers, and to which volumes innumerable have been devoted. Within the limited space of a single chapter all that can be attempted is a brief glance at the influence on design by which furniture and woodwork were affected. Perhaps the simplest way of understanding the changes which occurred, first in Italy, and subsequently in other countries, is to divide the chapter on this period into a series of short notes arranged in the order in which Italian influence would seem to have affected the designers and craftsmen of several European nations.

Towards the end of the fifteenth century there appears to have been an almost universal rage for classical literature, and we believe that some attempt was made to introduce Latin as a universal language; it is certain that Italian Art was adopted by nation after nation, until the whole of Western Europe was subject to this new and powerful influence.

As regards Architecture and Woodwork the Renaissance may very shortly be defined as the style of decoration which was engrafted on the Classical in Italy, and upon the Pointed style in other European countries.

As we look back upon the history of Art, assisted by the numerous examples in our Museums, one is struck by the want of novelty in the imagination of mankind. The glorious antique has always been our classic standard, and it seems only to have been a question of time as to when and how a return was made to the old designs of the Greek artists, then to wander from them awhile, and again to return when the world, weary of over-abundance of ornament, longed for the repose of simpler lines on the principles which governed the Athenian artists of old.

THE RENAISSANCE IN ITALY

Italy was the birthplace of the Renaissance. Leonardo da Vinci and Raffaelle may be said to have guided, or led the natural artistic instincts of their countrymen to discard the Byzantine-Gothic which, as M. Bonnaffé has said, was adopted by the Italians not as a permanent institution, but " faute de mieux " as a passing fashion.

It is difficult to say with any certainty when the first commencement of a new era actually takes place, but there is an incident related in Michael Bryan's biographical notice of Leonardo da Vinci which gives us an approximate date. Ludovico Sforza, Duke of Milan, had appointed this great master Director of Painting and Architecture in his academy in 1494, and says Bryan who obtained his information from contemporary writers, " Leonardo no sooner entered on his office, than he banished all the Gothic principles established by his predecessor, Michaelino, and introduced the beautiful simplicity and purity of the Grecian and Roman styles."

A few years after this date, Pope Julius II. commenced to build the present magnificent Church of St. Peter's, designed by Bramante d'Urbino, kinsman and friend of Raffaelle, to whose superintendence Pope Leo X. confided the work on the death of the architect in 1514. Michael Angelo had the charge committed to him some years after Raffaelle's death.

These dates give us a very fair idea of the time at which this important revolution in taste was taking place in Italy, from the end of the fifteenth to the commencement of the following century, and carved woodwork followed the new direction.

Leo X. was Pope in 1513. The period of peace which then ensued after war, which for so many decades had disturbed Italy, as France or

REPRODUCTION OF DECORATION BY RAFFAELLE

In the Loggie of the Vatican.

PERIOD: ITALIAN RENAISSANCE.

SALON OF M. EDMOND BONNAFFÉ.

DECORATED AND FURNISHED IN THE RENAISSANCE STYLE.

Germany had in turn striven to acquire her fertile soil, gave the princes and nobles leisure to rebuild and adorn their palaces; and the excavations which were then made, brought to light many of the Works of Art which had remained buried since the time when Rome was mistress of the world. Leo X. was a member of that remarkable and powerful family the Medicis, the very mention of which is to suggest the Renaissance, and under his patronage, and with the co-operation of the reigning dukes and princes of the different Italian states, artists were given encouragement and scope for the employment of their talents. Michael Angelo, Titian, Raffaelle Sanzio, Andrea del Sarto, Correggio and many other great artists were raising up monuments of everlasting fame; Palladio

CHAIR IN CARVED WALNUT.
Found in the house of Michael Angelo.

was re-building the palaces of Italy, which were then the wonder of the world; Benvenuto Cellini and Lorenzo Ghiberti were designing those marvellous *chefs d'œuvre* in gold, silver and bronze which are now so rare; and a host of illustrious artists were producing work which has made the sixteenth century famous for all time.

The circumstances of the Italian noble caused him to be very amenable to Art influence. Living chiefly out of doors, his climate rendered him less dependent on the comforts of small rooms to which more northern people were attached, and his ideas would naturally incline towards pomp and elegance, rather than to home life and utility. Instead of the warm chimney corner and the comfortable seat, he preferred furniture of a more palatial character for the adornment of the lofty and spacious saloons of his palace, and therefore we find the buffet elaborately carved with a free treatment of the classic antique and frequently "garnished" with the beautiful majolica of Urbino, of Pesaro and of Gubbio. The sarcophagus, or *cassone* of oak, or more commonly of chestnut or walnut, sometimes painted and gilded, sometimes carved with scrolls and figures; the cabinet designed with architectural outline, and fitted inside with steps and pillars like a temple; chairs which are wonderful to look upon as guardians of a stately doorway, but uninviting as seats; tables inlaid, gilded and carved, with slabs of marble or of Florentine mosaic work, but which from their height are

VENETIAN CENTRE TABLE, CARVED AND GILT.
(*In the Victoria and Albert Museum*).

as a rule impossible to use for any domestic purpose; mirrors with richly carved and gilded frames : these are all so many evidences of a style which is palatial rather than domestic, in design as in proportion.

The walls of these handsome saloons or galleries were hung with rich velvet of Genoese manufacture, or with stamped and gilt leather. A composition ornament was also applied to woodwork, and then gilded and painted, a kind of decoration termed "gesso work."

A rich effect was produced on the carved console tables, chairs, stools and frames intended for gilding, by the method employed by the Venetian and Florentine craftsmen, who laid gold leaf on a red preparation, and then burnished the chief portions. There are in

MARRIAGE COFFER IN CARVED WALNUT.

(Collection of Comte de Briges).

PERIOD: RENAISSANCE (XVI. CENTURY) VENETIAN.

the Victoria and Albert Museum several specimens of such work, and
now that time and wear have caused this red groundwork to show

PAIR OF ITALIAN CARVED BELLOWS, IN WALNUT WOOD.
(In the Victoria and Albert Museum).

through the faded gold, the harmony of colour is very satisfactory.
Other examples of fifteenth century Italian carving, such as the old

cassone fronts, are picked out with gold, the remainder of the work displaying the rich warm colour of the walnut or chestnut wood.

Of the smaller articles of furniture, the "bellows" and wall brackets of this period deserve mention; the carving of these is very carefully finished, and is frequently very elaborate. The illustration on page 66 is that of a pair of bellows in the Victoria and Albert collection. In the famous Magniac Collection, which was sold in July, 1892, a pair of very finely carved Venetian bellows of this description realised the high price of 450 guineas. There are two pairs very similar to be seen in the Wallace Collection.

Mirror frames of carved wood were not known in Italy until the beginning of the sixteenth century. In 1507 two glass makers of Murano invented a method of making mirrors of crystal glass and were granted a

TWO CARVED WALNUT WOOD FRAMES, ITALIAN. SEVENTEENTH CENTURY.
(In the Victoria and Albert Museum).

monopoly for twenty years: nearly fifty years later in 1564, mirror makers formed themselves into a distinct guild. The plates were not larger than four to five feet square, and were generally bevelled at the edges. The frames were carved with free Renaissance designs, soft woods being generally used, though the harder Italian walnut was also favoured. Venice and Florence were famous for these carved mirror frames and the two illustrations given are representative of late seventeenth century Florentine work.

The enrichment of woodwork by means of inlaying deserves mention. In the chapter on Ancient Furniture we have seen that ivory was used as an inlaid ornament as early as six centuries before Christ, but its revival and development in Europe probably commenced in Venice about the end of the thirteenth century, in copies of geometrical designs, let into ebony and brown walnut, and into a wood something like rosewood; parts of boxes and chests of these materials are still in existence. Mr. Maskell tells us in his Handbook on "Ivories," that probably owing to the difficulty of procuring ivory in Italy, bone of fine

CARVED ITALIAN MIRROR FRAME. SIXTEENTH CENTURY.
(In the Victoria and Albert Museum).

quality was frequently used in its place. All this class of work was known as "Tarsia," "Intarsia" or "Certosina," a word supposed to be derived from the name of the well-known religious community—the Carthusians—on account of the dexterity of those monks at this work.

The panels of the high screen or back to the stalls in "La Certosa di Pavia" (a Carthusian Monastery suppressed by Joseph II.) are famous examples of early intarsia. In an essay on the subject written by Sir T. G. Jackson, R.A., they are said to be the work of one Bartolommeo, an Istrian artist, and to date from 1486. The same writer mentions still more elaborate examples of pictorial "intarsia" in the choir stalls of Sta. Maria Maggiore in Bergamo.

Towards the end of the fourteenth century, makers of ornamental furniture began to copy marble mosaic work by making similar patterns

A Sixteenth Century "Coffre-fort."

of different woods, and subsequently this branch of industrial Art developed from such modest beginnings as the simple pattern of a star, or bandings of different kinds of wood in the panel of a door, to elaborate picture making, in which landscapes, views of churches, houses and picturesque ruins were copied, figures and animals being also introduced. This work was naturally facilitated and encouraged by increasing commerce between different nations, which rendered available a greater variety of woods. In some of the early Italian "intarsia" the decoration was cut into the surface of the panel, piece by piece. As artists became more skilful, veneers were applied, and the effect was heightened by burning with hot sand the parts requiring shading, the lines caused by the thickness of the sawcuts being filled in with black wood or stained glue, in order to define the design more clearly.

The "mounting" of articles of furniture with metal enrichments doubtless originated in the iron corner pieces and hinge plates which were used to strengthen the old chests, of which mention has been made, and as the artificers began to render their productions decorative as well as useful, what more natural progress than that the iron corners, bandings or fastenings should be of ornamental forged or engraved iron. In the sixteenth century metal workers reached a point of excellence which has never been surpassed, and those marvels of mountings in steel, iron and brass were produced in Italy and Germany which are far more important as works of Art than the plain and unpretending productions of the coffer maker, which are their *raison d'être*. The woodcut on page 69 represents a very good example of a "Coffre-fort" in the Victoria and Albert collection. The decoration is bitten in with acids so as to present the appearance of its being damascened, and the complicated lock, shown on the inside of the lid, is characteristic of those safeguards for valuable documents at a time when the modern burglar-proof safe had not been invented.

The illustration on the following page is from an example in the same Museum showing a different decoration, the oval plaques of figures and coats-of-arms being of carved ivory let into the surface of the coffer. This is an early specimen, and belongs as much to the period treated in the previous chapter as to that now under consideration.

"Pietra-dura," as an ornament, was first introduced into Italy during the sixteenth century and became a fashion. This was an inlay of highly polished rare marbles, agates, hard pebbles, lapis lazuli and other stones; ivory was also carved and applied as a bas-relief, as well as inlaid in arabesques of the most elaborate designs; tortoise-shell, brass, mother-of-pearl and other costly materials were introduced as enrichments in the decoration of cabinets and of caskets. Silver plaques embossed and engraved were pressed into the service as the native princes of Florence, Urbino, Ferrara and other independent cities vied with Rome, Venice and Naples in sumptuousness of ornament and lavishness of expense, until the inevitable period of decline supervened by reason of exaggeration of ornament and prodigality of decoration.

Edmond Bonnaffé, contrasting the latter period of Italian Renaissance with that of sixteenth century French woodwork, has pithily remarked: *" Chez eux, l'art du bois consiste à le dissimuler chez nous à le faire valoir."*

Mr. Ruskin, in his "Stones of Venice," alludes to this over-ornamentation of the later Renaissance in severe terms. After describing the progress of Art in Venice from Byzantine to Gothic, and from Gothic to Renaissance, he sub-divides the latter period into three classes :—1. Renaissance grafted on Byzantine. 2. Renaissance grafted

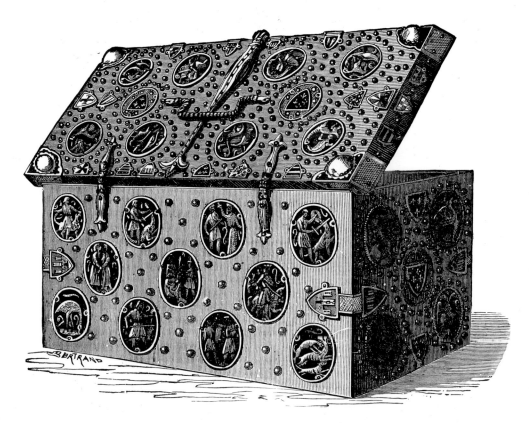

ITALIAN COFFER WITH MEDALLIONS OF IVORY. FIFTEENTH CENTURY.
(Victoria and Albert Museum).

on Gothic. 3. Renaissance grafted on Renaissance ; and this last the veteran Art critic calls " double darkness," one of his characteristic terms of condemnation which many of us cannot follow but the spirit of which we can appreciate.

Speaking generally of the character of ornament, we find that whereas in the furniture of the Middle Ages, the subjects for carving were taken from the lives of the saints or from metrical romance, the Renaissance carvers illustrated scenes from classical mythology and allegories, such as representations of the elements, seasons, months, the cardinal virtues or the battles scenes and triumphal processions of earlier times.

The outlines and general designs of the earlier Renaissance cabinets were apparently suggested by the old Roman triumphal arches and sarcophagi; afterwards these were modified and became varied, elegant and graceful, but latterly as the period of decline was marked, the

CARVED WALNUT WOOD ITALIAN CHAIRS. LATE SIXTEENTH CENTURY.
(From Drawings of the Originals in the Victoria and Albert Museum).

outlines as shown in the two chairs illustrated on this page, became confused and dissipated by over-decoration.

The illustrations given of specimens of furniture of Italian Renaissance render lengthy descriptions unnecessary. So far as it has been possible to do so, a selection has been made to represent the different classes of

EBONY CABINET.

With marble mosaics, and bronze gilt ornaments. Florentine work.

PERIOD: XVII. CENTURY.

work, and as there are in the Victoria and Albert Museum numerous examples of *cassone* fronts, panels, chairs and cabinets which can be examined, it is easy to form an idea of the decorative woodwork made in Italy during the period that we had been considering.

VENETIAN STATE CHAIR.
Carved and Gilt Frame, Upholstered with Embroidered Velvet. Date about 1670.
(*In the possession of H.M. the King at Windsor Castle*).

THE RENAISSANCE IN FRANCE

From Italy the great revival of industrial Art travelled to France. Charles VIII., who for two years had held Naples (1494-96), brought among other artists from Italy, Bernadino de Brescia and Domenico de Cortona, and Art which at this time was in a feeble languishing state in France, began to revive. François I. employed an Italian architect to build the Chateau of Fontainebleau, which had hitherto been but an old-fashioned hunting-box in the middle of the forest, and Leonardo da Vinci and Andrea del Sarto came from Florence to decorate the interior. Guilio Romano, who had assisted Raffaelle to paint the *loggie* of the Vatican, exercised an influence in France, which was transmitted by his pupils for generations. The marriage of Henri II. with Catherine de Medicis increased the influence of Italian Art, and the subsequent union of Marie de Medicis with Henri Quatre continued that influence. Diane de Poictiers, mistress of Henri II., was the patroness of artists and Fontainebleau has been well said to "reflect the glories of gay and splendour-loving kings, from François Premier to Henri Quatre."

Besides Fontainebleau, François I. built the Chateau of Chambord, that of Chenonceaux on the Loire, the Chateau de Madrid with others, and commenced the Louvre.

Following their King's example, the more wealthy of his subjects rebuilt or altered their chateaux and hotels, decorated them in the Italian style, and furnished them with cabinets, chairs, coffers, armoires, tables and various other articles, designed after the Italian models.

The character of the woodwork naturally accompanied the design of the building. Fireplaces, which until the end of the fifteenth century had been of stone, were now made of oak, richly carved and ornamented with the armorial bearings of the "*seigneur.*" The *Prie dieu* chair, which Viollet le Duc tells us came into use in the fifteenth century, was now made larger and more ornate, in some cases becoming what might almost be termed a small oratory, the back being carved in the form of an altar, and the utmost care was lavished on the work. It must be remembered that in France, until the end of the fifteenth century, there were no benches or seats in the churches, and therefore prayers were said by the aristocracy in the private chapel of the chateau, and by the middle classes in the chief room of the house.

The large high-backed chair of the sixteenth century "*chaire à haut dossier,*" the arm chair "*chaire à bras,*" "*chaire tournante,*" for domestic use, are all of this time, and some illustrations will show the highly finished carved work of Renaissance style which prevailed.

Besides the "*chaire,*" which was reserved for the "*seigneur,*" there were smaller and more convenient stools, the ⅄ form supports of which were also carved.

Cabinets were made with an upper and lower part; sometimes the latter was in the form of a stand with caryatides figures like the famous cabinet in the Chateau Fontainebleau, a vignette of which forms the initial letter of this chapter; and sometimes it was enclosed by doors generally decorated with carving. The upper part had richly carved panels, which when opened disclosed drawers with fronts minutely carved.

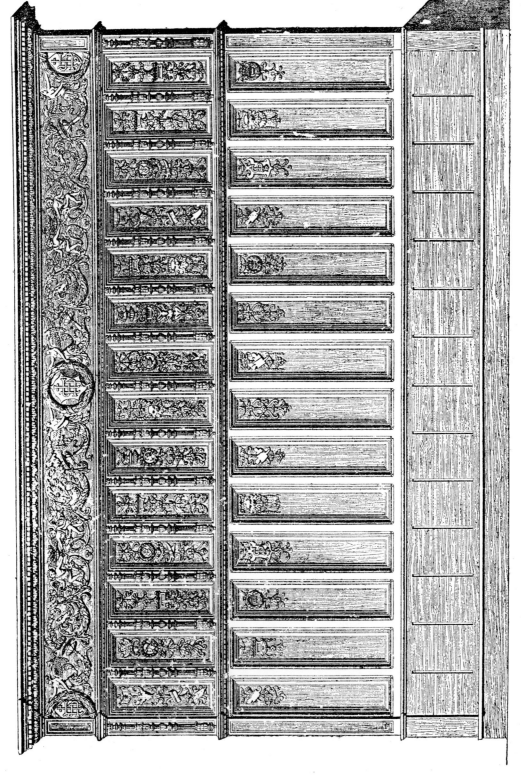

ORNAMENTAL PANELLING IN ST. VINCENT'S CHURCH, ROUEN.

PERIOD: EARLY FRENCH RENAISSANCE. TEMP. FRANÇOIS I.

M. Edmond Bonnaffé, in his work on the sixteenth century furniture of France, gives no less than 120 illustrations of "*tables, coffres, armoires, dressoirs, sieges et bancs,*" manufactured at Orleans, Anjou, Maine, Touraine, Le Berri, Lorraine, Burgundy, Lyons, Provence, Auvergne, Languedoc and other towns and districts, besides the Capital, which excelled in the reputation of her "menuisiers," certain articles of furniture being particularised in old documents as "*fait a Paris.*"

CARVED OAK PANEL, DATED 1577.
FRENCH RENAISSANCE.

He also mentions that Francis I. preferred to employ native workmen, and that the Italians were retained only to furnish the designs and lead the new style ; and in giving the names of the most noted French cabinet makers and carvers of this time, he adds that Jacques Lardant and Michel Bourdin received no less than 15,700 livres for a number of "*buffets de salles,*" "*tables garnies de leur trèteaux,*" "*chandeliers de bois*" and other articles.

The bedstead, of which there is given an illustration on page 79, is a good representation of French Renaissance. It formed part of the contents of the Chateau of Pau, and belonged to Jeanne d'Albret, mother of Henri Quatre, who was born at Pau in 1553. The bedstead is of oak, and by time has acquired a rich warm tint, the details of the carving remaining sharp and clear. On the lower cornice moulding, the date 1562 is carved.

This like other furniture and contents of palaces in France, forms part of the State or National Collection, of which there are excellent illustrations and descriptions in M. Williamson's "Mobilier National," a valuable contribution to the literature of this subject which should be consulted.

FAC SIMILES OF ENGRAVINGS ON WOOD.
By J. Amman, in the sixteenth century, showing interiors of Workshops of the period.

Another example of four-post bedsteads of French sixteenth century work is the one in the Cluny Museum, which is probably some years later than the one at Pau, and in the carved members of the two lower posts has more resemblance to our English Elizabethan work.

An important collection of carved furniture of French Renaissance was exhibited in *l'exposition rétrospective de Lyons*, held in that city in 1877, and M. J. B. Giraud, *conservateur* of the Archæological Museums of Lyons, has reproduced some fifty of the more important specimens in his valuable work,* published in 1880, giving the name of the lender of each example and other details. The "Spitzer" Collection, sold in Paris in

* "Meubles en bois sculpté ayant figuré à l'exposition rétrospective de Lyons en 1877," par J. B. Giraud.

CARVED OAK BEDSTEAD OF JEANNE D'ALBRET.

From the Chateau of Pau. (Collection " Mobilier National.")

PERIOD: FRENCH RENAISSANCE (Date 1562).

FRENCH CARVED OAK CABINET.

In the Musée du Louvre. (Collection Sauvageot).

PERIOD: EARLY XVI. CENTURY.

(Reproduced by permission of Messrs. Boussod Valadon et Cie.)

ARMOIRE OF WALNUT WOOD.
In Two Sections.
Carvings in relief after Jean Goujon; the panels represent Hercules and Antaeus and Mars and Venus.
French: Late Renaissance.   Second Half of Sixteenth Century.   (Wallace Collection.)

1893, contained several fine examples of French Renaissance oak furniture which realised high prices.

The fine armoire in the Wallace Collection, which is illustrated on the preceding page, is a good example of late French Renaissance.

Hardwick Hall, the historic mansion built and furnished by Elizabeth Countess of Shrewsbury, the famous Bess of Hardwick, during the reign of Elizabeth, contains at least three very remarkable specimens of French furniture of this period. These are generally described to the visitor as of English manufacture, but there can be no doubt of their French origin. The famous cabinet or "side-board" as it is generally termed in the Museum catalogues is certainly a representative example of the later French Renaissance and it is unfortunate that owing to indifferent light the photograph obtained does not permit of a more satisfactory illustration.

The second cabinet of architecturally composed and finely carved design, which stands in the library, is also of walnut wood and deserves the most careful attention of the student of this period of French carving. The spandrels and outside panels are finely inlaid with landscapes and floral ornament. The third most noteworthy specimen of this period is the "drawing" table supported by four mythical sea horses, which stands in the same apartment.

Towards the latter part of the reign of Henri IV. the style of decorative Art in France became debased and inconsistent. Construction and ornamentation were guided by no principle, but followed the caprice of the individual. Meaningless pilasters, entablatures and contorted cornices replaced the simpler outline and subordinate enrichment of the time of Henri II., and until the great revival of taste under the "*grand monarque*," there was in France a period of richly ornamented but ill-designed decorative furniture. An example of this can be seen at South Kensington in a plaster cast of a large chimney-piece from the Chateau of the Seigneur de Villeroy near Menecy, by German Pillon who died in 1590. In this the failings mentioned above will be readily recognised and also in another example, namely that of a carved oak door from the Church of St. Maclou Rouen by Jean Goujon, in which the work is very fine but somewhat overdone with enrichment.

During the "Louis Treize" period, chairs became more comfortable than those of an earlier time. The word "chaise," as a diminutive of "chaire," found its way into the French vocabulary to denote the less thronelike seat which was in more ordinary use, and instead of being at this period entirely carved, it was upholstered in velvet, tapestry or needlework ; the frame was covered, and only the legs and arms were visible and slightly carved. In the illustration on page 85, the King and his courtiers are seated on chairs such as have been described. Marqueterie was more common; large armoires, chests of drawers and knee-hole writing tables were covered with an inlay of vases of flowers and birds of a brownish wood, with enrichments of bone and ivory, inserted in a black ground of stained wood, very much like the Dutch inlaid furniture of some years later, but with less colour in the various veneers than is

CABINET OF CARVED WALNUT WOOD.
FRENCH: LATE RENAISSANCE.   TEMP. HENRI IV.
(*In the Library of Hardwick Hall.*)

found in the Dutch work. Mirrors became larger, the decoration of rooms had ornamental friezes with lower portions of the walls panelled, and the bedrooms of ladies of position began to be more luxuriously furnished.

Cardinal Richelieu was the King's chief Minister of State and spent vast sums rebuilding the Palais Royal and the Chateau Rueil; his lavish expenditure in the collection of Art treasures is said to have caused the jealousy of his Royal Master, to appease which he presented him with a considerable portion of his collection.

CENTRE-PIECE OF SIDEBOARD.

Of Walnut, elaborately carved, and enriched with plaques of coloured marble.
FRENCH: LATE RENAISSANCE. TEMP. HENRI IV.
(*In the Presence Chamber of Hardwick Hall.*)

Cabinets of this period were designed upon architectural lines, ebony ornamented with columns and slabs of *lapis-lazuli*, jasper and agate, the columns mounted with gilt bronze caps and bases, and not infrequently having as decoration statuettes of allegorical figures also in gilt bronze. There is a cabinet in the Louvre which has the arms of France supported by angels, with a gilt bronze statue of the King, and another which has a gilt bronze statue of Queen Marie Thérèse figuring as Pallas, with *lapis-lazuli* columns and rich mounts. The work of André Charles Boulle which will be considered in Chapter VI. was the continuation and development of this grand and stately kind of furniture.

LOUIS XIII. AND HIS COURT IN A HALL WITNESSING A PLAY.
(From a Miniature dated 1643.)

During this reign there was a great advance in the manufacture of rich textiles for covering the more expensive furniture, and of silks, velvets, brocades, elaborate fringes and gimps for upholstery. The console table appears in inventories for the first time, and the *gueridon* a small round table supported on a column ending in a tripod foot, finds a place in the furniture of the smaller rooms of the period.

It is somewhat singular that while Normandy very quickly adopted the new designs in her buildings and furniture, and Rouen carvers and joiners became famous for their work, the neighbouring province Brittany was conservative of her earlier designs. The sturdy Breton has through all changes of style preserved much of the rustic quaintness of his furniture, and when some years ago the writer was stranded in a sailing trip up the Rance, owing to the shallow state of the river, and had an opportunity of visiting some of the farm-houses in the country district a few miles from Dinan, there were still to be seen many examples of this quaint rustic furniture. Curious beds, consisting of shelves for parents and children, form a cupboard in the wall and are shut in during the day by a pair of lattice doors of Moorish design, with the wheel pattern and spindle perforations. These, with the armoire of similar design, and the "huche" or chest with relief carving of a pattern part Moorish part Byzantine, used as a step to mount to the bed and also as a table, are still the *garniture* of a good farm-house in Brittany.

The earliest date of this quaint furniture is about the middle of the fifteenth century, and has been handed down from father to son by the more well-to-do farmers. The manufacture of armoires, cupboards, tables and doors, is still carried on near St. Malo, where some of the old specimens may still be found.

THE RENAISSANCE IN THE NETHERLANDS

In the Netherlands the reigning princes of the great House of Burgundy had prepared the ground for the Renaissance, and by the marriage of Mary of Burgundy with the Archduke Maximilian, the countries which then were called Flanders and Holland passed under Austrian rule. This influence was continued by the taste and liberality of Margaret of Austria, who being appointed "Governor" of the Low Countries in 1507, seems to have introduced Italian artists and to have encouraged native craftsmen. We are told that Corneille Floris introduced Italian ornamentation and grotesque borders; that Pierre Coech architect and painter adopted and popularised the designs of Vitruvius and Serlio. Wood carvers multiplied and embellished churches and palaces, houses of Burgomasters, Town Halls and residences of wealthy citizens.

Oak, at first almost the only wood used, became monotonous, and as a relief, ebony and other rare woods, introduced by the increasing commerce with the Indies, were made available for the embellishments of furniture and woodwork of this time.

One of the most famous examples of rich wood carving is the well-known hall and chimney-piece at Bruges with its group of cupidons and armorial bearings, amongst an abundance of floral detail. This over-ornate *chef d'œuvre* was designed by Lancelot Blondel and Guyot de Beauregrant, and its carving was the combined work of three craftsmen celebrated in their day, Herman Glosencamp, André Rash and Roger de Smet. There is in the Victoria and Albert Museum a full-sized plaster cast of this gigantic chimney-piece, the lower part being coloured black to indicate the marble of which it was composed, with panels of alabaster carved in relief, while the whole of the upper portion of the richly carved ceiling of the room is of oak. This chimney-piece is noteworthy, not only artistically but historically, as being a monument in its way, in celebration of the victory gained by Charles V. over Francis I. of France, in 1525,

An Ebony Armoire, Richly Carved. Flemish Renaissance.
(In the Victoria and Albert Museum.)

at Pavia, the victorious sovereign being at this time not only Emperor of Germany, but also enjoying amongst other titles those of Duke of Burgundy, Count of Flanders, King of Spain and the Indies, etc., etc. The large statues of the Emperor, of Ferdinand and Isabella, with some thirty-seven heraldic shields of the different royal families with which the conqueror claimed connection, are prominent features in the intricate and elaborate design.

There is in the same part of the Museum a cast of the oak door of the Council Chamber of the Hotel de Ville at Oudenarde, of a much less elaborate character. Plain mullions divide sixteen panels carved in the orthodox Renaissance style, with cupids bearing tablets, from which are depending floral scrolls, and at the sides the supports are columns, with the lower parts carved and standing on square pedestals. The date of this work is 1534, somewhat later than the Bruges carving, and is a representative specimen of the Flemish work of this period.

The clever Flemish artist so thoroughly copied the models of his different masters that it has become exceedingly difficult to speak positively as to the identity of much of the woodwork, and to distinguish it from German, English or Italian, although as regards the latter we have seen that walnut wood was employed very generally, whereas in Flanders oak was nearly always used for figure work.

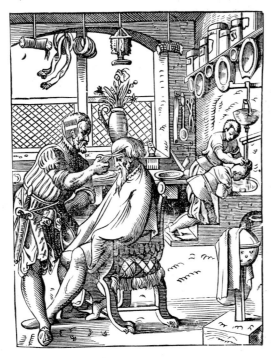
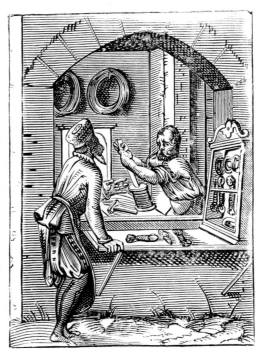

A BARBER'S SHOP.   A FLEMISH WORKSHOP.
Showing Furniture of the time.
(From Wood Engravings by J. Amman.   SIXTEENTH CENTURY.)

After the period of the purer forms of the first Renaissance, the best time for carved woodwork and decorative furniture in the Netherlands was probably the seventeenth century, when the Flemish designers and craftsmen had ceased to copy the Italian patterns, and had established the style which we recognise as "Flemish Renaissance."

Lucas Faydherde architect and sculptor (1617-1694)—whose boxwood group of the death of John the Baptist is in the Victoria and Albert Museum--both the Verbruggens, and Albert Bruhl, who carved the choir work of St. Giorgio Maggiore in Venice, are amongst the most celebrated Flemish wood carvers of this time. Vriedman de Vriesse and Crispin de Passe, although they worked in France, belong to Flanders and to the century. Some of the most famous painters—Frans Hals, Jordaens, Rembrandt, Metsu, Van Mieris—all belong to this time, and in some of the fine interiors represented by these Old Masters, in which embroidered curtains and rich coverings relieve the sombre colours of the dark carved oak furniture, there is a richness of effect which the artist could scarcely have imagined, but which he must have observed in the houses of the rich burghers of prosperous Flanders.

There is a kind of cabinet produced in Holland about this period which deserves notice. It is generally made of ebony with two outer doors, opening to disclose an interior fitted with several small doors and sometimes a recess in the centre; the fronts of these doors being decorated with well-executed paintings of figure subjects or landscapes. The lower part or stand has spirally turned legs connected by a stretcher. Occasionally we find cabinets of a similar character but without the two enclosing doors, the front of the cabinet being divided into several panels which are the drawer fronts, and these are also well painted, sometimes on copper, by skilful Dutch seventeenth century artists.

Lord De L'Isle and Dudley possesses a very fine cabinet of this description at Penshurst, with a carved and gilt stand in the Louis XIV. style. The date of this cabinet is about 1690.

In the chapter on Jacobean furniture, we shall see the influence and assistance which England gained from Flemish wood workers; and the similarity of the treatment in both countries will be noticed in some of the Victoria and Albert Museum specimens of English marqueterie, made at the end of the seventeenth century. The figure work in Holland has always been of high order, and although as the seventeenth century advanced this became less refined, the proportions have always been well preserved, and the attitudes of the figures free and unconstrained.

A very characteristic article of seventeenth century Dutch furniture is the large and massive wardrobe, with the doors handsomely carved, not infrequently having three columns, one in the centre and one at each side, generally forming part of the doors, which are also enriched with square panels, carved in the centre and finished with mouldings. There are specimens in the Victoria and Albert Museum of these, and also of some of earlier Flemish work when the Renaissance was purer in style and, as has been observed, of less national character.

Two full-page illustrations are good examples of these respective styles. In general design and in some of the carved ornament they

CARVED OAK ARMOIRE.

SIMILAR TO OUR ENGLISH ELIZABETHAN STYLE.

FLEMISH RENAISSANCE. LATE SIXTEENTH OR EARLY SEVENTEENTH CENTURY.

(Victoria and Albert Museum.)

CARVED OAK ARMOIRE.

ORNATE STYLE OF LATE FLEMISH RENAISSANCE.

LATE SEVENTEENTH CENTURY.   (*Victoria and Albert Museum.*)

resemble our Elizabethan oak furniture, but a careful observation of details and comparison with authenticated examples of English sixteenth or early seventeenth century work should enable a correct attribution to be made.

The marqueterie of this period is extremely rich, the designs are less severe, but the colouring of the woods is varied, and the effect is heightened by the addition of small pieces of mother-of-pearl and ivory. Later, this marqueterie became florid, badly finished and the colouring of the veneers crude and gaudy. Old pieces of plain mahogany furniture were decorated with a thin layer of highly coloured veneering, a meretricious ornamentation altogether lacking refinement.

In Chapter IV., on Jacobean furniture, there are some notes on the importation into England of lacquered furniture from Holland, and this chapter on the Renaissance in Holland should not omit some mention of this type of decorative woodwork. The Dutch East India Company existed long before ours, and their trade with the East was very extensive. Lacquered screens, cabinets and chests were made in China and Japan for the Dutch market and copied in Holland.

There is a peculiarity and character about some of the furniture of North Holland, in the towns of Alkmaar, Hoorn and others in this district, which is worth noticing. The treatment has always been more primitive and quaint than in the Flemish cities to which allusion has been made—and it was here that the old farm-houses of the Nord-Hollander were furnished with the rush-bottomed chairs painted green, with three-legged tables, and dower chests painted in flowers and figures of a rude description; the colouring being chiefly green and bright red, a combination which is extremely effective.

A FLEMISH CITIZEN AT MEALS.
(From a Sixteenth Century MS.)

THE RENAISSANCE IN SPAIN

We have seen that Spain, as well as Germany and the Low Countries, was under the rule of the Emperor Charles V., and therefore it is unnecessary to look further for the sources of influence which carried the wave of Renaissance to the Spanish carvers and cabinet makers.

The Low Countries from the time of the Van Eycks had been famous for their school of painting, for their tapestry and for their woodwork.

French artists also found employment in Spain, and the older Gothic became superseded as in other countries. Berruguete, a Spaniard, who

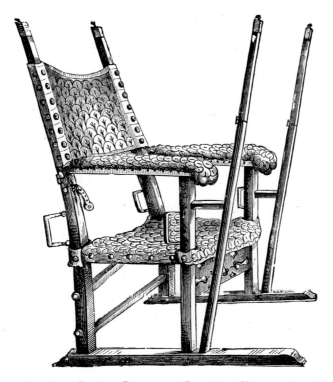

SEDAN CHAIR OF CHARLES V.

Probably made in the Netherlands. Arranged with movable back and uprights to form a canopy when desired.

(*In the Royal Armoury, Madrid.*)

had studied in the atelier of Michael Angelo, returned to his own country with the new influence strong upon him, and the vast wealth and resources of Spain at this period of her history enabled her nobles to indulge their tastes in cabinets richly ornamented with repoussé plaques of silver, and later of tortoise-shell, of ebony and of scarce woods from her Indian possessions, though in a more general way chestnut was still a favourite medium.

CHAIR OF WALNUT OR CHESTNUT WOOD.

Covered in Leather, with embossed pattern. Spanish. (Collection of Baron de Vallière.)

PERIOD: EARLY XVII. CENTURY.

WOODEN COFFER.

With wrought iron mounts and falling flap, on carved stand. Spanish.
(Collection of M. Monbrison.)

Period: XVII. Century.

In many Spanish cabinets the influence of Moorish Art is very
dominant ; these have generally a plain exterior, the front is hinged as
a fall-down flap, and discloses a decorative effect which reminds one
of some of the Alhambra work—quaint arches inlaid with ivory, of a
somewhat bizarre colouring of blue and vermilion—altogether a rather
barbarous but rich and effective treatment.

Contemporary with decorative woodwork of Moorish design there was
also a great deal of carving and of furniture made after designs brought
from Italy and the North of Europe; and Mr. J. H. Pollen, quoting
a trustworthy Spanish writer, Señor J. F. Riaño, says:—" The brilliant
epoch of sculpture (in wood) belongs to the sixteenth century, and was
due to the great impulse it received from the works of Berruguete and
Felipe de Borgoñu. The former was the chief promoter of the Italian
style, and the choir of the Cathedral of Toledo, where he did so much
work, is the finest specimen of the kind in Spain. Toledo, Seville and
Valladolid were at the time great productive and artistic centres."

The same writer, after discussing the characteristic Spanish cabinets
decorated outside with fine ironwork and inside with columns of bone
painted and gilt, which were called " Vargueños," says:—" The other
cabinets or escritoires belonging to that period (sixteenth century) were to
a large extent imported from Germany and Italy, while others were
made in Spain in imitation of these, and as the copies were very similar
it is difficult to classify them. . . . .

" Besides these inlaid cabinets, others must have been made in the
sixteenth century, inlaid with silver. An Edict was issued in 1594,
prohibiting with the utmost rigour, the making and selling of this kind
of merchandise, in order not to increase the scarcity of silver." The
Edict says that " no cabinets, desks, coffers, braziers, shoes, tables
or other articles decorated with stamped, raised, carved or plain silver
should be manufactured."

Examples of native woodwork are to be seen in many old buildings
of Spanish cities, and the change from Gothic to Renaissance which we
have noticed in other countries can be recognised.

Although not strictly within the period treated of in this chapter,
it is convenient to observe that much later, in the seventeenth and
eighteenth centuries, one finds the Spanish cabinet maker ornamenting
his productions with an inlay of ivory let into tortoise-shell, representing
episodes in the history of *Don Quichotte,* and scenes from the national
pastime of bull-fighting. These cabinets generally have simple rectangular
outlines with numerous drawers, the fronts of which are decorated in
the manner described, and when the stands are original they are formed
of turned legs of ebony or stained wood.

To the seventeenth century also belonged the high-backed Spanish and Portuguese chairs, of dark brown leather, stamped with numerous figures, birds and floral scrolls, studded with brass nails and ornaments, while the legs and arms are alone visible as woodwork. They are made of chestnut, with some leafwork or scroll carving. There is a good woodcut of one of these chairs.

Until Baron Davillier wrote his work on Spanish Art, very little was known of the various peculiarities by which we can now distinguish examples of woodwork and furniture of that country from many Italian or Flemish contemporary productions. Some of the Museum specimens will assist the reader to mark these characteristics, and it may be observed generally that in the treatment of figure subjects in the carved work, the attitudes are somewhat strained and as has been noted, the outlines of the cabinets are without any special feature. Besides the Spanish chestnut (noyer), which is singularly lustrous and was much used, one also finds cedar, cypress wood and pine.

In the Chapel of St. Bruno, attached to the Carthusian convent at Granada, the doors and interior fittings are excellent examples of inlaid Spanish work of the seventeenth century ; the monks of this order at a somewhat earlier date are said to have produced the " tarsia," or inlaid work, to which allusion has already been made. Copies of Chippendale furniture are also to be found in Spain, made no doubt in imitation of articles imported from England in the eighteenth century.

THE RENAISSANCE IN GERMANY

German Renaissance may be said to have made its début under Albrecht Dürer. There was already in many of the German cities a disposition to copy Flemish artists, but under Dürer's influence this new departure became developed in a high degree, and, as the sixteenth century advanced the Gothic designs of an earlier period were abandoned in favour of the more free treatment of figure ornament, scrolls, enriched panels and mouldings, which mark the new era in all Art work.

Many remarkable specimens of German carving are to be met with in Augsburg, Aschaffenburg, Berlin, Cologne, Dresden, Gotha, Munich, Mannheim, Nuremberg, Ulm, Regensburg and other old German towns.

Although made of steel, the celebrated chair at Longford Castle in Wiltshire is worthy of some notice as a remarkable specimen of German Renaissance. It is fully described in Richardson's " Studies from Old English Mansions." It was the work of Thomas Rukers, and was presented by the city of Augsburg to the Emperor of Germany in 1577.

THE STEEL CHAIR.

At Longford Castle, Wiltshire.

The city arms are at the back, and also the bust of the Emperor. The other minute and carefully finished decorative subjects represent various events in history; a triumphal procession of Cæsar, the Prophet Daniel explaining his dream, the landing of Æneas and other historical and mythical events. The Emperor Rudolph placed the chair in the City of Prague, Gustavus Adolphus plundered the city and removed it to Sweden, whence it was brought by Mr. Gustavus Brander more than a hundred years ago, and sold by him to Lord Radnor.

As is the case with Flemish wood-carving, it is often difficult to identify German work, but its chief characteristics may be described as an exuberant realism and a fondness for minute detail. M. Bonnaffé has described this work in a telling phrase: "*l'ensemble est tourmenté, laborieux, touffu tumultueux.*"

There is a remarkable example of rather late German Renaissance oak carving in the private chapel of S. Saviour's Hospital, in Osnaburg Street, Regent's Park, London. The choir stalls, some thirty-one in number, and the massive doorway, formed part of a Carthusian monastery at Buxheim Bavaria, which was sold and brought to London after the monastery had

GERMAN CARVED OAK BUFFET. SEVENTEENTH CENTURY.
(From a Drawing by Prof. Heideloff.

been secularised and had passed into the possession of the territorial landlords, the Bassenheim family. At first intended to ornament one of the Colleges at Oxford, it was afterwards re-sold and purchased by the author and fitted to the interior of S. Saviour's, and, so far as the proportions of the chapel would admit of such an arrangement, the relative positions of the different parts are maintained. The figures of the twelve apostles—of David, Eleazer, Moses, Aaron and of the eighteen saints at the back of the choir stalls, are skilfully carved and the whole must have been a harmonious and well-considered arrangement of ornament. The work, executed by the monks themselves, is said to have been commenced in 1600, and to have been completed in 1651, and though a little later than, according to some authorities the best time of the Renaissance, is so good a representation of German work of this period that it will well repay an examination. This work of reconstruction was carried out in 1885-6 when the chapel was attached to a private hospital for the treatment of cancer by a special process, and was controlled by a lady who was the head of an Anglican religious order. Since that time the property has changed hands.

THE RENAISSANCE IN DENMARK

The work of the Danish cabinet maker and carver has received scant notice by writers on Continental woodwork, and yet some distinctive features deserve a few words of description. Closely akin to German work, it is generally attributed to that origin, and may be said to have changed from the Gothic of the fifteenth century to the Renaissance which came about in the last decade or two of that century and continued into the sixteenth century and later. Like other countries in which we have described this change, Denmark received its inspiration from Italy but it arrived through the medium of Germany and Holland.

In an article written by George Brochner for " The Connoisseur " of February, 1921, there are some descriptions and illustrations of Danish cabinets with authenticated dates running from 1500-1530 to about 1650, which show the conquest of this Renaissance influence over the Gothic, and the two illustrations which, by the courtesy of the publishers of " The Connoisseur," are given with these notes, will indicate this change. The cabinet of Renaissance outline and fluted pilasters and supports has three panels of an earlier date, the coats-of-arms being those of Otto Krumpen and his wife. He was a Danish statesman, the uncle of Ellen Rostrup who was married in 1568, and this is probably the date of the panels which show some signs of late Gothic treatment. The

OAK CABINET OF DANISH WORK.

Date about 1600.

With panels made some thirty years earlier.

(From " The Connoisseur," by permission.)

OAK CHEST OF DANISH WORK.

DATE ABOUT 1650.

With four panels representing Faith, Hope, Love and Peace and Native Inscription.

(From "The Connoisseur," by permission.)

second illustration is that of a chest, a great many of which were made in Denmark in the sixteenth and seventeenth centuries. The subdivision of the design of this chest-front into richly carved panels, in each of which there is a figure of one of the Virtues, separated by pilasters handsomely carved with terminal figures, is characteristic of the Danish work of this time (seventeenth century), and the lettering which is so often seen on pieces of this character helps us materially to classify the work as Danish. In this instance the inscriptions may be translated as indicating Faith, Hope, Love and Peace.

Inscriptions in similar lettering, which are invariably in plain Roman characters, $1\frac{1}{4}$ inches high, carved in high relief, will be observed beneath the cornice of the cabinet illustrated.

When Biblical scenes, which are the most frequently depicted, are not favoured, we find armorial bearings of old Danish families or conventional ornaments with a head in a medallion as centre of the design: linenfold panels are also seen in Danish late fifteenth and early sixteenth century work. The wrought iron hinges, handles and lock plates which are mounted on Danish cabinets and chests are often of German workmanship and it is known that the German smiths exported to foreign countries great quantities of these wrought iron mounts. Herr Brochner considers that the best time of Danish cabinet work was during the latter part of the reign of Frederick II., and the earlier part of that of Christian IV., a time of peace and prosperity in Denmark, when the Arts flourished and noblemen spent money on the decoration and more sumptuous furnishings of their castles. He says that Holland played an important part in this development by sending eminent craftsmen to Denmark as to other foreign Courts and countries, and that the native cabinet makers and carvers not only copied the work of their foreign masters but instilled into their designs and workmanship an individuality which was sometimes an improvement and at others a naïve and imperfect rendering. As architectural principles made themselves felt the designs of furniture improved. The carved work described above was generally in oak, finished a rather dark colour with the old-fashioned wax polish. Gold and colour was also applied to Danish carving, particularly in some of the Church decorations.

THE RENAISSANCE IN ENGLAND

England under Henry the Eighth was peaceful and prosperous, and the King was ambitious to outvie his French contemporary, François I., in the sumptuousness of his palaces. John of Padua, Holbein, Havernius of Cleves and other artists, were induced to come to England and to introduce the new style. It however was of slow growth, and we have in the mixture of Gothic, Italian and Flemish ornament, the style which is known as "Tudor."

It has been well said that "Feudalism was ruined by gunpowder." The old-fashioned feudal castle was certainly no longer proof against cannon, and with the new order of things, threatening walls and serried battlements gave way as if by magic to the pomp and grace of the Italian mansion. High-roofed gables, rows of windows and glittering oriels looking down on terraced gardens, with vases and fountains, mark the new epoch.

CARVED OAK CHEST IN THE STYLE OF HOLBEIN.

The joiner's work plays a very important part in the interior decoration of the castles and country seats of this time, and the roofs were magnificently timbered with native oak, which was available in longer lengths than that of foreign growth. The Great Hall in Hampton Court Palace, which was built by Cardinal Wolsey and presented to the King, the halls of Oxford and many public buildings which remain to us, are examples of fine woodwork in the roofs. Oak panelling was largely used to line the walls of the great halls, the "linen scroll pattern" being a favourite form of ornament. This term describes a panel carved to represent a napkin folded in close convolutions, and appears to have been adopted from German work; specimens of this can be seen at Hampton Court and in old churches decorated in the early part of the sixteenth century. There is also some fine panelling of this date in King's College, Cambridge.

In this class of work, which accompanied the style known in architecture as the "Perpendicular," some of the finest specimens of ornamented interiors are to be found, that of the roof and choir stalls in the beautiful Chapel of Henry VII. in Westminster Abbey being world famous. The

CHAIR SAID TO HAVE BELONGED TO ANNA BOLEYN, HEVER CASTLE.
(From the Collection of Mr. Godwin, F.S.A.)

carved enrichments of the under parts of the seats, or "misericords," are remarkably minute, the subjects apparently being taken from old German engravings. This work was done in England before architecture and wood carving had altogether flung aside their Gothic trammels. Some of the best examples of these carved "misericords" are in Exeter Cathedral.

There are in the British Museum some interesting records of contracts made in the ninth year of Henry VIII.'s reign for "joyner's" work at

Hengrave, in which the making of "livery" or service cupboards is specified.

> "Ye cobards they be made ye facyon of livery y^t is wthout
> doors."

These were fitted up by the ordinary house carpenters, and consisted of three stages or shelves standing on four turned legs, with a drawer for table linen. They were at this period not enclosed, but the mugs or drinking vessels were hung on hooks, and were taken down and replaced after use; a ewer and basin was also part of the complement of a livery cupboard for cleansing these cups. In Harrison's description of England in the latter part of the sixteenth century the custom is thus described:

> "Each one as necessitie urgeth, calleth for a cup of such drinke as him liketh, so when he hath tasted it, he delivereth the cup again to some one of the standers by, who maketh it clean by pouring out the drinke that remaineth, restoreth it to the cupboard from whence he fetched the same."

It must be borne in mind, in considering the furniture of the earlier part of the sixteenth century, that the religious persecutions of the time, together with the general break up of the feudal system, had gradually brought about the disuse of the old custom of the master of the house taking his meals in the large hall or "houseplace," together with his retainers and dependents; and a small room leading from the great hall was fitted up with a "dressoir" or "service cupboard," for the drinking vessels in the manner just described, with a bedstead and a chair, some benches and the board on trestles, which formed the table of the period. This room called a "parler" or "privee parloir," was the part of the house where the family enjoyed domestic life, and it is a singular fact that the Clerics of the time, and also the Court party, saw in this tendency towards private life so grave an objection that in 1526 this change in fashion was the subject of a Court ordinance, and also of a special pastoral from Bishop Grosbeste. The text runs thus: "Sundrie noblemen and gentlemen and others doe much delighte to dyne in corners and secret places," and the reason given was that it was a bad influence, dividing class from class; the real reason was probably that by more private and domestic life, the power of the Church over her members was weakened. In spite however of opposition in high places, the custom of using the smaller rooms became more common, and we shall find the furniture, as time goes on, designed accordingly.

In the Victoria and Albert Museum there is a very remarkable cabinet, the decoration of which points to its being made in England at this time—that is, about the middle or during the latter half of the sixteenth century; but the highly finished and intricate marqueterie and carving would seem to prove that Italian or German craftsmen had

TUDOR CABINET IN THE VICTORIA AND ALBERT MUSEUM.

executed the work. It should be carefully examined as a very interesting specimen. The Tudor arms, the rose and portcullis, are inlaid on the stand. The arched panels in the folding doors and at the ends of the cabinet are in high relief, representing battle scenes, and bear some resemblance to Holbein's style. The general arrangement of the design reminds one of a Roman triumphal arch. The woods employed are chiefly pear tree, inlaid with coromandel and other woods. Its height is 4ft. 7in. and width 3ft. 1in., but there is in it an immense amount of careful detail which could only be the work of the most skilful craftsmen of the day, and it was evidently intended for a room of moderate dimensions where the intricacies of design could be observed. Mr. Hungerford Pollen has described this cabinet fully, giving the subjects of the ornament, the Latin mottoes and inscriptions and other details, which occupy over four closely printed pages of his Museum catalogue. It cost the nation £500, and was a very judicious purchase.

Chairs were very scarce articles during the first half of the sixteenth century, and as we have seen with other countries, only used for the master or mistress of the house. The chair which is said to have belonged to Anna Boleyn, of which an illustration is given on page 105, is from the collection of the late Mr. Geo. Godwin, F.S.A., formerly editor of *The Builder*, and was part of the contents of Hever Castle, in Kent. It is of carved oak, inlaid with ebony and boxwood, and was probably made by an Italian workman. "Settles" were largely used, and both these and such chairs as then existed, were dependent for richness of effect upon the loose cushions with which they were furnished.

If we attempt to gain a knowledge of the designs of the tables of the sixteenth and the early part of the seventeenth centuries, from interiors represented in paintings of this period, the visit to the picture gallery will be almost in vain, for in nearly every case the table is covered by a cloth. As these cloths or "carpets," as they were then termed, to distinguish them from the "tapet" or floor covering, often cost far more than the articles they covered, a word about them may be allowed.

Most of the old inventories from 1590, after mentioning the "framed" or "joyned" table, name the "carpett of Turky werke" which covered it, and in many cases there was still another covering to protect the best one, and when Frederick Duke of Wurtemburg visited England in 1592, he noted a very extravagant "carpett" at Hampton Court, which was embroidered with pearls and cost 50,000 crowns.

The cushions or "quysshens" for the chairs, of embroidered velvet, were also very important appendages to the otherwise hard oaken and ebony seats, and as the actual date of the will of Alderman Glasseor quoted below is 1589, we may gather, from the extract given, something of the character and value of these ornamental accessories which would probably have been in use for some five-and-twenty or thirty years previously.

"Inventory of the contents of the parler of St. Jone's, within the cittie of Chester," of which place Alderman Glasseor was vice-chamberlain:—

"A drawinge table of joyned work with a frame," valued at "xl shillings."
Two formes covered with Turkey work to the same belonginge xiij shillings and iiij pence.
A joyned frame xvj*d*.
A bord ij*s*. vj*d*.
A little side table with a frame ij*s*. vj*d*.
A pair of virginalls with the frame xxx*s*.
Sixe joyned stooles covr'd with nedle werke xv*s*.
Sixe other joyned stooles vj*s*.
One cheare of nedle werke ij*s*. iiij*d*.
Two little fote stooles iiij*d*.
One longe carpett of Turky werke vil*d*.
A shortte carpett of the same work xij*s*. iiij*d*.
One cupbord carpett of the same x*s*.
Sixe quysshens of Turkye xij*s*.
Sixe quysshens of tapestree xx*s*.
And others of velvet "embroidered wt gold and silver armes in the middesle."
Eight pictures xl*s*.   Maps, a pedigree of Earl Leicester in "joyned frame" and a list of books.

This Alderman Glasseor was apparently a man of taste and culture for those days; he had "casting bottles" of silver for sprinkling perfumes after dinner, and he also had a country house "at the sea," where his parlour was furnished with a "canapy bedd."

As the century advances, and we get well into Elizabeth's reign, wood carving becomes more ambitious, and although it is impossible to distinguish the work of Flemish carvers, who had settled in England, from that of our native craftsmen, these doubtless had acquired from the former much of their skill. In the costumes and in the faces of figures or busts, produced in the highly ornamental oak chimney-pieces of the time, or in the carved portions of the fourpost bedsteads, the national characteristics are preserved, and with a certain grotesqueness introduced into the treatment of accessories, assist us to distinguish the English school of Elizabethan ornament from other contemporary work.

Knole, Longleat, Burghley, Hatfield, Hardwick and Audley End are familiar instances of the change in interior decoration which accompanied that in architecture; terminal figures, that is pedestals diminishing toward their bases, surmounted by busts of men or women, elaborate interlaced strap work carved in low relief, trophies of fruit and flowers, take the place of the more Gothic treatment formerly in vogue. The change in the design of furniture naturally followed, for when Flemish or Italian carvers were not employed, the actual execution was often by the hand of the house carpenter, who was influenced by what he saw around him.

The great chimney-piece in Speke Hall, near Liverpool, portions of the staircase at Hatfield and of other English mansions before mentioned, are good examples of the wood carving of this period, and the illustrations from authenticated examples which are given, will assist the reader to follow these remarks.

There is a mirror frame at Goodrich Court of early Elizabethan work, carved in oak and partly gilt ; the design is in the best style of the Renaissance and more like Italian or French than English work. Architectural mouldings, wreaths of flowers, cupids and an allegorical figure of Faith are harmoniously combined in the design, the size of the whole frame being 4ft. 5in. by 3ft. 6in. It bears the initials R.M., and is dated 1559, the year in which Roland Meyrick became Bishop of Bangor ; it is still in the possession of the Meyrick family. A careful drawing of this frame was made by Henry Shaw, F.S.A.,

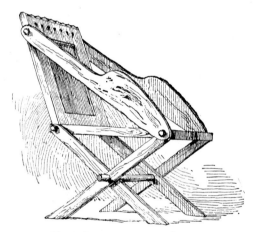

THE GLASTONBURY CHAIR.
(In the Palace of the Bishop of Bath and Wells.)

and published in " Specimens of Ancient Furniture drawn from existing Authorities," in 1836.   This valuable work of reference also contains finished drawings of other noteworthy examples of the sixteenth century furniture and woodwork.   Amongst these is one of the Abbot's chair at Glastonbury, temp. Henry VIII., the original of the chair familiar to us now in the chancel of many churches ; also a chair in the State-room of Hardwick Hall Derbyshire, covered with crimson velvet embroidered with silver tissue, and others very interesting to refer to because the illustrations are all drawn from the articles themselves, and their descriptions are written by an excellent antiquary and collector, Sir Samuel Rush Meyrick.

The mirror frame just described was probably one of the first of its size and kind in England.   It was the custom, as has been already stated, to paint the walls with subjects from history or Scripture, and there are many precepts in existence from early times until about the beginning of Henry VIII.'s reign, directing how certain walls were to be decorated. The discontinuance of this fashion brought about the framing of pictures, and some of the paintings by Holbein, who came to this country about 1511, and received the patronage of Henry VIII. some fourteen or fifteen years later, are probably the first pictures that were framed in England. There are some two or three of these at Hampton Court Palace, the ornament being a scroll in gold on a black background, the width of the frame very narrow in comparison with its canvas. Some of the old wall

CARVED OAK ELIZABETHAN BEDSTEAD.

paintings were on a small scale, and, where long stories were represented, the subjects, instead of occupying the whole flank of the wall, had been divided into rows some three feet or less in height, these being separated by battens, and therefore the first frames would appear to be really little more than the addition of vertical sides to the horizontal top and bottom which such battens had formed. Subsequently frames became more ornate and elaborate. After their application to pictures, their use for mirrors was but a step in advance, and the mirror in a carved and gilt or

OAK WAINSCOTING.

From an old house in Exeter. Victoria and Albert Museum.

PERIOD: ENGLISH RENAISSANCE (ABOUT 1550-75).

decorated frame, probably at first imported and afterwards copied, came to replace the older mirror of very small dimensions which had been used for toilet purposes.

Until early in the fifteenth century, mirrors of polished steel in the antique style, framed in silver and ivory, had been used; in the wardrobe account of Edward I. the item occurs: "A comb and a mirror of silver gilt," and we have an extract from the privy purse of expenses of Henry VIII. which mentions the payment "to a Frenchman for certayne loking glasses," which would probably be a novelty then brought to his Majesty's notice.

There was no glass used for windows* previous to the fifteenth century, the substitute being shaved horn, parchment and sometimes mica, let into the shutters which enclosed the window opening.

The oak panelling of rooms during the reign of Elizabeth was very handsome, and in the example at South Kensington, of which there is here an illustration, the Nation possesses an excellent representative specimen. This was removed from an old house in Exeter, and its date is given by Mr. Hungerford Pollen as from 1550-75. The pilasters and carved panels under the cornice are very rich, and in the best style of Elizabethan Renaissance, while the panels themselves being plain, afford repose and bring the ornament into relief. The entire length is 52ft., and average height 8ft. 3in. If this panelling could be arranged as it was fitted originally in the house of one of Elizabeth's subjects, with models of fireplace, moulded ceiling and accessories added, we should then have an object lesson of value, and be able to picture a contemporary of Drake or Raleigh in his West of England home.

A later purchase by the Science and Art Department, which was added to the Museum in 1891 for the extremely moderate price of £1,000, is the panelling of a room some 23ft. square and 12ft. 6in. high from Sizergh Castle, Westmorland. The chimney-piece was unfortunately not purchased, but the Department has arranged the panelling as a room with a plaster model of the extremely handsome ceiling. The panelling is of richly figured oak entirely devoid of polish, and is inlaid with black bog oak and holly in geometrical designs, being divided at intervals by tall pilasters with flutings of bog oak and having Ionic capitals. The work was probably done locally, and from wood grown on the estate, and is one of the most remarkable examples in existence. The date is about 1560 to 1570, and it was described in local literature nearly two hundred years ago.

* Dr. Jacob von Falké states that the first mention of glass as an extraordinary product occurs in a register of 1239.

While we are on the subject of panelling, it may be worth while to point out that with regard to old English work of this date, one may safely take it for granted that where, as in the Victoria and Albert (Exeter) example, the pilasters, frieze and frame-work are enriched, and the panels

DINING HALL IN THE CHARTERHOUSE.
Showing Oak Screen and front of Minstrels' Gallery, dated 1571.
PERIOD: ELIZABETHAN.

plain, the work was designed and made for the house, but when the panels are carved and the rest plain, they were bought, and then fitted up by the local carpenter.

 **Dudley**

 Self Service

Wednesday, June 29, 2011 - 13:18

You have returned 2 items

Title	Fee
Antiques price guide 2004	None
Closer look at antiques	None

Thank you for using this service

Self Service

Dudley

Wednesday, June 29 2011 - 13:13

You have returned 2 item...

Title	Fee
Antiques price guide 2004	£3.95
Closer look at antiques	None

Thank you for using this service

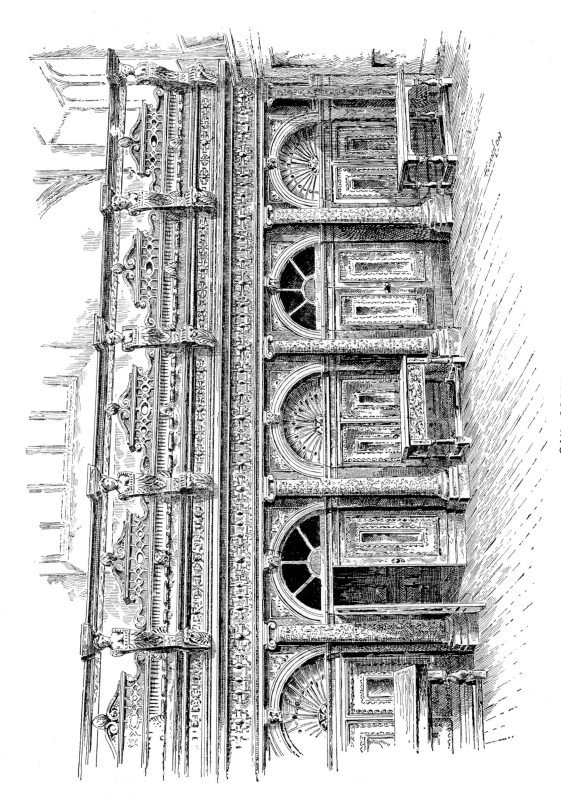

OAK SCREEN.

IN THE HALL OF GRAY'S INN. SHOWING FURNITURE AT THAT END OF THE HALL.

Another Museum specimen of Elizabethan carved oak is a fourpost bedstead, with the arms of the Countess of Devon, which bears date 1593, and has all the characteristics of the time.

There is also a good example of Elizabethan woodwork in part of the interior of the Charterhouse, immortalised by Thackeray, when as "Greyfriars," in the "Newcomes," he described it as the old school "where the colonel and Clive and I were brought up," and it was here that, as a "poor brother," the old colonel had returned to spend the evening of his gentle life, and, to quote Thackeray's pathetic lines,

COURT CUPBOARD OF CARVED OAK. ELIZABETHAN.
The property of Lord Fisher.
(*The Geffrye Museum.*)

"when the chapel bell began to toll, he lifted up his head a little, and said 'Adsum!' It was the word we used at school when names were called."

This famous relic of Old London, which fortunately escaped the Great Fire in 1666, was formerly an old monastery which Henry VIII. dissolved in 1537, and the house was given some few years later to Sir Edward, afterwards Lord North, from whom the Duke of Norfolk purchased it in 1565, and the handsome staircase, carved with terminal figures and Renaissance ornament, was probably built either by Lord

North or his successor. The woodwork of the Great Hall, where the pensioners still dine every day, is very rich, the fluted columns with Corinthian capitals, the interlaced strap work and other details of carved oak are characteristic of the best sixteenth century woodwork in England; the shield bears the date of 1571. This was the year when the Duke of Norfolk, who was afterwards beheaded, was released from the Tower on a kind of furlough, and probably amused himself with the enrichment of his mansion, then called Howard House. In the old Governors' room, formerly the drawing room of the Howards, there is a

HALL OF GRAY'S INN.
Showing Tables and Benches.

specimen of the large wooden chimney-piece of the end of the sixteenth century, painted instead of carved. After the Duke of Norfolk's death, the house was granted by the Crown to his son, the Earl of Suffolk, who sold it in 1611 to the founder of the present hospital, Sir Thomas Sutton, a citizen who was reputed to be one of the wealthiest of his time. Some of the furniture given by him will be found noticed in the chapter on the Jacobean period.

Large garderobes or armoires, buffets, Court cupboards, chests, tables, chairs and benches were made in great numbers about this time.

The illustration on page 116 is from the photograph of a Court cupboard which is ornamented with carving undoubtedly English of the Elizabethan period and may be compared with the illustrations which accompany the writer's remarks on Dutch Renaissance to enable the reader to appreciate the difference in treatment.

There are in London many other excellent examples of Elizabethan oak carving. Amongst those easily accessible and valuable for reference, are the Hall of Gray's Inn, built in 1560, the second year of the Queen's reign, and Middle Temple Hall, built in 1570-72. By permission of Mr. William R. Douthwaite, librarian of "Gray's Inn," and author of "Gray's Inn, its History and Associations," we are enabled to give illustrations of the interior of the Hall, and also of the carved screen supporting the Minstrels' Gallery. The interlaced strap work, generally found in Elizabethan carving, encircles the shafts of the columns as a decoration. The table in the centre has also some low relief carving on the drawer front, but the straight and severe style of leg leads us to place its date at some fifty years later than the Hall. The desk on the left, and the table on the right, are probably of a still later period. It may be mentioned here that the long table which stands at the opposite end of the Hall on the daïs, said to have been presented by Queen Elizabeth, is not of the design with which the furniture of her reign is associated by experts; the heavy cabriole legs, with bent knees, corresponding with the legs of the chairs (also on the daïs) are of unmistakable Dutch origin, and so far as the writer's observations lead to a conclusion, were probably introduced into England about the time of William III.

The same remarks apply to a table in Middle Temple Hall, also said to have been there during Elizabeth's time. Mr. Douthwaite alludes to the rumour of the Queen's gift in his book, and endeavoured to substantiate it from the records at his command, but in vain. The authorities at Middle Temple are also, as far as we have been able to ascertain, without any documentary evidence to prove the claim of their table to any greater age than the end of the seventeenth century.

The carved oak screen of Middle Temple Hall is magnificent, and no one should miss seeing it. Terminal figures, fluted columns, panels broken up into smaller divisions and carved enrichments of various devices, are all combined in a harmonious design, rich without being overcrowded, and its effect is enhanced by the rich colour given to it by age, by the excellent proportions of the Hall, by the plain panelling of the three other sides, and above all by the grand oak roof, which is certainly one of the finest of its kind in England. Some of the tables and forms are of a much later date, but an interest attaches even to this furniture from the fact of its having been made from oak grown close to the Hall; and as one of the tables has a slab composed of an oak plank nearly thirty inches wide, we can imagine what fine old trees once grew and flourished close to the now busy Fleet Street and the bustling Strand. There are frames, too, in Middle Temple made from the oaken timbers which once formed the piles in the Thames on which rested "the Temple Stairs."

In Mr. Herbert's "Antiquities of the Inns of Court and Chancery" there are several facts of interest in connection with the woodwork of Middle Temple. He mentions that the screen was paid for by contributions from each bencher of twenty shillings, each barrister of ten shillings and every other member of six shillings and eightpence; that the Hall was founded in 1562 and furnished ten years later, the screen being put up in 1574; and that the memorials of some two hundred and fifty

PANEL IN A CARVED OAK CHEST.
A MAN TRAINING TWO BEARS. ENGLISH: TIME OF HENRY VIII.
(*From "The Connoisseur," by permission.*)

"Readers" which decorate the otherwise plain oak panelling, date from 1597 to 1804, the year in which Mr. Herbert's book was published. Referring to the furniture, he says:—"The massy oak tables and benches with which this apartment was anciently furnished, still remain, and so may do for centuries, unless violently destroyed, being of wonderful strength." Mr. Herbert also mentions the masks and revels held in this famous Hall in the time of Elizabeth; he also gives a list of quantities and prices of materials used in the decoration of Gray's Inn Hall.

In the Hall of the Carpenters' Company, in Throgmorton Avenue, are three curiously carved oak panels, worth noticing here, as they are of a date bringing them well into this period. They were formerly in the old Hall, which escaped the Great Fire, and in the account books

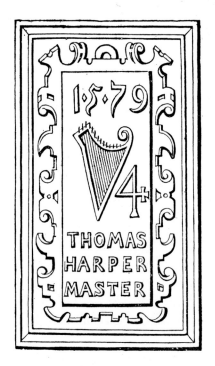

THREE CARVED OAK PANELS.

Now in the Court Room of the Hall of the Carpenters' Company. Removed from the former Hall.

PERIOD: ELIZABETHAN.

of the Corporation is the following record of the cost of one of these panels :—

"Paide for a planke to carve the arms of the Companie   iijs."

"Paide to the Carver for carving the arms of the Companie xxiijs. iiijd."

The price of material (3s.) and workmanship (23s. 4d.) was certainly not excessive. All three panels are in excellent preservation, and the design of a harp, being a rebus of the Master's name, is a quaint relic of old customs. Some other oak furniture in the Hall of this ancient Company will be noticed in the following chapter. Mr Jupp, a former Clerk of the Company, has written an historical account of the "Carpenters," which contains many facts of interest. The office of King's Carpenter or Surveyor, the powers of the Carpenters to search, examine and impose fines for inefficient work, and the trade disputes with the

PART OF AN ELIZABETHAN STAIRCASE.

"Joyners," the "Sawyers" and "Woodmongers" are all entertaining reading and throw many side-lights on the woodwork of the sixteenth and seventeenth centuries.

The illustration of Hardwick Hall shows oak panelling and decoration of a somewhat earlier and also somewhat later time than Elizabeth, while the carved oak chairs are of Jacobean style. At Hardwick is still kept the historic chair in which it is said that William, fourth Earl of Devonshire, sat when he and his friends compassed the downfall of James II. In the curious little chapel, hung with ancient tapestry and containing the original Bible and Prayer Book of Charles I., are other quaint chairs covered with cushions of sixteenth or early seventeenth century needlework.

THE ENTRANCE HALL, HARDWICK HALL.

Period of Furniture: Iacobean. XVII. Century.

Some of the greatest treasures in furniture still remaining in this historic house are not of English origin, and therefore have been noticed in the earlier part of the present chapter, which deals with the later period of French Renaissance, corresponding with our Elizabethan time, when Hardwick was built and furnished by Elizabeth Countess of Shrewsbury. The third husband of this remarkable woman was a Cavendish, and it is owing to this marriage that Hardwick is now one of the possessions of the Duke of Devonshire.

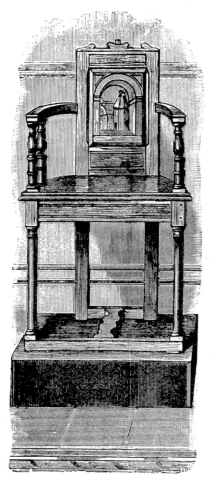

SHAKESPEARE'S CHAIR.
(See note on page 124.)

The famous long table of oak, with elaborate inlay, representing various sports and a procession which has a Latin inscription, is one of the most remarkable pieces of English furniture of Elizabethan times, and it is unfortunate that a photograph taken for the purpose of illustration in these pages was not sufficiently clear for reproduction.

Hardwick contains many relics of English work of this period of great interest to our readers and by the Duke's courtesy visitors are permitted to see it when the family is not in residence.

Before concluding the remarks on this period of English woodwork and furniture, further mention should be made of Penshurst Place, to which there has been already some reference in the chapter on the period of the Middle Ages. It was here that Sir Philip Sydney spent much of his time and produced his best literary work during the period of his retirement when he had lost the favour of Elizabeth; and in the room known as the "Queen's Room," illustrated on page 126, some of the furniture is of this period. The crystal chandeliers are said to have been given by Lord Leicester to his Royal Mistress and some of the chairs and tables were sent down by the Queen and presented to Sir Henry Sydney (Philip's father) when she stayed at Penshurst during one of her Royal progresses. The room, with its vases and bowls of old Oriental china and the contemporary portraits on the walls, gives us a good idea of the very best effect that was attainable with the material then available.

Richardson's "Studies" contains, amongst other examples of furniture and carved oak decorations of English Renaissance, interiors of Little Charlton, East Sutton Place, Stockton House Wilts, Audley End Essex, and the Great Hall Crewe, with its beautiful hall screens and famous carved "parloir," all notable mansions of the sixteenth century.

To this period of English furniture belongs the celebrated "Great Bed of Ware," of which there is an illustration. This was formerly at the "Saracen's Head" at Ware, but it has been removed to Rye House, about two miles away. Shakespeare's allusion to it in the "Twelfth Night" has identified the approximate date and gives the bed a character. The following are the lines :—

> Sir Toby Belch.—And as many lies as shall lie in thy sheet of paper altho' the sheet were big enough for the Bed of Ware in England, set em down, go about it.

Another illustration (see page 123) shows the chair which is said to have belonged to William Shakespeare: it may or may not be the actual one used by the poet, but it is most probably a genuine specimen of about his time, though perhaps not made in England. There is a manuscript on its back which states that it was known in 1769 as the Shakespeare Chair, when Garrick borrowed it from its owner, Mr. James Bacon of Barnet, and since that time its history is well known. The carved ornament is in low relief and represents a rough idea of the dome of S. Marc and the Campanile Tower.

We have now briefly and roughly traced the advance of what may be termed the flood-tide of Art from its birthplace in Italy, to France, the Netherlands, Spain, Germany, Denmark and England; and by explanation and description, assisted by illustrations, have endeavoured to show how

THE GREAT BED OF WARE.

Formerly at the Saracen's Head, Ware, but now at Rye House, Broxbourne, Herts.

PERIOD: XVI. CENTURY.

the Gothic of the latter part of the Middle Ages gave way before the revival of classic forms and arabesque ornament, with the many details and peculiarities characteristic of each different nationality which had adopted the general change. During this period the "bahut" or chest has become a cabinet with infinite varieties; the simple *prie dieu* chair, as a devotional piece of furniture, has been elaborated into almost an oratory;

THE "QUEEN'S ROOM," PENSHURST PLACE.

(Reproduced from "Historic Houses of the United Kingdom," by permission of Messrs. Cassell & Co., Limited.)

tables have, towards the end of the period, become more ornate, and made as solid pieces of furniture, instead of the planks and trestles which we found when the Renaissance commenced. Chimney-pieces, which in the fourteenth century were merely stone smoke-shafts or hoods supported by corbels, have been replaced by handsome carved oak erections, ornamenting the hall or room from floor to ceiling, and the English livery cupboard,

CARVED OAK CHIMNEY-PIECE.

In Speke Hall, near Liverpool.   Period : Elizabethan.

with its foreign contemporary the buffet, is the forerunner of the side-board of the future.

Carved oak panelling has replaced the old arras and ruder wood lining of an earlier time, and with the departure of the old feudal customs and the indulgence in greater luxuries by the more wealthy nobles and merchants in Italy, Flanders, France, Germany, Spain and England, we have the elegances and grace with which Art, and increased means of gratifying taste, enabled the sixteenth century virtuoso to adorn his home.

CHAPTER IV

Jacobean Furniture

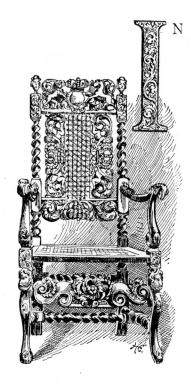

IN the chapter on "Renaissance" the great Art revival in England has been noticed; in the Elizabethan oak work of chimney-pieces, panelling and furniture are to be found varying forms of the free classic style which the Renaissance had brought about. These fluctuating changes in fashion continued in England from the time of Elizabeth until the middle of the eighteenth century, when, as will be shown presently, a distinct alteration in the design of furniture took place.

The domestic habits of Englishmen were getting more established. We have seen how religious persecution during preceding reigns, at the time of the Reformation, had encouraged private domestic life of families in the smaller rooms and apart from the gossiping retainer, who might at any time bring destruction upon the household by giving information about items of conversation he had overheard. There is a quaint passage in one of Sir Henry Wotton's letters written in 1600 which shows that this home life was now becoming a settled characteristic of his countrymen:—

"Every man's proper mansion house and home, being the theatre of his hospitality, the seate of his selfe fruition, the comfortable part of his own life, the noblest of his son's inheritance, a kind of private princedom, nay the possession thereof an epitome of the whole world may well deserve by these attributes, according to the degree of the master, to be delightfully adorned."

Sir Henry Wotton was Ambassador in Venice in 1604 and is said to have been the author of the well-known definition of an ambassador's calling, namely, "an honest man sent to lie abroad for his country's good." This offended the piety of James I. and caused him for some time

OAK CHIMNEY-PLACE IN SIR WALTER RALEIGH'S HOUSE, YOUGHAL, IRELAND.
Said to be the work of a Flemish Artist, who was brought over for the purpose of
executing this and other carved work at Youghal.

to be in disgrace. He also published some twenty years later " Elements of Architecture," and being an antiquary and man of taste, sent home many specimens of the famous Italian wood carving.

It was during the reign of James I. and that of his successor that Inigo Jones, our English Vitruvius, was making his great reputation; he had returned from Italy full of enthusiasm for the Renaissance of Palladio and his school, and of knowledge and taste gained by a diligent study of the ancient classic buildings of Rome. His influence would be speedily felt in the design of woodwork fittings for the interiors of his edifices. There is a note in his own copy of Palladio, now in the library of Worcester College, Oxford, which is worth quoting :—

" In the name of God : Amen. The 2 of January, 1614, I being in Rome compared these desines following, with the Ruines themselves.—INIGO JONES."

In the following year he returned from Italy on his appointment as King's Surveyor of Works and until his death in 1652 was full of work, although unfortunately for us much that he designed was never carried out and much that he carried out has been destroyed by fire. The Banqueting Hall of Whitehall; St. Paul's, Covent Garden; the old water-gate originally intended as the entrance to the first Duke of

CHIMNEY-PIECE IN BYFLEET HOUSE.
EARLY JACOBEAN.

Buckingham's Palace, close to the Embankment Garden at Charing Cross; Nos. 55 and 56, on the south side of Great Queen Street, Lincoln's Inn; and one or two monuments and porches, are amongst the examples that remain to us of this great master's work.

The woodcut on page 132 shows a portion of the King's room in Ford Castle which still contains souvenirs of Flodden Field according to an article in the *Magazine of Art.* The room is in the northernmost tower, which still preserves externally the stern grim character of the border fortress; and the rooms in that tower look towards the famous battle-field. The chair shows a date 1638 and there is another of Dutch design of about fifty or sixty years later; but the carved oak bedstead, with tapestry hangings, and the oak press, which the writer of the article mentions as forming part of the old furniture of the room, scarcely appear in the illustration.

THE KING'S CHAMBER, FORD CASTLE.

Mr. Hungerford Pollen tells us that the majority of so-called Tudor houses were actually built during the reign of James I., and this may probably be accepted as an explanation of there being much in the architecture and woodwork known to be of this time which would seem to belong to the earlier period.

The illustration of wooden chimney-pieces will show this change. There are in the Victoria and Albert Museum some three or four chimney-pieces of stone, having the upper portions of carved oak, the dates of which have been ascertained to be about 1620; these were removed from an old house in Lime Street, City, and give us an idea of the interior decoration of a residence of a London merchant of the time. The one illustrated on page 135 is somewhat richer than the others; the carving of the panels of all of them is in less relief and simpler in character than those which occur in the latter part of Elizabeth's time.

The earliest dated piece of Jacobean furniture which has come under the writer's observation is the octagonal table belonging to the Carpenters' Company. The illustration, taken from Mr. Jupp's book referred to in the last chapter, hardly does the table justice; it is really a very handsome piece of furniture and measures about 3 feet 3 inches in

CARVED OAK CENTRE TABLE.
In the Hall of the Carpenters' Company.

diameter. In the spandrels of the arches between the legs are the letters R.W., G.I., J.R., and W.W., being the initials of Richard Wyatt, George Isack, John Reeve, and William Willson, who were Master and Wardens of the Company in 1606, which date is carved in two of the spandrels. While the ornamental legs show some of the characteristics of Elizabethan work, the treatment is less bold, the large acorn-shaped member has become more refined and attenuated and the ornament is altogether more subdued. This is a remarkable specimen of early Jacobean furniture and is the only one of the shape and kind known to the writer; it is in excellent preservation, save that the top is split. It shows signs of having been made with considerable skill and care.

Our Science and Art Department keep for reference an album containing photographs, not only of many of the specimens in the different museums under its control, but also of some of those which have been lent for a temporary exhibition. The illustration of the two chairs overleaf is taken from this source, the album having been placed at the writer's disposal by the courtesy of the head of the Photographic Department. The left-hand chair, from Abingdon Park, is said to have belonged to Lady Barnard, Shakespeare's grand-daughter, and the other may still be seen in the Hall of the Carpenters' Company.

In the Hall of the Barbers' Company in Monkswell Street, the Court Room, which is lighted with an octagonal cupola, was designed by Inigo Jones, as a Theatre of Anatomy, when the Barbers and Surgeons were one corporation. There are some three or four tables of this period in the

CARVED OAK CHAIR.　　　　　　CARVED OAK CHAIR.
From Abingdon Park.　　　　　　In the Carpenters' Hall.
EARLY XVII. CENTURY.　ENGLISH.
(From Photos in the Victoria and Albert Museum Album.)

Hall having four legs connected by stretchers, quite plain; the moulded edges of the table tops are also without enrichment. These plain oak slabs and also the stretchers have been renewed, but in exactly the same style as the original work; the legs however are the old ones and are simple columns with plain turned capitals and bases. Other tables of this period are to be found in a few old country mansions; there is one in Longleat, which, the writer has been told, has a small drawer at the end to hold the copper coins with which the retainers of the Marquis of

OAK CHIMNEY-PIECE.

Removed from an old house in Lime Street, City.

PERIOD: JAMES I.

(*Victoria and Albert Museum.*)

Bath's ancestors used to play a game of shovel penny. In the Chapter House in Westminster Abbey there is also one of these plain substantial James I. tables, which is singular in being nearly double the width of those which were usually made at this time. As the Chapter House was, until comparatively recent years, used as a room for the storage of records, this table was probably made, not as a dining table, but for some other purpose requiring greater width.

OAK SIDEBOARD IN THE VICTORIA AND ALBERT MUSEUM.
PERIOD: JAMES II.

In the chapter on the Renaissance there was an allusion to the Charterhouse, which was purchased for its present purpose by Thomas Sutton in 1611, and in the chapel may be seen to-day the original Communion table placed there by the founder. It is of carved oak with a row of legs running lengthways underneath the middle, and four others at the corners; these, while being cast in the simple lines already noticed in describing the tables in the Barbers' Hall and the Chapter House in Westminster Abbey, are enriched by carving from the base to the third of the height of the leg, and the frieze of the table is also carved in low relief. The rich carved wood screen which supports the organ loft is also of Jacobean work.

There is in the Victoria and Albert Museum a carved oak chest with a centre panel representing the Adoration of the Magi, of about this date, 1615-20; it is mounted on a stand with three feet in front and two behind, which are much more primitive and quaint than the ornate supports of Elizabethan carving ; while the only ornaments on the drawer fronts which form the frieze of the stand are moulded panels, in the centre of each of which there is a turned knob by which to open the drawer. This chest and the table which forms its stand were probably not intended for each other. The illustration opposite shows the stand, which is a good representation of the carving of this time, *i.e.*, early seventeenth century. The applied ornaments on the upper parts of two of the legs, and also between and beneath the geometrical panels, should be noticed. These ornaments turned by the lathe, then split and applied to the cabinet or table are a mark of Stuart times.

There is no greater storehouse for specimens of furniture in use during the Jacobean period than Knole, that stately mansion of the Sackville family, then the property of the Earls of Dorset. In the King's Bedroom, which is said to have been specially prepared and furnished for the visit of King James I., the public, owing to the courtesy and public spirit of the present Lord Sackville, can still see the bed, originally of crimson silk, but now much faded, elaborately embroidered with gold. It is said to have cost £8,000, also the chairs and seats, which are believed to have formed part of the original equipment of the room are in much the same position as they originally occupied.

In the carved work of this furniture we cannot help thinking that the hand of the Venetian craftsman is to be traced and it is probable that they were copied from patterns brought from Venice for the purpose. A suite of furniture of that time appears to have consisted of six stools and two arm chairs, almost entirely covered with velvet, having the ȣ form supports, a design which, so far as the writer's investigations have gone, appears to have come from Venice. In the "Leicester" gallery at Knole, which is panelled with oak and furnished with Elizabethan and Jacobean chairs and tables, there is a portrait of King James the First, painted by Mytens, seated on such a chair, and just below the picture is placed the chair which is said to be identical with the one portrayed. It is similar to the one reproduced on page 139 from a drawing of Mr. Charles Eastlake's.

In the same gallery also are three sofas or settees upholstered with crimson velvet and one of these has an accommodating rack, by which either end can be lowered at will to make a more convenient lounge.

This excellent example of Jacobean furniture has been described and sketched by Mr. Charles Eastlake in "Hints on Household Taste." He

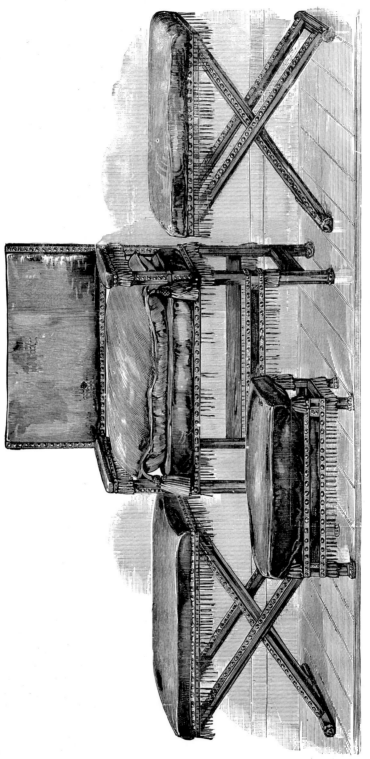

SEATS AT KNOLE.
Covered with Crimson Silk Velvet.
PERIOD: JAMES I.

says: "The joints are properly 'tenoned' and pinned together in such a manner as to ensure its constant stability. The back is formed like that of a chair, with a horizontal rail only at its upper edge, but it receives additional strength from the second rail, which is introduced at the back of the seat." In Marcus Stone's well-known picture of "The Stolen Keys" this is the sofa portrayed. The arm chair illustrated is part of the same suite of furniture. The furniture of another room at Knole is said to have been presented by King James to the first Earl of Middlesex, who had married into the Dorset family. The author has been furnished with a photograph of this room; and the illustration overleaf from this will give the reader a better idea than a lengthy description.

ARM CHAIR.
Covered with Velvet, trimmed with Fringe, and studded with Copper Nails.
EARLY XVII. CENTURY.
(*From a Drawing of the Original at Knole, by Mr. Charles Eastlake.*)

It seems from a comparison of the Knole furniture with the designs of some of the tables and other woodwork produced during the same reign, and bearing the impress of the more severe style of Inigo Jones, that there were then in England two styles of decorative furniture. One of these, simple and severe, showing a reaction from the grotesque freedom of Elizabethan carving, and the other, copied from Venetian ornamental woodwork, with cupids on scrolls forming the supports of stools, having these ornamental legs connected by stretchers, the design of which is, in

THE "SPANGLE" BEDROOM AT KNOLE.

The Furniture of this room was presented by James I. to the Earl of Middlesex.

the case of those in the King's Bedchamber at Knole, a couple of cupids in a flying attitude holding up a crown. This kind of furniture was generally gilt and under the black paint of those at Knole, traces of the gold are still to be seen.

Mr. Eastlake visited Knole and made a careful examination and sketches of the Jacobean furniture there and has well described and illustrated it in his book just referred to; he mentions that he found there a slip of paper tucked beneath the webbing of a settle, with an inscription in Old English characters which fixed the date of some of the furniture at 1620. Lord Sackville has confirmed this date in a letter to the author, by a reference to the heirloom book, which also bears out the author's opinion that some of the more richly carved furniture of this time was imported from Italy.

In the Lady Chapel of Canterbury Cathedral there is a monument to Dean Boys, who died in 1625. This represents the Dean seated in his library at a table with turned legs, over which there is a tapestry cover. Books line the walls of the section of the room shown in the stone carving; it differs little from the sanctum of a literary man of the present day. There are many other monuments which represent furniture of this period and amongst the more curious is that of a child of King James I., in Westminster Abbey, close to the monument of Mary Queen of Scots. The child is sculptured about life size, in a carved cradle of the time.

Holland House, Kensington, is a good example of a Jacobean mansion. The chief interest, inseparable from this house, is, of course, associated with the memory of the third Lord Holland, "nephew of Fox and friend of Grey," who gathered round him within its walls the most brilliant and distinguished society of the day, presiding over it with that genial courtesy which was the rich inheritance of his family.

Macaulay, at the conclusion of his essay on Lord Holland, has, with his unrivalled power of description, told us of the charm and fascination of "that circle in which every talent and accomplishment, every art and science, had its place"—enumerating also the names of many of those who formed it, and expatiating on "the grace and the kindness, far more admirable than grace, with which the princely hospitality of that ancient mansion was dispensed." Princess Liechtenstein has also preserved for us, in "Holland House," a charming record of many of the historical associations of this famous old place.

There are in the house also many objects of great interest, of various periods, which, by the courtesy of Lady Ilchester, the writer has been allowed to examine. Our business however is with the seventeenth century and we must now return to a consideration of the furniture and woodwork of that time.

COUCH, ARM CHAIR AND SINGLE CHAIR.

CARVED AND GILT.

Upholstered in Rich Silk Velvet.   Part of Suite at Penshurst Place.

Also an Italian Cabinet.

PERIOD: CHARLES II.

The Holland House of the time of James I. was originally built in the year 1607, as " Cope Castle," by Sir Walter Cope, who then owned the extensive " Manor " of Kensington. Cope's daughter married Sir Henry Rich, who became Earl of Holland in 1624 and was executed by the Parliamentarians in 1649. He it was who added to the house the wings and arcades. Princess Liechtenstein tells us the story of " the solitary ghost of its first lord, who, according to tradition, issues forth at midnight from behind a secret door, and walks slowly through the scenes of his former triumph with his head in his hand."

There is some good old woodwork of the early part of the seventeenth century and the panelling and chimney-piece of the famous " white parlour " are of the times of James I., the work, still in good preservation, being in the best Jacobean taste. The panels are formed by bold uncarved mouldings, separated at intervals by flat pilasters with fluted shafts and carved capitals ; the panels in the frieze, between the trusses, which support a " dentilled " cornice, are enriched with fretwork ornaments in relief, and the whole has a simple but decorative architectural effect of the best English rendering of the Renaissance. The " gilt room," where the ghost is said to commence its nocturnal promenade, was decorated by Francesco Cleyn, an Italian, who also worked for the King.* The room was prepared for a ball which was purposed to be given in honour of the marriage of Prince Charles to Henrietta Maria. There are now on the chief staircase of Holland House two chairs with their backs carved as shells and with legs shaped and ornamented with scrollwork and masks with swags of foliage which are also attributed to Cleyn. Horace Walpole, in a reference to Holland House, has mentioned these chairs in " Anecdotes of Painters." " Two chairs, carved and gilt, with large shells for backs . . . were undoubtedly from his designs, and are evidences of his taste." Walpole also mentions a garden seat of similar design by Cleyn. A drawing of one of these chairs forms the tail piece of this chapter.

There is another Jacobean house of considerable interest, the property of Sir T. G. Jackson, R.A. An account of it has been written by him and was read to some members of the Surrey Archæological Society who visited Eagle House, Wimbledon, in 1890. It appears to have been the country seat of a London merchant who lived early in the seventeenth century. Sir T. G. Jackson bears witness to the excellence of the work-

---

* The present decorations of the room were painted either actually by Watts or under his directions, when, as favourite artist to the fourth Lord Holland, he did so much to beautify the house and made so many additions to its store of portraits. His work is fully described in " Holland House," by Princess Marie Liechtenstein. London, 1874.

manship and expresses his opinion that the carved and decorated enrichments were executed by native and not by foreign craftsmen. He gives an illustration in his pamphlet of the sunk " Strap Work, " which, though Jacobean in its date, is also found in the carved ornament of Elizabeth's time.

It is very probable that had the reign of Charles I. been less troublous this would have been a time of much progress in the domestic Arts in England. The Queen was a Medici on her mother's side, Italian literature was in vogue and Italian artists therefore would probably have been encouraged to come over and instruct our workmen. The King himself was an excellent mechanic and boasted that he could earn his living at almost any trade save the making of hangings. His father had established the tapestry works at Mortlake; he himself had bought the Raffaelle Cartoons to encourage the work—and much was to be hoped from a monarch who had the taste and judgment to induce a Vandyke to settle in England. The Civil War, whatever it has achieved for our liberty as subjects, certainly hindered by many years our progress as an artistic people.

But to consider some of the furniture of this period in detail. Until the sixteenth century was well advanced the word " table " in our language meant an index or pocket book (tablets), or a list, *not* an article of furniture. The table was, as we have noticed in the time of Elizabeth, composed of boards generally hinged in the middle for convenience of storage, and supported on trestles which were sometimes ornamented by carved work. The word trestle, by the way, is said to be derived from the " threstule," *i.e.,* three-footed supports, and these three-legged stools and benches formed in those days the seats for everyone except the master of the house. Chairs were, as we have seen, scarce articles; sometimes there was only one, a throne-like seat for an honoured guest or for the master or mistress of the house, and doubtless our present phrase of " taking the chair " is a survival of the high place a chair then held amongst the household gods of a gentleman's mansion. Shakespeare possibly had the boards and trestles in his mind when, about 1596, he wrote in " Romeo and Juliet ":—

> Come, musicians, play!
> A hall! a hall! give room and foot it girls.
> More light, ye knaves, and turn the tables up."

In the play of " King Henry the Fourth " he gives "table" its earlier meaning, for the Archbishop of York is made to say :—

> " . . . . The King is weary
> Of dainty and such picking grievances;
> And therefore will he wipe his tables clean,
> And keep no tell-tale to his memory."

Mr. Maskell, in his handbook on " Ivories," tells us that the word " table " was also used in the fourteenth and fifteenth centuries to denote the religious carvings and paintings in churches; and he quotes Chaucer to show that the word was also used to describe the game of draughts.

" They dancen and they play at chess and tables."

Now however at the time of which we are writing, chairs were becoming more plentiful and the table was a definite article of furniture. In inventories of the time and for some twenty years previous, as has been already noticed in the preceding chapter, we find mention of " joyned table," framed table, " standing " and " dormant " table, and the word " board " had gradually disappeared. It remains to us however as a souvenir of the past in the name we still give to a body of men meeting for the transaction of business, and in connection with social life in the phrase " the festive board." The width of these earlier tables had been about 30 inches and guests sat on one side only with their backs to the wall in order, it may be supposed, to be the more ready to resist any sudden raid which might be made on the house during the relaxation of the supper hour, and this custom remained in use long after there was any necessity for its observance.

In the time of Charles the First the width was increased, and a contrivance was introduced for doubling the area of the top when required, by drawing out two flaps from either end, and by means of a wedge-shaped arrangement, the centre or main table top was lowered, and the whole table, thus increased, became level. Illustrations taken from Mr. G. T. Robinson's article on furniture in the *Art Journal* of 1881 represent a " drawinge " table, which was the name by which these " latest improvements " were known. The black lines were of stained pear tree, let into the oak : the acorn shaped member of the leg is an imported Dutch design, which became very common about this time, and was applied to the supports of cabinets, sometimes, as in the illustration overleaf, plainly turned, but frequently carved. Another table of this period was the " folding table," which was made with twelve, sixteen or with twenty legs, as shown in the illustration of this example and which, as its name implies, would shut up into about one-third of its extended size. There is one of these tables in the Stationers' Hall. They are now termed " gate-legged " tables : the date generally accepted of the introduction of the gate-legged table is about 1650. Although card-playing was common during the Tudor and early Stuart times, there does not appear to have been any special table for the purpose until towards the end of the seventeenth century.

It was probably in the early part of the seventeenth century that the couch became known in England.   It was not common, nor quite

FOLDING TABLE AT PENSHURST PLACE.
PERIOD: CHARLES II. TO JAMES II.

"DRAWINGE" TABLE WITH BLACK LINES INLAID.
PERIOD: CHARLES II.

in the form in which we now recognise that luxurious article of furniture, but was probably a carved oak settle, with cushions so arranged as to form a resting lounge by day.   Shakespeare speaks of the "branch'd velvet gown" of Malvolio having come from a "day bed," and there is also an allusion to one in "Richard the Third." The following passage occurs in one of Beaumont and Fletcher's plays :—

"Is the great couch up, the Duke of Medina sent?" to which the duenna replies, "'Tis up, and ready"; and then Marguerite asks, "And day beds in all chambers?" receiving in answer, "In all, lady."

In a volume of *Notes and Queries* there is a note which would show that the lady's wardrobe of this time (1622) was a very primitive article of furniture. Mention is made there of a list of articles of wearing

THEODORE HOOK'S CHAIR.

SCROWLED CHAIR IN CARVED OAK.

apparel belonging to a certain Lady Elizabeth Morgan, sister to Sir Nathaniel Rich, which, according to the old document there quoted, dated the 13th day of November, 1622, "are to be found in a great bar'd chest in my Ladie's Bedchamber." To judge from this list, Lady Morgan was a person of fashion in those days. We may also take it for granted that beyond the bedstead, a prie-dieu chair, a bench, some chests and the indispensable mirror there was not much else with which to furnish a lady's bedroom in the reign of James I. or that of his successor.

The "long settle" and "scrowled chair" were two other kinds of seats in use from the time of Charles I. to that of James II. The illustrations are taken from authenticated specimens in the collection of Mr. Dalton, of Scarborough. They are most probably of Yorkshire manufacture, about the middle of the seventeenth century. The ornament in the panel of the back of the chair is inlaid with box or ash, stained with a greenish black to represent green ebony and with a few small pieces

CHAIR USED BY KING CHARLES I. DURING HIS TRIAL.

of rich red wood then in great favour. Mr. G. T. Robinson, to whose article already referred to we are indebted for the description, says that this wood was "probably brought by some buccaneer from the West." He also mentions another chair of the Stuart period, which formed a table and subsequently became the property of Theodore Hook, who carefully preserved its pedigree. It was purchased by its late owner, Mr. Godwin, editor of *The Builder*. A woodcut of this appears on page 147.

Another chair to which there is an historical interest attached, is that in which Charles I. sat during his trial; this was exhibited in the Stuart Exhibition in London in 1889. The illustration is taken from a print in the *Illustrated London News* of the time.

SETTLE OF CARVED OAK.

Probably made in Yorkshire.

PERIOD: CHARLES II.

SETTEE UPHOLSTERED IN CRIMSON VELVET.

Richly Trimmed and Embroidered in Gold, with the Monogram of Charles I. and Henrietta Maria. Frame Carved and Gilt.

HOLYROOD PALACE : TIME OF CHARLES I.

In addition to the chairs of oak, carved, inlaid and plain, which were in some cases rendered more comfortable by having cushions tied to the backs and seats, the upholstered chair, which we have seen had been brought from Venice in the early part of the reign of James I., now came into general use. Few have survived, but there are still to be seen in

AN UPHOLSTERED CHAIR OF THE TIME OF CHARLES I.
HOLYROOD PALACE.

pictures of the period, chairs represented as covered with crimson velvet, studded with copper nails, the seat being trimmed with fringe, similar to that at Knole, illustrated on page 139.

At Holyrood Palace there still remain, fortunately not restored or regilt, but in a condition which, if rather dilapidated is much more satisfactory than if the ravages of time had been more or less obliterated by new work, a very handsome settee and an upholstered chair, of which there are illustrations on pages 150 and 151. The back cushions of the settee are embroidered with the crown and monogram of King Charles I. and Queen Henrietta Maria and therefore there can be little doubt as to

CARVED OAK CHAIR, WITH CROWN AND THISTLE ORNAMENTS,
INDICATING SCOTTISH ORIGIN.
TIME OF CHARLES I.   HOLYROOD PALACE.

their date. The velvet and handsome fringe, as well as the rich carving and faded gilding, are all witnesses of the great improvement in upholstered furniture which took place about this time, an improvement which has been generally ascribed by writers on the subject to the later period of Charles II.

The improvement in the manufacture of rich materials for covering the more luxurious kinds of furniture may be traced to the Huguenots who fled to this country from the persecution in France.

In 1681 letters of naturalisation were granted to these industrious refugees, and in 1689 there were 40,000 families settled here engaged in various textile trades such as the weaving of silk, velvet and other fabrics, and in the manufacture of costly fringes and gimps of a most elaborate kind. A great many of these materials were used for the expensive furniture ordered by the Court and by wealthy noblemen and merchants. It is interesting to note that about this time there were two

CARVED OAK TABLE, DATE ABOUT 1600.
HOLYROOD PALACE.

royal proclamations, the one forbidding the purchase of silk and velvet not of English manufacture, and another forbidding the mixture of cotton with silk. The exquisite quality of these old materials which are still covering the upholstered furniture at Knole, Holyrood, Drayton and other great houses bear testimony to the effect of these old enactments.

Very large sums were spent by the rich noblemen, the King's ministers and his mistresses upon furniture during the reign of Charles II. The cost of £8,000 for the Queen's bedstead at Hampton Court has already been mentioned. Sir Dudley North (1641-91) is said to have

spent £4,000 in furnishing his stately rooms in Basinghall Street, and
there are many mentions of the extravagance of the time in the " Verney
Memoirs," the diaries of Evelyn and Pepys, of Celia Fiennes and other
contemporary writers.

A great deal of the furniture at Holyrood Palace has no particular
connection with the history of Mary Queen of Scots, with the tragedy
of whose life the Palace is generally associated, but has been supplied by
noblemen who have occupied the position of Keeper of the Palace. Some
of this furniture dates from the time of Charles I. and has a peculiar

CARVED OAK TABLE WITH ARCADED SUPPORT AND EXTENDING TOP.
EARLY XVII. CENTURY.   HOLYROOD PALACE.

interest from the fact of its being of Scottish manufacture; the chair,
of which a reproduction is given on page 152, has the crown and thistles,
the Scottish emblem, on the top of the back of the chair and also in the
carved ornament of the stretcher, while on the ornamental uprights of the
back the thistle is again introduced in the centre of the two scrolls.

The carved oak table illustrated on page 153, also at Holyrood
Palace, is an excellent example of the "fixed top" table in use at the
commencement of the seventeenth century; it is in excellent condition
and a beautiful rich brown colour. On the same floor in which this

table is exhibited there is a good example of another kind of table of the same period with an extending top and an arcaded support, of which we also give an illustration on page 154.

For those who are especially interested in Scottish woodwork and furniture of the sixteenth and seventeenth centuries there is an excellent monograph by John William Small, architect, with descriptions and very carefully executed drawings, giving all the details of carved ornament.

CARVED OAK CHAIR.

Said to have been used by members of Cromwell's family.
(*The original in the possession of T. Knowles Parr, Esq.*)

CARVED OAK CHAIR, JACOBEAN STYLE.

(*The original in the Author's possession.*)

The examples illustrated by him are taken from the old Palaces of Linlithgow, Stirling, Dunfermline, Culross, Holyrood and some of the most interesting old houses in Edinburgh, and include fine specimens of the chairs, old presses, tables, pulpits and ornamental panelling and woodwork from these historic houses.

There is in the Historical Portrait Gallery in Bethnal Green Museum, a painting by an unknown artist, but dated 1642, of Sir William Lenthall, who was Speaker of the House of Commons on the memorable occasion

when, on the 4th January in that year, Charles I. entered the House
to demand the surrender of the five members. The chair on which Sir
William is seated is of a very similar description to the one used by
Charles I. (illustrated on page 148).

The importation of scarce foreign woods gave an impetus to inlaid
work in England, which had been crude and rough in the time of
Elizabeth. In the marqueterie of Italy, France, Holland, Germany and
Spain considerable excellence had already been attained. Mahogany had
been discovered by Sir Walter Raleigh as early as 1595 but did not come
into general use until the first quarter of the eighteenth century was passed.

STAIRCASE IN GENERAL IRETON'S HOUSE, DATED 1630.

During the year 1891, owing to the extension of the Great Eastern
Railway premises at Bishopsgate Street, an old house of antiquarian
interest was pulled down, and generously presented by the Company to
the Victoria and Albert Museum. This has been erected so as to enable
the visitor to see a good example of the exterior as well as some of the
interior woodwork of a quaint house in the middle of the seventeenth
century. It was the residence of Sir Paul Pindar, during the time of
Charles I., and the carved oak chimney-piece with some other good
ornamental woodwork of this period is worth attention.

In the illustration of a child's chair, which is said to have been
used by members of Cromwell's family, can be seen an example of carved

oak of this time; it was lent to the writer by its present owner, in whose family it is an heirloom, one of his ancestors having married the Protector's daughter. The ornament has no particular style and it may be taken for granted that the period of the Commonwealth was not marked by any progress in decorative Art. The illustration of a staircase on the preceding page proves that there were exceptions to the prevalent

OAK CHAIR COVERED WITH RED LEATHER.
Jacobean: Middle of Seventeenth Century.
(*Victoria and Albert Museum*).

Puritan objection to figure ornament. In one of Mrs. S. C. Hall's papers, " Pilgrimages to English Shrines," contributed in 1849 to the *Art Journal*, she describes the interior of the house which was built for Bridget the Protector's daughter who married General Ireton. The handsome oak staircase had the newels surmounted by carved figures, representing different grades of men in the General's army—a captain, common soldier, piper, drummer, etc., etc., while the spaces between the balustrades were filled in with devices emblematical of warfare, the ceiling being decorated in the fashion of the period.   At the time Mrs. Hall wrote the house bore Cromwell's name.

We may date from the Commonwealth the more general use of chairs; people sat as they chose, and no longer regarded the chair as the lord's place. A style of chair we still recognise as Cromwellian was imported from Holland about this time—plain square backs and seats covered with brown leather, studded with brass nails. The legs, which are now generally turned with a spiral twist, were in Cromwell's time plain or but slightly carved.

The residence of Charles II. abroad had accustomed him and his friends to the much more luxurious furniture of France and Holland. With the Restoration came a foreign Queen, a foreign Court, French manners and French literature. Cabinets, chairs, tables and couches were imported into England from the Netherlands, France, Spain and Portugal; and our craftsmen profited by new ideas and new patterns and an increased demand for decorative articles of furniture. The King of Portugal had ceded Bombay, one of the Portuguese Indian Stations, to the new Queen of England and there is a chair of this Indo-Portuguese work, carved in ebony, now in the Ashmolean Museum at Oxford, which was given by Charles II. either to Elias Ashmole or to Evelyn. The chair is very similar to one at Penshurst; it is grouped (see page 159) with a settee of like design, together with a small folding chair which Mr. G. T. Robinson, in his article on "Seats," has described as Italian, but which we take the liberty of pronouncing to be Flemish, judging by a similar one now in the Victoria and Albert Museum.

In connection with this Indo-Portuguese furniture it would seem that spiral turning became known and fashionable in England during the reign of Charles II. and in some chairs of English make which have come under the writer's notice, the legs have been carved to imitate the effects of spiral turning—an amount of superfluous labour which would scarcely have been incurred but for the fact that the country house-carpenter of this time had an imported model which he copied without knowing how to produce by means of the lathe the effect which had just come into fashion. There are, too, in certain illustrations in Shaw's " Ancient Furniture," some lamp-holders in which this spiral turning is overdone, a fault which is frequently to be met with when any particular kind of ornament comes into vogue.

The suite of furniture at Penshurst Place (illustrated), which comprises thirteen pieces, was probably imported about this time; two of the

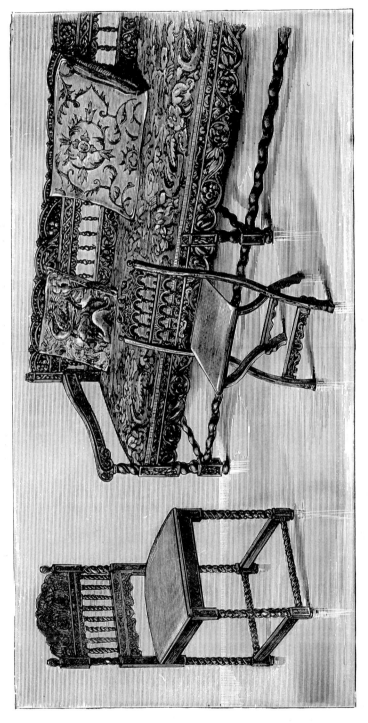

SETTEE AND CHAIR.

In carved ebony, part of the Indo-Portuguese Suite at Penshurst Place, with Flemish Folding Chair.

PERIOD: CHARLES II.

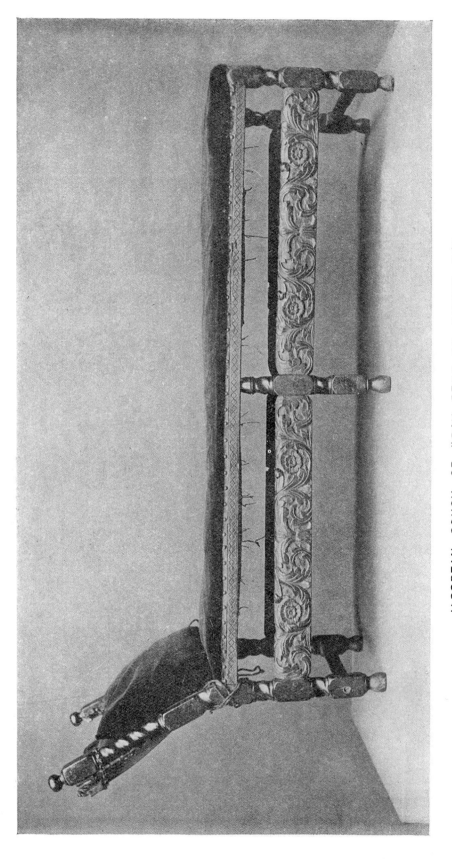

JACOBEAN COUCH OR "DAY BED" OF CARVED OAK.

MIDDLE OF SEVENTEENTH CENTURY.

(Victoria and Albert Museum).

smaller chairs appear to have their original cushions, the others have been re-covered by the late Lord de l'Isle and Dudley. The spindles of the backs of two of the chairs are of ivory; the carving, which is in solid ebony, is much finer on some than on others.

We gather a good deal of information about the furniture of this period from the famous diary of Evelyn. He thus describes Hampton Court Palace as it appeared to him at the time of its preparation for the reception of Catherine of Braganza, the bride of Charles II., who spent the royal honeymoon in this historic building, which had in its time sheltered for their brief spans of favour the six wives of Henry VIII., and the sickly boyhood of Edward VI.

"It is as noble and uniform a pile as Gothic architecture can make it. There is incomparable furniture in it, especially hangings designed by Raphael, very rich with gold. Of the tapestries I believe the world can show nothing nobler of the kind than the stories of Abraham and Tobit.* . . . . . The Queen's bed was an embroidery of silver on crimson velvet, and cost £8,000, being a present made by the States of Holland when his Majesty returned. The great looking-glass and toilet of beaten massive gold were given by the Queen Mother. The Queen brought over with her from Portugal such Indian cabinets as had never before been seen here." Evelyn wrote, of course, before Wren made his Renaissance additions to the Palace.

There are many references by Evelyn to the costliness and splendour of furniture of this time. Recording a visit to Lady Arlington at Goring House in 1763, he mentions the bed, the glasses, silver, cabinets and vases "and such rich furniture as is seldom seen." In another entry he speaks of the "wantonness and profusion."

We are able to illustrate some examples of furniture of this time which are in the Victoria and Albert Museum. The couch or "day bed," with carved oak frame, has an adjustable back fitted with an iron rack on a similar principle to the one already described in the couch at Knole. The date of this day bed is about 1660. The four single chairs illustrated are probably some few years later and are considered by the Museum authorities of South Kensington to be of provincial make— two being of Lancashire origin and the other two from Yorkshire or Derbyshire. It will be observed that these chairs are without upholstery. The cushions of the period were loose and fastened to the chair by being tied with tapes. In some of the old wills and inventories these cushions of "Turkey cloth" or velvet were mentioned separately from the chairs.

* This tapestry is still in the Great Hall at Hampton Court Palace.

After the Great Fire which occurred in 1666 and destroyed some 13,000 houses and no fewer than eighty-nine churches, Sir Christopher Wren was given an opportunity, almost unprecedented in history, of displaying his genius for design and reconstruction. Writing of this great architect, Macaulay says, " The austere beauty of the Athenian portico, the gloomy sublimity of the Gothic arcade, he was, like most of his contemporaries, incapable of emulating and perhaps incapable of appreciating ; but no man born on our side of the Alps has imitated with so much success the magnificence of the palace churches of Italy.   Even the superb

JACOBEAN OAK CHAIRS (LANCASHIRE), ABOUT 1670.
(Victoria and Albert Museum.)

Louis XIV. has left to posterity no work which can bear a comparison with St. Paul's."

Wren's great masterpiece was commenced in 1675 and completed in 1710, and its building therefore covers a period of thirty-five years, carrying us through the reign of James II., William III. and Mary and well on to the end of Anne's reign.   The admirable work which he did during this time and which has effected so much for the adornment of our Metropolis, had a marked influence on the ornamental woodwork of the second half of the seventeenth century : in the additions which he made to Hampton

Court Palace, in Bow Church, in the Hospitals of Greenwich and of Chelsea, there is a sumptuousness of ornament in stone and marble, which show the influence exercised on his mind by the desire to rival the grandeur of Louis XIV., the Fountain Court at Hampton being in direct imitation of the Palace of Versailles. The carved woodwork of the choir of St. Paul's, with fluted columns supporting a carved frieze; the richly carved panels and the beautiful figure work on both organ lofts afford evidence that the oak enrichments followed the marble and stone ornament. The swags of fruit and flowers, the cherubs' heads with folded wings, and

JACOBEAN OAK CHAIRS (YORKSHIRE OR DERBYSHIRE), ABOUT 1670.
(*Victoria and Albert Museum.*)

other details of Wren's work, closely resemble the designs executed by Gibbons, whose carving will be noticed later on.

It may be mentioned here that amongst the few Churches in the City of London which escaped the Great Fire and contained woodwork of particular note, are St. Helen's, Bishopsgate, and the Charterhouse Chapel, which contain the original pulpits of about the sixteenth century.

The famous Dr. Busby, who for fifty-five years was head master of Westminster School, was a great favourite of King Charles, and a picture, painted by Sir Peter Lely, is said to have been presented to

Sedes, ecce tibi! quæ tot produxit alumnos,
Quot gremio nutrit Granta, quot Isis habet.

From the Original by Sir Peter Lely, presented to Dʳ Busby by King Charles

"SEDES BUSBIANA,"

PERIOD: CHARLES II.   (*From an old Print.*)

the Doctor by his Majesty; it is called " Sedes Busbiana." Prints from this old picture are scarce and the writer was indebted to the late Mr. John C. Thynne for the loan of his copy, from which the illustration is taken. The portrait in the centre, of the Pedagogue aspiring to the mitre, is that of Dr. South, who succeeded Busby and whose monument in Westminster Abbey is next to his. The illustration is interesting, as although it may not have been actually taken from a chair itself, it shows a design in the mind of a contemporary artist.

Of the Halls of the City Guilds there is none more quaint and in greater contrast to the bustle of the neighbourhood than the Hall of the Brewers' Company in Addle Street, City. This was partially destroyed, like most of the older Halls, by the Great Fire, but was one of the first to be restored and refurnished. In the kitchen are still to be seen the remains of an old trestle and other relics of an earlier period, but the hall or dining room and the Court Room are original, with very slight additions, since the date of their interior equipment in 1670 to 1673. The Court Room has a richly carved chimney-piece in oak, nearly black with age, the design of which is a shield with a winged head, palms and swags of fruit and flowers, while on the shield itself is an inscription stating that this room was wainscoted by Alderman Knight, Master of the Company and Lord Mayor of the City of London, in the year 1670. The room itself is exceedingly quaint, with its high wainscoting and windows, reminding one of the portholes of a ship's cabin, while the chief window looks out on to the old-fashioned garden, giving the beholder altogether a pleasing illusion, carrying him back to the days of Charles II.

The chief room or Hall is still more handsomely decorated with carved oak of this time. The actual date, 1673, is over the doorway on a tablet which bears the names, in the letters of the period, of the master, " James Reading, Esq.," and the Wardens, " Mr. Robert Lawrence," " Mr. Samuel Barber " and " Mr. Henry Sell."

The names of other Masters and Wardens are also written over the carved escutcheons of their respective arms and the whole room is one of the best specimens in existence of the oak carving of this date. At the western end is the Master's chair, of which by the courtesy of Mr Higgins, a former Clerk to the Company, we are able to give an illustration overleaf; the shield-shaped back, the carved drapery and the coat-of-arms with the Company's motto, are all characteristic features, as are also the Corinthian columns and arched pediments in the oak decorations of the room. The broken swan-necked pediment, which surmounts the cornice of the room over the doors, is probably a more recent addition, this ornament having come in about thirty years later.

There are also the old dining tables and benches: these are as plain and simple as possible. In the Court Room is a table, which was formerly in the Company's barge; it has some good inlaid work in the arcading which connects the two end standards and some old carved lions' feet; the top and other parts have been renewed. There is also an oak fire-screen of about the end of the seventeenth century.

THE MASTER'S CHAIR.
Hall of the Brewers' Company.   (*From a Pen and Ink Sketch by H. Evans*).

Another City hall, the interior woodwork of which dates from just after the Great Fire, is that of the Stationers' Company, in Ave Maria Lane, close to Ludgate Hill. Mr. Charles Robert Rivington, the present Master to the Company, has written a pamphlet, full of very interesting records of this ancient and worshipful corporation, from which the following

A COURT CUPBOARD OF OAK.

ENGLISH (JACOBEAN).   SEVENTEENTH CENTURY.

(Victoria and Albert Museum.)

paragraph is a quotation:—"The first meeting of the court after the fire, was held at Cook's Hall, and the subsequent courts, until the hall was rebuilt, at the Lame Hospital Hall, *i.e.*, St. Bartholomew's Hospital. In 1670 a committee was appointed to rebuild the hall and in 1674 the Court agreed with Stephen Colledge (the famous Protestant joiner) to wainscot the hall ' with well-seasoned and well-matched wainscot, according to a model delivered in for the sum of £300.' His work is now to be seen in excellent condition."

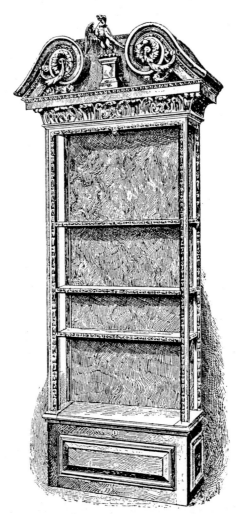

CARVED OAK LIVERY CUPBOARD.
In the Hall of the Stationers' Company.   Made in 1674, the curved pediment
added later, probably in 1788.

Mr. Rivington read his paper to the London and Middlesex Archæological Society in 1881 and the writer can with pleasure confirm his statement as to the condition, in 1889, of this fine specimen of seventeenth century work. Less ornate and elaborate than the Brewers' Hall, the panels are only slightly relieved with carved mouldings, but the end of the room, or main entrance, opposite the place of the old daïs (long since removed), is somewhat similar to that in the Brewers' Hall, and presents a fine architectural effect, which will be observed in the illustration below.

There is on page 168 an illustration of one of the two livery cupboards which formerly stood on the daïs and these are good examples of the cupboards for display of plate of this period. The lower part was formerly the receptacle for unused viands, which were distributed to the poor after the feast. In their original state these livery cupboards finished with a

CARVED OAK SCREEN.
In the Hall of the Stationers' Company, erected in 1674; the Royal Coat-of-Arms has since been added.

straight cornice, the broken pediments with the eagle (the Company's crest) having most probably been added when the Hall was, to quote an inscription on a shield, "repaired and beautified in the mayoralty of the Right Honourable William Gill, in the year 1788," when Mr. Thomas Hooke was Master and Mr. Field and Mr. Rivington (the present Master's grandfather) Wardens.

There is still preserved in a lumber room one of the old benches of seventeenth century work—now replaced in the hall by modern folding chairs. This is of oak with turned skittle-shaped legs slanting outwards

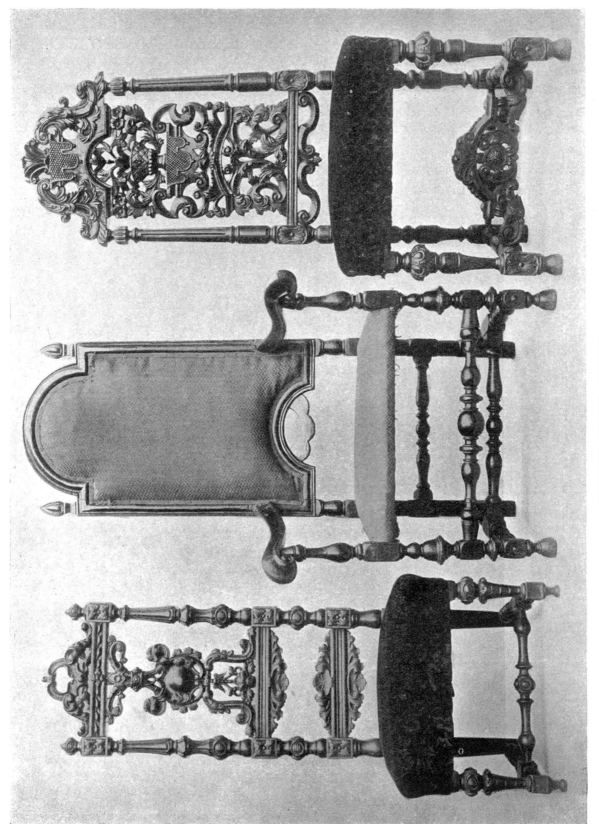

WALNUT WOOD CHAIRS.

Formerly in the Old Palace, Richmond.   Date about 1690 (William and Mary.)

(Victoria and Albert Museum.)

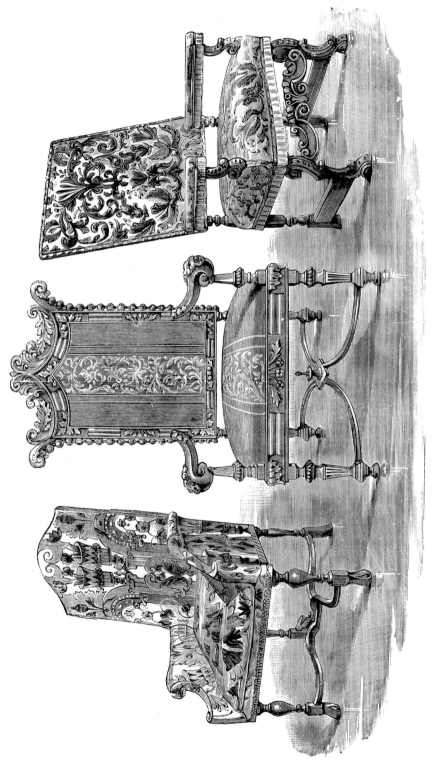

ARM CHAIRS.

Chair upholstered in Spitalfields silk.   Carved and upholstered Chair.   Chair upholstered in Spitalfields silk.

HAMPTON COURT PALACE.   HARDWICK HALL.   KNOLE, SEVENOAKS,

PERIOD: WILLIAM III. TO QUEEN ANNE.

and connected and strengthened by plain stretchers. The old tables are still in their original places.

Another example of seventeenth century oak panelling is the handsome chapel of the Mercers' Hall—the only City Company possessing their own chapel—but only the lining of the walls and the reredos are of the original work, the remainder having been added some fifty years ago, when some of the original carving was made use of in the new work. Indeed, in this magnificent hall, about the most spacious of the old City Corporation palaces, there is a great deal of new work mixed with old—new chimney-pieces and old overmantels—some of Grinling Gibbons' carved enrichments, so painted and varnished as to have lost much of their character; these have been applied to the oak panels in the large dining hall.

The Hall of the Vintners' Company, in Upper Thames Street, E.C., contains some fine oak panelling of this period, and the Hall of the Goldsmiths' Company, which was built and furnished about 1830, has the lobby and two of the upstairs rooms panelled with the oak lining of the former hall, which was destroyed by fire. There are large panels with Corinthian columns and over-door enrichments, probably the work of the latter part of the reign of James II.

Towards the end of the seventeenth century the fashion was for much larger panels than formerly, and besides the examples quoted, which are accessible, there are numerous old country houses where the original panelling still remains.

The interior decoration of living rooms had been undergoing changes since the commencement of the period of which we are now writing. In 1638 a man named Christopher had taken out a patent for enamelling and gilding leather, which was used as a wall decoration over the oak panelling. This decorated leather had hitherto been imported from Holland and Spain. When this was not used, and tapestry, which was very expensive, was not obtainable, the plaster was roughly ornamented. Somewhat later than this, pictures were let into the wainscot to form part of the decoration, for in 1669 Evelyn, when writing of the house of the Earl of Norwich, in Epping Forest, says, " A good many pictures put into the wainscot, which Mr. Baker, his lordship's predecessor, brought from Spaine." Indeed, subsequently the wainscot became simply the frame for pictures, and the same writer deplores the disuse of timber, and expresses his opinion that a sumptuary law ought to be passed to restore the " ancient use of timber." Although no law was enacted on the subject, yet, some twenty years later, the whirligig of fashion brought about the revival of the custom of lining rooms with oak panelling.

It is said that about 1670 Evelyn found Grinling Gibbons in a small thatched house on the outskirts of Deptford, and introduced him to the King, who gave him an appointment on the Board of Works, and patronised him with extensive orders. The character of his carving is well known. Generally using lime-tree as the vehicle of his designs, his life-like birds and flowers, groups of fruit and heads of cherubs are easily recognised. One of the rooms in Windsor Castle is decorated with the work of his chisel, which can also be seen in St. Paul's Cathedral, Hampton Court Palace, Chatsworth, Burghley and perhaps his best in Petworth House in Sussex. He also sculptured in stone. The base of King Charles' statue at Windsor, the font of St. James', Piccadilly (round the base of which are figures of Adam and Eve), are his work, as is also the lime-tree border of festoon work over the Communion table. Gibbons was an Englishman, but appears to have spent his boyhood in Holland, where he was christened "Grinling." He died in 1721. His pupils were Samuel Watson, a Derbyshire man, who did much of the carved work at Chatsworth, Drevot of Brussels, and Lawreans of Mechlin. Gibbons and his pupils founded a school of carving in England which has been continued by tradition to the present day.

LACQUERED FURNITURE IN ENGLAND

In the latter half of the seventeenth century lacquered furniture was very fashionable. In Chapter V. on Eastern furniture there are some notes upon this method of decorating woodwork, and in Chapter VI. mention has been made of its introduction into France and its use by their *ébenistes.*

There are many references to what was at that time a new fashion, in letters and documents of the seventeenth century. Horace Walpole writing to Sir Horace Mann in 1743 mentions his visit to a factory where he witnessed the "new and curious process of japanning upon wood."

There are several examples of English and Dutch lacquer in the Victoria and Albert Museum. The earliest of these is attributed to the time of Charles II., and the carved and gilt or sometimes the silvered stands of these cabinets are in the style of Grinling Gibbons who was employed by the King and Court of Charles. No doubt a great deal of lacquer was imported from Holland about the time of William the Third's accession to the English throne, and it is impossible to distinguish some of the Dutch work from that made in this country.

The tall clock cases or grandfather clocks were very often decorated with lacquer in various colours such as black, red, brown and occasionally green and buff; the ornament, nearly always of a Chinese character, was executed in gold, some portions being in slight relief. Many of these clocks bear the names and dates of the clockmaker so that we have

CABINET OF RED LACQUER.

With Chinese landscapes in gold and silver, mounted with engraved gilt metal hinges, on a stand carved with female mask and decorated with foliage on a red ground.

ENGLISH: PERIOD OF QUEEN ANNE. Sold at Christies' in the Duke of Leeds Collection June 10th, 1920.

(From a Photo supplied by Messrs. Christie.)

reliable data as to the time of their productions. Mr. Francis Lenygon in his " English Furniture, 1660-1760 " has illustrated several with the dates and makers' names running from 1695 to 1750, and there are many good illustrations of English lacquer in Mr. Percy Macquoid's "History of English Furniture."

Besides cabinets and clock cases, linen chests, tables of different shapes, sets of chairs and various other articles of furniture were made in lacquer. "Chequers" the beautiful old sixteenth century Buckingham-shire mansion which Lord and Lady Lee of Fareham have presented to the Prime Ministers of England, contains many good examples of English lacquer, besides some examples in which panels of Chinese lac form parts of old seventeenth century cabinets and chests of English manufacture.

Within the last ten to fifteen years there has been in England a greatly increased appreciation of lacquered furniture. Cabinets of the square box-like form, having two doors opening and disclosing an interior arrangement of various small doors, which, twenty to twenty-five years ago could be purchased for £30 to £50, now realise some five or six times those amounts and exceptional examples bring sensational prices, the red variety being that which is in most favour. In July, 1920, at Christies' a cabinet of this description mounted on a Chippendale lacquered stand realised 950 guineas, and a month earlier at a sale of the Duke of Leeds' furniture, a remarkably fine and well-preserved cabinet realised the record price of £2,331. The stand of this fine cabinet is of a design very seldom seen, and this no doubt to some extent influenced the price. By per-mission of Messrs. Christie and of Mr. M. Harris, the purchaser, an illustration is given of this cabinet.

The fashion in England for the manufacture and importation of lacquer may be said to have commenced during the reign of Charles II., to have increased and developed during the time of William and Mary, and gradually declined after the middle of the eighteenth century.

The important immigration of French workmen which occurred about this time has already been referred to, and these refugees bringing with them their skill, their patterns and ideas, influenced the carving of our ornamental frames and the designs of some of our furniture. This influence is to be traced in some of the contents of Hampton Court Palace, particularly in the carved and gilt centre tables and the *torchères* of French design but of English workmanship. They introduced the manufacture of crystal chandeliers and founded our Spitalfields silk industry and other trades until then little practised in England.

The beautiful silver furniture at Knole belongs to this time, having been made for one of the Earls of Dorset, in the reign of James II. The illustration is from a photograph taken by Mr. Corke, of Sevenoaks. Electrotypes of the originals are in the Victoria and Albert Museum.

SILVER FURNITURE AT KNOLE.

(From a Photo by Mr. Corke, of Sevenoaks.)

From two other suites at Knole, consisting of a looking-glass, a table and a pair of *torchères*, in the one case of plain walnut wood and in the other of ebony with silver mountings, it would appear that a toilet suite of furniture of the time of James II. generally consisted of articles more or less costly, according to circumstances, but of a similar pattern to those shown in the illustration. The silver table bears the English Hall mark of the reign.

Knole also contains several other articles made by the silversmiths of Charles the Second's time and, although not strictly coming within the

SILVER TABLE PRESENTED TO WILLIAM III. BY THE CORPORATION OF THE CITY OF LONDON.
LATE SEVENTEENTH CENTURY.   WINDSOR CASTLE.

category of furniture, deserve mention here. There are twenty-six wall sconces, some of which have lately been adapted for the electric lighting of the Colonnade, a toilet service which was a wedding present to Lady Frances Cranfield, Countess of Dorset, and bears her monogram, a pair of very handsome fire-dogs, besides some urns, bowls and a handsome ewer and basin. The majority of these fine specimens of old English silver bear the Hall mark of the period. Mr. Lionel Sackville-West, now Lord Sackville, published a well-illustrated book giving many interesting particulars of this wonderful house and its valuable contents.

OAK PANELLING WITH APPLIED CARVINGS IN CEDAR.

FROM CLIFFORD'S INN, LONDON.   ENGLISH, C. 1686-88.

(*Victoria and Albert Museum.*)

Windsor Castle is also rich in specimens of sumptuously rich silver furniture. In Sir Guy Laking's work entitled "The Furniture of Windsor Castle," there are detailed descriptions of a table, a mirror and some *torchères*, bearing the crown and cypher of Charles II., with the Hall marks and makers' names of the time.

A very handsome table of later workmanship is illustrated on page 177. This was presented to William III. by the Corporation of the City of London and bears the initials of its maker, Andrew Moore, a celebrated silversmith, of Bridewell.

THE TIME OF WILLIAM AND MARY

Two famous storehouses of beautiful furniture of this time are Ham House, Petersham, and Drayton Manor, Northamptonshire, the residence of the Earl of Peterborough, a contemporary of the Duke of Lauderdale. The former house can be seen if special permission is obtained and the student of late seventeenth century English furniture should avail himself of the privilege so courteously granted by the Earl of Dysart.

Built by Sir Thomas Vavasour in 1610, it was for a time the residence of Prince Henry, eldest son of James I. In 1643 Charles I. gave it to his friend, William Murray, whom he created Earl of Dysart, and the title passed to his eldest daughter Elizabeth, and from her first marriage sprang the family which now owns the place; her second husband was the too famous Duke of Lauderdale, and the State rooms furnished by the Duke and Duchess have remained practically unaltered. The Duke died in 1682, but Elizabeth lived until 1698, and this accounts for so much of the furniture in the house being of the time of William and Mary.

That period of furniture in England has been called "the Age of Walnut." This wood which had been occasionally used during the reigns of Elizabeth and James I., came into more general use both for veneers and for solid work. An attractive feature of the former was the peculiar figuring which is known as "oyster shells" from the resemblance which the natural markings of the wood bear to the shell of an oyster. Marqueterie was very fashionable, the designs generally being vases of different coloured flowers and scrolls inlaid on a groundwork of walnut wood. The legs of tables were either spirally turned and connected by a flat stretcher or turned somewhat like the balusters of a staircase with cup-like ornaments, varied by legs formed as "S" scrolls. Cabinets and tables of ebony and of lignum vitæ, ornamented with plaques of embossed silver, are also a feature of this time, and there are several of these at

Drayton Manor. As a rule they were made to the order of wealthy noblemen and were enriched with coats-of-arms. Mirror frames were also ornamented with silver. Hangings and draperies were very rich, and the State bed at Drayton is a striking example of the wonderful needlework adapted to this use. Queen Mary stimulated the art of embroidery by her example, and there is a letter of Bishop Burnet from which the following extract is significant: " sometimes with so constant a diligence as if she had to earn her bread by it. It was no new thing, and looked like a sight, to see a Queen work so many hours a day." Cross stitch and tent stitch and *petit point* embroideries were very much the vogue among Court ladies, and in the coverings of some of the chairs and settees of this time we have preserved to us many beautiful examples of their skill and industry. Sir George Donaldson, in his private museum at Hove, has a fine collection of this kind of needlework.

As the seventeenth century came to its end, furniture of a more domestic character seems to have been made in great quantities, and the walnut wood cabinets, double chests of drawers, called tallboys, tables of a useful and not ornamental kind, a greater variety of chairs and other articles of domestic furniture came into general use.

For the first time we have cabinets for the display of china of which Queen Mary was an enthusiastic collector, as was also her sister Queen Anne, and the bill of Garrett Johnson's, quoted below, appears to have been for a cabinet made for the purpose of displaying specimens of old china.

The fashion for a number of small tables for guests at a dinner party, which has obtained in England during recent years, is not altogether a novelty. In the inventory of the contents of Ham House made in 1679, there are three small cedar wood tables for dining, and in later years there were eight of these tables. The fashion is said to have come in after the Restoration.

The process of decorating furniture with Gesso-work has been mentioned in Chapter III. as an Italian fashion, but at the end of the seventeenth century it was very much the vogue in England. Ornamental centre and side tables, gueridons and mirror frames were coated with a preparation made with whitening and boiled parchment shavings, afterwards carved with scroll and figure designs, and then gilt. It may be mentioned here that a century later Robert Adam designed a great deal of Gesso-work, but his process was more mechanical, as his designs were produced by pressing from moulds. There are several examples of seventeenth century Gesso-work at Hampton Court Palace.

Very few names of the makers of furniture of this time have been handed down to us. Pepys in his diary under the date 27th August,

1666, mentions "the new presses for my books made by Mr. Sympson, joyner." These he bequeathed to Magdalene College, Cambridge, where they can still be seen; they have handsomely carved cornices and surbase mouldings.

Another name has been quoted by Mr. Lenygon from an old bill of £200 for a "wrighting table with a cabinet to set over it, and a large

MAHOGANY DRESSING TABLE, MIRROR, AND FOUR INLAID BOXES.
ENGLISH: ABOUT 1680—1700.
(Victoria and Albert Museum.)

glas case upon a cabinet with door finely inley'd for the closit, at Whitehall, for Her Majesty in 1694." This was from Garrett Johnson, cabinet maker.

In Sir George Donaldson's collection there is a fine cabinet of an architectural design, the front door having two fluted pilasters with carved caps and the cornice surmounted by a scroll pediment. Inside the door the name of the maker is inlaid, " Saml. Bennett, London, fecit," in plain half inch letters.

As an instance of the interest which in the seventeenth century was taken in artistic furniture, the following quotation from Pepys' diary is of interest. The diarist had called upon a Mr. Povy and in recording his visit wrote "most extraordinary fine house, at work with a cabinet maker on a new inlaid table."

The full page illustration on page 178 shows the interior of a room which has been reconstructed by the Victoria and Albert Museum experts, and represents panelling and doors of oak and cedar with some contemporary furniture. The old house in Clifford's Inn from which these examples were removed was built for John Penhallow, 1686-88, and remained without material alterations until his death in 1716.

Specimens of English furniture, dating from about 1680 to 1700, distinctly show the influence of Flemish design. The Stadtholder, King William III., with his Dutch friends, imported many of their household gods and our English craftsmen seem to have copied these very closely. The chairs and settees in the Victoria and Albert Museum and at Hampton Court Palace have the shaped back, with a wide inlaid or carved upright bar; the cabriole leg and the carved shell ornament on the knee of the leg, and on the top of the back, which are still to be seen in the furniture of many old Dutch houses.

There are many examples of furniture of this date, which it is difficult to distinguish from Flemish, but in some others there is a characteristic decoration in marqueterie, which may be described as a seaweed scroll in holly or box wood, inlaid on a pale walnut ground, which enables us to recognise it as English work. A good example of this is to be seen in the upright "grandfather's clock" in the Victoria and Albert Museum, the effect being a pleasing harmony of colour.

On opposite page is an illustration of a walnut wood and marqueterie centre table at Ham House, from a photograph in the Victoria and Albert Museum album. This has been described by the Museum authorities as Dutch, and, like many other pieces of this time which have been found in old English houses, it is difficult to decide whether such a piece was imported from Holland, or made in this country by Dutch workmen, or copied from similar furniture which had been brought over. We are inclined in this case to think that the table is of English manufacture and the date about 1700 to 1720.

A French artist who designed furniture, named Daniel Marot, was a protégé of William III. and from his drawings some of the State furniture at Hampton Court Palace, including the King's bedstead, was made.

Marot's style was an elaborate rendering of late Louis XIV. designs. He was undoubtedly a versatile artist of great ability, and influenced the design of furniture in this country at the end of the seventeenth and the early part of the eighteenth century. Chippendale is said to have adopted some of his designs when he produced his *Director* some half-a-century later.

As we have observed with regard to French furniture of this time, mirrors came more generally into use and the frames were both carved

MARQUETERIE TABLE FROM HAM HOUSE.
PROBABLY ENGLISH (DUTCH STYLE), ABOUT 1700.

and inlaid. There are several of these at Hampton Court Palace, all with bevel-edged plate glass; some have frames entirely of glass, the short lengths which make the frame having the joints over-laid by rosettes of blue glass or a narrow moulding of gilt work on both sides of the frame. In one room (the Queen's Gallery) the frames are painted in colours and relieved by a little gilding.

These notes on the furniture, which was in use during the reign of William and Mary, should indicate how great was the variety of material

MARQUETERIE TABLE TOP.

English work showing Dutch influence. Time of William and Mary.

(From "The Connoisseur," by permission.)

available for the furnishing of the homes of people of moderate means. Dutch furniture, lacquered cabinets and screens imported or manufactured in England, Gesso-work tables and mirrors of great variety, rich upholstery and beautiful needlework were combined with Oriental porcelain, the collection of which had become fashionable; there were besides examples of the excellent work of the silversmiths of this time. Portraits of Lely, Kneller and many contemporary artists both English and Continental, tapestries and eastern rugs were all accessories which the person of taste and means was able to procure. We have in many old documents such as inventories, wills and diaries, evidence that there was a striving for artistic effects in the home.

THE TIME OF QUEEN ANNE

The style of decoration in furniture and woodwork which we recognise as " Queen Anne," apart from the marqueterie just described, appears, so far as the writer's investigations have gone, to be due to the designs of some eminent architects of the time. Sir James Vanbrugh was building Blenheim Palace for the Queen's victorious general, and also Castle Howard. Nicholas Hawksmoor had erected the church of St. George's, Bloomsbury, and James Gibbs, a Scotch architect and antiquary, the church of St. Martin's-in-the-Fields and the Radcliffe Library at Oxford. A ponderous style characterises the woodwork interiors of these buildings.

The furniture made in England during this reign scarcely belongs to the Jacobean period and an apology or explanation seems necessary for including these notes in a chapter dealing with that period of taste. It may be said however that from the end of the seventeenth century, say from the accession of William III. until the time of Chippendale, we were, in this country, passing through a time of transition, which strongly reflects the Dutch and French influence which dominated our cabinet makers' work. Some of the illustrations on the last few pages of this chapter are examples of this influence, and in the rooms at Hampton Court Palace the reader will find many pieces of furniture which will assist him to understand the phase of taste through which we were passing during the early years of the eighteenth century.

The material mostly used was walnut and the salient ornaments by which we recognise what is called the Queen Anne style are some of those which have already been referred to. The " swan-necked " pediment, the cabriole leg with clubbed foot and the carved scallop-shell ornament on the knees of the legs of chairs and tables, a partiality for numerous

CABINET IN WALNUT WOOD.

With panels of '' Seaweed '' Marqueterie.

The property of the Duke of Northumberland.   QUEEN ANNE PERIOD.

(*From '' The Connoisseur,'' by permission.*)

small drawers to the cabinets, is noticeable, and mirror frames of walnut wood have some carved ornaments relieved by gilding. The peculiar seaweed scroll marqueterie has already been described and generally speaking the decoration by inlay, of this time, is modest and restrained, generally only one colour, that of the yellow box or stained holly on a groundwork of walnut. Laburnum wood of different shades was also used in the marqueterie, and the legs of tables were occasionally turned out of yew

CARD TABLE OF WALNUT WOOD.
A typical piece of furniture of Queen Anne period.
(*From " The Connoisseur," by permission.*)

tree wood. Ivory stained green was also used as an inlay. Corner cupboards, double chests of drawers, tray-topped tables, grandfather clocks and quaint card and side tables are still to be found of this period.

Although the practice of card playing had been the fashion in Tudor and early Stuart times, and was indulged in during the reign of James I. to pass the time while the scenes at the theatre were being "set," no tables for the special purpose of card playing appear to have been made. So far as the writer's observations have gone the first card tables were those of walnut wood of the time of Queen Anne, and the foregoing illustration is a representative example. Some have very delicately carved enrichments on the front of the tables, and they generally have sunk circles where the silver candlesticks of the period were to stand and others have places for the counters. Those of this early eighteenth century period are invariably well made as regards joinery and materials.

The first mention of corner cupboards appears to have been made in an advertisement of a Dutch joiner in the *Postman* of March 8th, 1711; these cupboards, with their carved pediments, being part of the modern fittings of a room of the time of Queen Anne.

The oak presses common to this and earlier times are formed of an upper and lower part, the former sometimes being three sides of an

CARVED AND GILT SEAT FROM HAM HOUSE.
English work, latter half of Seventeenth Century.

octagon with the top supported by columns, while the lower half is straight and the whole is carved with incised ornament. These useful articles of furniture, in the absence of wardrobes, are described in inventories of the time (1680-1720) as "press cupboards," "great cupboards," "wainscot" and "joyned cupboards."

Nearly all writers on the subject of furniture and woodwork are agreed in considering that the earlier part of the period discussed in this chapter—namely, the seventeenth century, gives us the best examples of English work. As we have seen in noticing some of the earlier Jacobean examples already illustrated and described, it was a period marked by increased refinement of design, through the abandonment of the more grotesque and often coarse work of Elizabethan carving, and by soundness of construction and thorough workmanship.

Furniture made in England during the seventeenth century is a credit to the painstaking craftsmen of those days and even upholstered furniture, like the couches and chairs at Knole, after more than 250 years' service, are fit for use. When we come to deal with furniture of the present day and the methods of production which are now in practice, a comparison will be made which must be to the credit of the Jacobean period.

*   *   *   *   *   *

In the foregoing chapters an attempt has been made to preserve, as far as possible, a certain continuity in the history of the subject matter of this work from the earliest times until after the Renaissance had been generally adopted in Europe. In this endeavour a greater amount of attention has been bestowed upon the furniture of a comparatively short period of English history than upon that of other countries and it is hoped that this arrangement will be approved by English readers.

It has now become necessary to interrupt this plan and before returning to the consideration of European design and work, to devote a short chapter to those branches of the Industrial Arts connected with furniture, which flourished in China and Japan, in India, Persia and Arabia, at a time anterior and subsequent to the Renaissance period in Europe.

SEVENTEENTH CENTURY CHAIR
IN HOLLAND HOUSE.

PATTERN OF A CHINESE LAC SCREEN (COROMANDEL LACQUER).

(*Victoria and Albert Museum.*)

CHAPTER V

The Furniture of Eastern Countries

CHINESE AND JAPANESE FURNITURE

WE have been unable to discover when the Chinese first began to use State or domestic furniture. Whether, like the ancient Assyrians and Egyptians, there was an early civilisation which included the arts of joining, carving and upholstering, we do not know; most probably there was; and from the plaster casts which one sees in our Indian Museum of the ornamental stone gateways of Sanchi Tope, in Bhopal, Central India, it would appear that, in the early part of our Christian era the carvings in wood of their neighbours and co-religionists, the Hindoos, represented figures of men and animals in the woodwork of sacred buildings or palaces. The marvellous dexterity in manipulating wood, ivory and stone which we recognise in the Chinese of to-day, is probably inherited from their early ancestors.

Sir William Chambers travelled in China in the early part of the eighteenth century. It was he who introduced the "Chinese style" into furniture and decoration which was adopted by Chippendale and other makers as will be noticed in the chapter dealing with that period of

English furniture. He gives us the following description of the furniture which he found in " The Flowery Land ":—

" The movables of the saloon consist of chairs, stools and tables ; made sometimes of rosewood, ebony or lacquered work and sometimes of bamboo only, which is cheap and nevertheless very neat. When the movables are of wood the seats of the stools are often of marble or porcelain, which, though hard to sit on, are far from unpleasant in a climate where the summer heats are so excessive. In the corners of the rooms are stands four or five feet high, on which they set plates of citrons and other fragrant fruits, or branches of coral in vases of porcelain, and glass globes containing goldfish, together with a certain weed somewhat resembling fennel ; on such tables as are intended for ornament only, they also place the little landscapes, composed of rocks, shrubs and a kind of lily that grows among pebbles covered with water. Sometimes, also, they have artificial landscapes made of ivory, crystal, amber, pearls and various stones. I have seen some of these that cost over three hundred guineas, but they are at least mere baubles, and miserable imitations of Nature. Besides these landscapes they adorn their tables with several vases of porcelain and little vases of copper, which are held in great esteem. These are generally of simple and pleasing forms. The Chinese say they were made two thousand years ago, by some of their celebrated artists, and such as are real antiques (for there are many counterfeits) they buy at an extravagant price, giving sometimes no less than £300 sterling for one of them.

" The bedroom is divided from the saloon by a partition of folding doors, which, when the weather is hot, are in the night thrown open to admit the air. It is very small and contains no other furniture than the bed and some varnished chests, in which they keep their apparel. The beds are very magnificent ; the bedsteads are made much like ours in Europe—of rosewood, carved, or lacquered work : the curtains are of taffeta or gauze, sometimes flowered with gold, and commonly either blue or purple. About the top a slip of white satin, a foot in breadth, runs all round, on which are painted, in panels, different figures—flower-pieces, landscapes and conversation pieces, interspersed with moral sentences and fables written in Indian ink and vermilion."

From old paintings and engravings which date from about the fourteenth or fifteenth century, one gathers an idea of such furniture as existed in China and Japan in earlier times. In one of these which is reproduced in Racinet's " Le Costume Historique," there is a Chinese princess reclining on a sofa which has a frame of black wood, visible and slightly ornamented ; it is upholstered with rich embroidery, for which these artistic people seem to have been famous from a very early period. A servant stands by her side to hand her the pipe of opium with which the monotony of the day was varied—one arm rests on a small wooden table or stand which is placed on the sofa and which holds a flower vase and a pipe stand. On another old painting two figures are seated on mats playing a game which resembles draughts, the pieces being moved about on a little table with black and white squares like a modern chessboard, with shaped feet to raise it a convenient height for the players; on the floor, cups of tea stand ready at hand. Such pictures are generally ascribed to the fifteenth century, the early period of the great Ming dynasty, which appears to have been the time of an improved culture and taste in China.

From this time and a century later (the sixteenth) also date those beautiful cabinets of lacquered wood enriched with ivory, mother-of-pearl, with silver and even with gold, which have been brought to England occasionally; but genuine specimens of this and of the seventeenth century are very scarce and extremely valuable.

The Chinese furniture which one sees generally in Europe dates from the eighteenth century and was made to order and imported by the Dutch; this explains the curious combination to be found of Oriental and European designs; thus there are screens with views of Amsterdam and other cities copied from paintings sent out for the purpose, while the frames of the panels are of carved rosewood of the fretted bamboo pattern characteristic of the Chinese. Elaborate bedsteads, tables and cabinets were also made, with panels of ash stained a dark colour and ornamented with hunting scenes, in which the representations of men and horses are of ivory, or sometimes with ivory faces and limbs while the clothes are chiefly of a brown coloured wood. In a beautiful table in the Victoria and Albert Museum, which is said to have been made in Cochin-China, mother-of-pearl is largely used and produces a rich effect.

The furniture brought back by the late Duke of Saxe-Coburg from China and Japan is of the usual character imported and the remarks hereafter made on Indian or Bombay furniture apply equally to this adaptation of Chinese detail to European designs.

LACQUER

The most highly prized work of China and Japan in the way of decorative furniture is the beautiful lacquer work, and in the notice on French furniture of the eighteenth century and also in the chapter dealing with the furniture of the time of Queen Anne, we shall see that the process was adopted in Holland, France and England with marked success.

It is worth while however to allude to it here a little more fully. The process as practised in China is thus described by M. Jacquemart:—

"The wood when smoothly planed is covered with a sheet of thin paper or silk gauze, over which is spread a thick coating made of powdered red sandstone and buffalo's gall. This is allowed to dry, after which it is polished and rubbed with wax, or else receives a wash of gum water, holding chalk in solution. The varnish is laid on with a flat brush, and the article is placed in a drying room, whence it passes into the hands of a workman, who moistens and again polishes it with a piece of very fine grained soft clay slate, or with the stalks of the horse-tail or shave grass. It then receives a second coating of lacquer, and when dry is once more polished. These operations are repeated until the surface becomes perfectly smooth and lustrous. There are never applied less than three coatings and seldom more than eighteen, though some old Chinese and some Japan ware are said to have received upwards of twenty. As regards China, this seems quite exceptional, for there is in the Louvre a piece with the legend 'lou-tinsg,' *i.e.*, six coatings, implying that even so many are unusual enough to be worthy of special mention."

There is as much difference between different kinds and qualities of lac as between different classes of marqueterie. The most highly prized is the LACQUER ON GOLD GROUND, and the first specimens of this work which reached Europe during the time of Louis XV. were presentation pieces from the Japanese princes to some of the Dutch officials. This lacquer on gold ground is rarely found in furniture and only as a rule in some of those charming little boxes, in which the luminous effect of the lac is heightened by the introduction of silver foliage on a minute scale, or of tiny landscape work and figures charmingly treated, partly with dull gold and partly with gold highly burnished. Small plaques of this beautiful ware were used for some of the choicest pieces of furniture made for Marie Antoinette and mounted by Gouthière.

AVANTURINE lacquer closely imitates in colour the sparkling mineral from which it takes its name and a less highly finished preparation of it is used as a lining for the small drawers of cabinets. Another lacquer has a black ground on which landscapes delicately traced in gold stand out in charming relief. Such pieces also were used by Riesener and mounted by Gouthière in some of the most costly furniture made for Marie Antoinette; specimens of such furniture are in the Louvre. It is this kind of lacquer in varying qualities that is usually found in cabinets, folding screens, coffers, tables, étagères and other ornamental articles. Enriched with inlay of mother-of-pearl, the effect of which is in some cases heightened and rendered more effective by transparent colouring on its reverse side, as in the case of a bird's plumage or of those beautiful blossoms which both Chinese and Japanese artists can represent so faithfully.

A very remarkable screen in Chinese lacquer of later date is in the Victoria and Albert Museum. It is composed of twelve folds, each ten feet high and measuring, when fully extended, twenty-one feet. This screen is very beautifully decorated on both sides with incised and raised ornaments painted and gilt on black ground, with a rich border ornamented with representations of sacred symbols and various other subjects. The price paid for it was £1,000. There are also in the Museum some very rich chairs of modern Chinese work, in brown wood, probably teak, very elaborately inlaid with mother-of-pearl; they were exhibited in Paris in 1867.

Of the very early history of Japanese Industrial Arts we know but little. We have no record of the kind of furniture which Marco Polo found when he travelled in Japan in the thirteenth century; and until the Jesuit missionaries obtained a footing in the sixteenth century and sent home specimens of native work, there was probably very little of Japanese manufacture which found its way to Europe. The beautiful lacquer work of Japan, which dates from the end of the sixteenth and the following century, leads us to suppose that a long period of probation must have occurred before these processes, which were probably learned from the Chinese, could have been so thoroughly mastered.

Of furniture—with the exception of the cabinets, chests and boxes, large and small—of this famous lac there appears to have been little. Until the Japanese developed a taste for copying European customs and manners, the habit seems to have been to sit on mats and to use small tables raised a few inches from the ground. Even the bedrooms contained no bedsteads, but a light mattress served for bed and bedstead.

The process of lacquering has already been described, and in the chapter on French furniture of the eighteenth century it will be seen how specimens of this decorative material reached France by way of Holland, and were mounted into the *meubles de luxe* of that time. With this exception, and that of the famous collection of porcelain in the Japan Palace at Dresden, probably but little of the Art products of this artistic people had been exported until the country was opened up by the expedition of Lord Elgin and Commodore Perry, in 1858-9, and subsequently by the antiquarian knowledge and research of Sir Rutherford Alcock, who has contributed so much to our knowledge of Japanese Industrial Art; indeed, it is scarcely too much to say that so far as England is concerned, he was the first to introduce the products of the Empire of Japan.

The Revolution and the break up of the feudal system which had existed in that country for some eight hundred years ended by placing the Mikado on the throne. There was a sale in Paris in 1867 of the famous collection of the Shôgun, who had sent his treasures there to raise funds for the civil war in which he was then engaged with the Daimios. This was followed by the exportation of other fine native productions to Paris and London; but the supply of old and really fine specimens has, since about 1874, almost ceased and in default the European markets have become flooded with articles of cheap and inferior workmanship imported to meet the modern demand. The Government of Japan, anxious to recover many of the masterpieces which were produced in the best time, under the patronage of the native princes of the old *régime*, have established a museum at Tokio, where many examples of fine lacquer work, which had been sent to Europe for sale, have been placed after re-purchase, to serve as examples for native artists to copy, and to assist in the restoration of the ancient reputation of Japan.

There is in the Victoria and Albert Museum a very beautiful Japanese chest of lacquer work made about the beginning of the seventeenth century, the best time for Japanese Art; it formerly belonged to Napoleon I., and was purchased at the Hamilton Palace sale for £722: it is some 3ft. 3in. long and 2ft. 1in. high, and was intended originally as a receptacle for sacred Buddhist books. There are, most delicately worked on to its surface, views of the interior of one of the Imperial Palaces of Japan, and a hunting scene. Mother-of-pearl, gold, silver and avanturine are all used in the enrichment of this beautiful specimen of inlaid work, and the lock plate is a representative example of the best kind of metal work as applied to this purpose.

The late Duke of Saxe-Coburg had several fine specimens of Chinese and Japanese lacquer work in his collection, about the arrangement of which the writer had the honour of advising His Royal Highness when it arrived many years ago at Clarence House. The earliest specimen is a reading desk presented to him by the Mikado, with a slope for a book, much resembling an ordinary bookrest, but charmingly decorated with lacquer in landscape subjects on the flat surfaces, while the smaller parts are diapered with flowers and quatrefoils in relief of lac and gold. This is of the sixteenth century. The Victoria and Albert Museum contains many good examples of Eastern lacquer from the seventeenth century to comparatively modern times.

The grotesque carving of the wonderful dragons and marvellous monsters introduced into furniture made by the Chinese and Japanese, and especially in the ornamental woodwork of the Old Temples, is thoroughly peculiar to those masters of elaborate design and skilful manipulation; and the low rate of remuneration, compared with our European notions of wages, enables work to be produced that would be impracticable under any other conditions. In comparing the ornamentation on Chinese with that of Japanese furniture, it may be said that more eccentricity is effected by the latter than by the former in their designs and general decoration. The Japanese joiner is unsurpassed, and much of the lattice work, admirable in design and workmanship, is so quaint and intricate that only by close examination can it be distinguished from finely cut fretwork.

INDIAN FURNITURE

European influence upon Indian Art and manufactures has been of long duration. It was first exercised by the Portuguese and Dutch in the early days of the United East India Company, afterwards by the French, who established a trading company there in 1664, and chiefly by the English, the first charter of the old East India Company dating as far back as 1600. This European taste dominated almost everything of an ornamental character until it became difficult to find a decorative article the design of which did not in some way or other show the predominance of European influence over native conception. Therefore it becomes important to ascertain what kind of furniture, limited as it was, existed in India during the period of the Mogul Empire, which lasted from 1505 to 1739, when the invasion of the Persians under Nadír Shah destroyed the power of the Moguls. The country formerly subject to them was then divided among sundry petty princes.

The thrones and State chairs used by the Moguls were rich with elaborate gilding; the legs or supports were sometimes of turned wood, with some of the members carved. The chair was formed like an hourglass, or rather like two bowls reversed, with the upper part extended to form a higher back to the seat. In M. Racinet's sumptuous work, "Le Costume Historique," published in Paris in twenty volumes (1876), there are reproduced some old miniatures from the collection of M. Ambroise Didot. These represent—with all the advantages of the most highly finished printing in gold, silver and colours—portraits of these native sovereigns seated on their State chairs with the umbrella as a sign of royalty. The panels and ornaments of the thrones are picked out with patterns of flowers, sometimes detached blossoms, sometimes the whole plant; the colours are generally bright red and green, while the ground of a panel or the back of a chair is in silver with arabesque tracery, the rest of the chair being entirely gilt. The couches are rectangular, with four turned and carved supports some eight or ten inches high, and also gilt. With the exception of small tables, which could be carried into the room by slaves and used for the light refreshments customary to the country, there was no other furniture. The ladies of the harem are represented as being seated on sumptuous carpets, and the walls are ornamented with gold and silver and colour, a style of decoration very well suited to the arched openings, carved and gilt doors, and brilliant costumes of the occupants of these Indian palaces.

After the break up of the Mogul power the influence of Holland, France and England brought about a mixture of taste and design which with the concurrent alterations in manners and customs, gradually led to the production of what is now known as the " Bombay Furniture." The elaborate minute carving of Indian design applied to utterly uncongenial Portuguese or French shapes of chairs and sofas, or to the familiar round or oval table, carved almost beyond recognition, are instances of this style. One sees these occasionally in the house of an Anglo-Indian, who has employed native workmen to make some of this furniture for him; the European chairs and tables having been given as models, while the details of the ornament have been left to native taste. There are in the Indian Museum at South Kensington several examples of this Bombay furniture and also some of Cingalese manufacture.

It is scarcely part of our subject to allude to the same kind of influence which has spoiled the quaint *bizarre* effect of native design and workmanship in silver, in jewellery, in carpets, embroideries and in pottery which was so manifest in the contributions sent to South Kensington at the Colonial Exhibition, 1886.

In the Jones Collection at the Victoria and Albert Museum there are two carved ivory chairs and a table, the latter gilded, the former partly gilded, which are a portion of a set taken from Tippo Sahib at the storming of Seringapatam. Warren Hastings brought them to England, and they were given to Queen Charlotte. After her death the set was divided: Lord Londesborough purchased part of it and this portion was formerly on loan at the Bethnal Green Museum.

Queen Victoria had also amongst her numerous Jubilee presents some very handsome ivory furniture of Indian workmanship, which may be seen at Windsor Castle. These, however, as well as the Jones Collection examples, though thoroughly Indian in character as regards the treatment of scrolls, flowers and foliage, show unmistakably the influence of French taste in their general form and composition. Articles such as boxes, stands for gongs, etc., are to be found carved in sandal wood, and in *dalburgia*, or black wood, with rosewood mouldings; and a peculiar characteristic of this Indian decoration, sometimes applied to such small articles of furniture, is the coating of the surface of the wood with red lacquer, the plain parts taking a high polish while the carved enrichment remains dull. The effect of this is precisely that of the article being made of red sealing wax, and frequently the minute pattern of the carved ornament and its general treatment tend to give an idea of an impression made in the wax by an elaborately cut die.

The larger examples of Indian carved woodwork are of teak; the finest and most characteristic specimens within the writer's knowledge are the two folding doors which were sent as a present by the Indian Government and are in the Indian Museum. They are of seventeenth century work and are said to have enclosed a library at Kerowlee. While the door frames are of teak, with the outer frames carved with bands of foliage in high relief, the doors themselves are divided into panels of fantastic shapes and yet so arranged that there is just sufficient regularity to please the eye. Some of these panels are carved and enriched with ivory flowers, others have a rosette of carved ivory in the centre and pieces of talc with green and red colour underneath, a decoration also found in some Arabian work. It is almost impossible to convey by words an adequate description of these doors; they should be carefully examined as examples of genuine native design and workmanship. Mr. Pollen has concluded a somewhat detailed account of them by saying :—" For elegance of shape and proportion and the propriety of the composition of the frame and sub-divisions of these doors, their mouldings and their panel carvings and ornaments, we can for the present name no other example so instructive. We are much reminded by this decoration of the pierced lattices at the S. Marco in Venice."

There is in the Indian Museum another remarkable specimen of native furniture—namely, a chair of the purest beaten gold of octagonal shape and formed of two bowls reversed, decorated with acanthus and lotus in repousée ornament. This is of eighteenth century workmanship and was formerly the property of Runjeet Sing. The precious metal is thinly laid on, according to the Eastern method, the wood underneath the gold taking all the weight. This throne was to have been used at the opening of the Imperial Institute by Queen Victoria, but at the last moment another seat was selected.

There is also a collection of plaster casts of portions of temples and palaces from a very early period until the present time, several having been sent over as a loan to the Indian and Colonial Exhibition of 1886.

A careful observation of the ornamental details of these casts leads us to the conclusion that the Byzantine style, which was dominant throughout the more civilised portion of Asia during the power of the Romans, had survived the great changes of the Middle Ages. As native work became subject more or less to the influence of the Indo-Chinese carvers of deities on the one side, and of the European notions of the Portuguese pioneers of discovery on the other, a fashion of decorative woodwork was arrived at which can scarcely be dignified by the name of a style, and which it is difficult to describe. Sir George Birdwood in his work on Indian Art points out that, about a hundred years ago, Indian designs were affected by the immigration of Persian designers and workmen. The result of this influence is to be seen in the examples in the Museum, a short notice of which will conclude these remarks on Indian work.

The copy in shishem wood of a carved window at Amritzar, in the Punjaub, with its overhanging cornice, ornamental arches supported by pillars and the surface covered with small details of ornament, is a good example of the sixteenth and seventeenth century work. The façades of dwelling-houses in teak wood, carved and still bearing the remains of paint with which part of the carving was picked out, represent the work of the contemporary carvers of Ahmedabad, famous for its woodwork.

Portions of a lacquer work screen similar in appearance to embossed gilt leather, with the pattern in gold, on a ground of black or red, and the singular Cashmere work called " mirror mosaic " give us a good idea of the Indian decoration of the eighteenth and early nineteenth centuries. This *bizarre* effect is produced by little pieces of looking-glass being introduced into the small geometrical patterns of the panels; these, when joined together, produce a very rich result.

The bedstead of King Theebaw, brought from Mandalay, is an example of this mixture of glass and wood, which can be made extremely effective. The wood is carved and gilt to represent the gold setting of numerous precious stones, which are counterfeited by small pieces of looking-glass and variously coloured pieces of transparent glass.

Some of the late King Edward's (at the time Prince of Wales) presents—namely, chairs with carved lions forming arms; tables of shishem wood, inlaid with ebony and ivory—show the European influence we have alluded to.

Amongst the modern ornamental articles in the Museum are many boxes, pen trays, writing cases and even photograph albums, of wood and ivory mosaic work, the inlaid patterns being produced by placing together strips of tin wire, sandal wood, ebony, and of ivory, white or stained green: these strips, when bound into a rod, either triangular or hexagonal, are cut into small sections, and then inlaid into the surface of the article to be decorated.

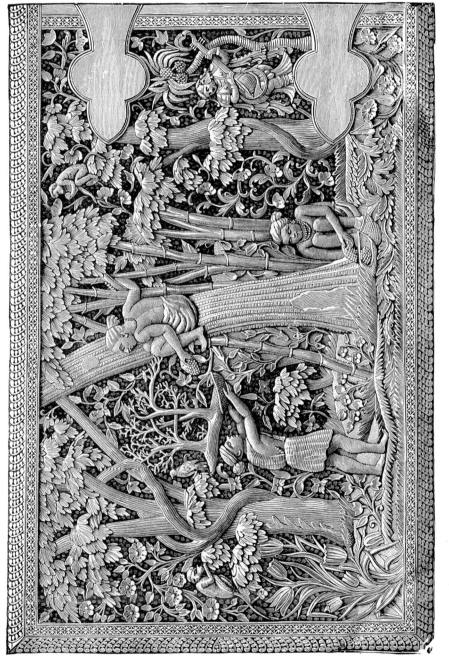

DOOR.

Of carved sandal wood, from Travancore. Indian Museum, South Kensington.
Period : Probably Late XVIII. Century.

Papier maché and lacquer work are also frequently found in small articles of furniture ; and the collection of drawings by native artists attest the high skill in design and execution attained by Indian craftsmen.

PERSIA

The Persians have from time immemorial been an artistic people, and their style of Art throughout successive generations has varied but little.

Major-General Murdoch Smith, R.E., a former Director of the branch of the Victoria and Albert Museum in Edinburgh, who resided for some years in Persia and had the assistance when there of M. Richard (a well-known French antiquary), made a collection of *objets d'art* some years ago for the Science and Art Department, which is now in the Kensington Museum, but it contains comparatively little that can be actually termed furniture ; and it is extremely difficult to meet with important specimens of ornamental woodwork of native workmanship. Those in the Museum and in other collections are generally small ornamental articles. The chief reason for this is doubtless that little timber is to be found in Persia, except in the Caspian provinces, where, as Mr. Benjamin has told us in " Persia and the Persians," wood is abundant ; and the Persian architect, taking advantage of his opportunity, has designed his houses with wooden piazzas—not found elsewhere—and with " beams, lintels and eaves quaintly, sometimes elegantly, carved and tinted with brilliant hues." Another feature of the decorative woodwork in this part of Persia is that produced by the large latticed windows, which are well adapted to the climate.

In the manufacture of textile fabrics—notably their famous carpets of Yezd and Ispahan and their embroidered cloths in hammered and engraved metal work and formerly in beautiful pottery and porcelain—they have excelled, and good examples will be found in the Victoria and Albert Museum. It is difficult to find a representative specimen of Persian furniture except a box or a stool and the illustration of a brass incense burner is therefore given to mark the method of native design, which was adopted in a modified form by the Persians from their Arab conquerors.

This method of design has one or two special characteristics which are worth noticing. One of these was due to the teaching of Mahomet forbidding animal representation in design—a rule which in later work has been relaxed ; another was the introduction of mathematics into Persia by the Saracens, which led to the adoption of geometrical patterns in design ; and a third, the development of " Caligraphy " into a fine art, which has resulted in the introduction of a text or motto into so many of the

Persian designs of decorative work. The combination of these three characteristics was the origin of the " Arabesque" form of ornament.

The general method of decorating woodwork is similar to the Indian method, and consists in either inlaying brown wood (generally teak) with ivory or mother-of-pearl in geometrical patterns, or in covering the wooden

INCENSE BURNER OF ENGRAVED BRASS.
(*Victoria and Albert Museum.*)

box or manuscript case with a coating of lacquer, somewhat similar to the Chinese or Japanese preparations. On this groundwork some good miniature painting was executed, the colours being, as a rule, red, green and gold, with black lines to give definition to the design.

The author of "Persia and the Persians," already quoted, had, during his residence in the country as American Minister, great opportunities of observation and in his chapter entitled "A Glance at the Arts of Persia" he has said a great deal about this mosaic work. Referring to the scarcity of wood in Persia he says: "For the above reason one is astonished at the marvellous ingenuity, skill and taste developed by the art of inlaid work, or mosaic in wood. It would be impossible to exceed the results achieved by the Persian artisans, especially those of Shiraz, in this wonderful and difficult art. . . . . Chairs, tables, sofas, boxes, violins, guitars, canes, picture frames, almost every conceivable object, in fact, which is made of wood, may be found overlaid with an exquisite casing of inlaid work, so minute sometimes that thirty-five or forty pieces may be counted in the space of a square eighth of an inch. I have counted four hundred and twenty-eight distinct pieces on a square inch of a violin, which is completely covered by this exquisite detail of geometric designs, in mosaic."

Mr. Benjamin—who, it will be noticed, is somewhat too enthusiastic over this kind of mechanical decoration—also observes that while the details will stand the test of a magnifying glass, there is a general breadth in the design which renders it harmonious and pleasing if looked at from a distance.

In the Victoria and Albert Museum there are several specimens of Persian lacquer work, which have very much the appearance of those papier maché articles that used to be so common in England some sixty years ago, save that the decoration is, of course, of Eastern character.

Of seventeenth century work there is also a fine coffer richly inlaid with ivory of the best description of Persian design and workmanship of this period, which reached the zenith of Persian Art during the reign of Shah Abbas. The numerous small articles of what is termed Persian marqueterie, are inlaid with tin wire and stained ivory, on a ground of cedar wood, very similar to the same kind of ornamental work already described in the Indian section of this chapter. These were purchased at the Paris Exhibition in 1867.

Persian Art of the present day may be said to be in a state of transition, owing to the introduction and assimilation of European ideas.

SARACENIC WOODWORK FROM CAIRO AND DAMASCUS

The changes of fashion in Western, as contrasted with Eastern, countries are comparatively rapid. In the former, the record of two or three centuries presents a history of great and well-defined alterations in manners, customs and therefore in furniture, while the more conservative Oriental has been content to reproduce, from generation to generation, the traditions of his forefathers; and we find that, from the time of the Moorish conquest and spread of Arabesque design, no radical change in Saracenic Art occurred until French and English energy and enterprise forced European fashions into Egypt. As a consequence the original quaintness and orientalism natural to the country are being gradually replaced by buildings, decoration and furniture of European fashion.

The carved pulpit, from a mosque in Cairo, which is in the Victoria and Albert Museum, was made for Sultan Kaitbeg, 1468-96. The side panels, of geometrical pattern, though much injured by time and wear, show signs of ebony inlaid with ivory and of painting and gilding; they are good specimens of the kind of work. The two doors, also from Cairo, the oldest parts of which are just two hundred years earlier than the pulpit, are exactly of the same style and so far as appearances go might just as well be taken for two hundred years later, so conservative was the Saracenic treatment of decorative woodwork for some four or five centuries. Pentagonal and hexagonal mosaics of ivory with little mouldings of ebony dividing the different panels, the centres of eccentric shapes of ivory or rosewood carved with minute scrolls, combine to give these elaborate doors a very rich effect, and remind one of the work still to be seen at the Alhambra in Granada.

The Victoria and Albert Museum has been fortunate in securing from the St. Maurice and Dr. Meymar collections a great many specimens which are well worth examination. The most remarkable is a complete room brought from a house in Damascus, which is fitted up in the Oriental style and gives one a good idea of an Eastern interior. The walls are decorated in colour and gold; the spaces are divided by flat pilasters; and there are recesses, or cupboards, for the reception of pottery, quaintly formed vessels and pots of brass. Oriental carpets, octagonal tables, such as the one which ornaments the initial letter of this chapter, hookas, incense burners, and cushions furnish the apartment; while the lattice window is an excellent representation of the " Mesherabijeh," or lattice work with which we are familiar since so much has been imported by Egyptian travellers. In the upper panels of the lattice there are inserted pieces of coloured glass and, looking outwards towards the light, the effect is very pretty. The date of this room is 1756, which appears at the foot of an Arabic inscription, of which a translation is appended to the exhibit. It commences :—" In the Name of God, the Merciful, the Compassionate," and concludes, " Pray therefore to Him morning and evening."

A number of bosses and panels, detached from their original framework, are also to be seen, and are good specimens of Saracenic design. A bedstead, with inlay of ivory, and numerous small squares of glass, under which are paper flowers, is also a fair sample of the more crude kind of native work.

The illustration on page 208 is of a carved wood door from Cairo, considered by the South Kensington authorities to be of Syrian work.

GOVERNOR'S PALACE, MANFALUT.

Showing a Window of Arab Lattice Work similar to that of the Damascus Room in the
Victoria and Albert Museum.

It shows the turned spindles, which the Arabs generally introduce into their ornamental woodwork; and the carving of the vase of flowers is a good specimen of its kind. The date is about the seventeenth century.

For those who would gain an extended knowledge of Saracenic or Arabian Art industry, "L'Art Arabe," by M. Prisse d'Aveunes should be consulted. There will be found in this work many carefully prepared illustrations of the cushioned seats, the projecting balconies of the lattice work already alluded to, of octagonal inlaid tables, and such other articles of furniture as were used by the Arabs. The South Kensington Handbook, "Persian Art," by Major-General Murdoch Smith, R.E., is also a very handy and useful work in a small compass.

While discussing Saracenic or Arab furniture it is worth noticing that our word "sofa" is of Arab derivation, the word "suffah" meaning "a place or couch for reclining before the door of Eastern houses."

SPECIMEN OF SARACENIC PANELLING OF CEDAR, EBONY AND IVORY.
(*Victoria and Albert Museum.*)

In Skeat's Dictionary the word is said to have first occurred in the *Guardian*, in the year 1713, and the phrase is quoted from No. 167 of that old periodical of the day—" He leapt off from the sofa on which he sat."

From the same source the word "ottoman," which Webster defines as "a stuffed seat without a back, first used in Turkey," is obviously obtained, and the modern low-seated upholsterer's chair of to-day is doubtless the development of a French adaptation of the Eastern cushion or "divan," this latter word having become applied to the seats which furnished the hall or council chamber in an Eastern palace, although its

A CARVED DOOR OF SYRIAN WORK.

(Victoria and Albert Museum.)

original meaning was probably the council or "court" itself, or the hall in which such was held.

Thus do the habits and tastes of different nations act and re-act upon each other. Western peoples have carried eastward their civilisation and their fashions, influencing Arts and industries with their restless energy and breaking up the crust of Oriental apathy and indolence; and have brought back in return the ideas gained from an observation of the association and accessories of Eastern life, to adapt them to the requirements and refinements of European luxury.

SHAPED PANEL OF SARACENIC WORK IN CARVED BONE OR IVORY.

BOULLE ARMOIRE.

Designed by Lebrun, formerly in the Hamilton Palace Collection,
sold at Christie's for £12,075 the pair.

PERIOD : LOUIS XIV,

CHAPTER VI

French Furniture

Palace of Versailles, "Grand" and "Petit Trianon"—The three Styles of Louis XIV., XV. and XVI.—The Wallace Collection—Berain, Lebrun and Colbert—André Charles Boulle and his Work—Carved and Gilt Furniture—Dalkeith Palace—Jean François Oeben—Hardwick Hall—Period of the Regency—The Work of Charles Cressent—Hotel Soubise—Jules Aurèle Meissonier. LOUIS XV. FURNITURE: Alteration in Condition of French Society—Watteau, Lancret and Boucher—Lacquered Furniture—Vernis Martin. The CAFFIERIS and their Work. PIERRE GOUTHIÈRE and his Work—Tapestry Furniture—Famous Suite at Chatsworth—Audry's Designs—"Bureau du Roi"—Oeben and Riesener. LOUIS XVI. AND MARIE ANTOINETTE: The Queen's Influence—Boudoir of the Marquise de Serilly—Simpler designs—Characteristic Ornaments of Louis XVI. Furniture—Work of Riesener and Gouthière—The Hamilton Palace Collection—Specimens in the Louvre—Upholstered Furniture—The Work of David Röntgen—Famous *Ebenistes* of the Period—J. F. Leleu—Martin Carlin—Claude Charles Saunier—J. Dubois—Jean Pafrat—Benemann—Weisweiller—The "Petit" Family—De la Fosse—Thomire—Gaudreaux—French Influence upon the Design of Furniture in other Countries—Middle-class Furniture—The Jones Collection—Extract from the *Times*.

HERE is something so distinct in the development of taste in furniture, marked out by the three styles to which the three monarchs have given the name of "Louis Quatorze," "Louis Quinze," and "Louis Seize," that it affords a fitting point for a new departure.

This will be evident to anyone who will visit, first the Palace of Versailles,* then the Grand Trianon, and afterwards the Petit Trianon. By the help of representative illustrations such a visit in the order given would greatly interest anyone having even a smattering of knowledge of the characteristic ornaments of these different periods. A careful examination would demonstrate how the one style gradually merged into that of its successor. Thus the massiveness and grandeur of the best Louis Quatorze *meubles de luxe* became in their later development too ornate and effeminate, with an elaboration of enrichment, culminating in the rococo style of Louis Quinze.

* The present decorations of the Palace of Versailles were carried out about 1830 under Louis Phillipe. "Versailles Galeries Historiques," par C. Gavard, is a work of thirteen vols. devoted to the illustration of the pictures, portraits, statues, busts and various decorative contents of the Palace.

Then we find in the Petit Trianon and also in the Château of Fontainebleau, the purer taste of Marie Antoinette dominating the Art productions of her time, which reached their zenith with regard to furniture in the production of such elegant and costly examples as have been preserved to us in the beautiful work-table and secretaire—sold some years since at the dispersion of the Hamilton Palace Collection— and in some other specimens which may be seen in the Musée du Louvre, in the Jones bequest in the Victoria and Albert Museum, the Wallace Collection and in other public and private collections. Several illustrations of these examples will be found in this chapter.

Since the earlier editions of this book were published we have inherited the priceless collection of old French furniture, china, pictures and *objets d'art* formed by the third and fourth Marquesses of Hertford, added to and re-organised by Sir Richard Wallace and bequeathed to the English nation by his widow who died in 1897. In mere money value this magnificent legacy has been estimated at from four to five millions sterling and it is impossible to say how much it would realise. Several notes and illustrations from this famous museum will be found in this chapter and the reader has the great advantage of being able to see these fine examples of French Art of the seventeenth and eighteenth centuries, not crowded and mingled with specimens of an alien character, but arranged with congenial surroundings which add so much to their artistic value. There is no other museum in the world where French furniture of the period treated in this chapter can be seen arranged with the pictures, bronzes, porcelain and other beautiful accessories by contemporary artists and craftsmen. It is also only due to the Trustees to acknowledge the material help and guidance which is rendered to the public by fully descriptive labels which are placed on nearly every article and by the excellent catalogues which are to be obtained for a nominal price.

We have to recollect that the reign of Louis XIV. was the time of the artists Berain, Lebrun and, later in the reign, of Watteau, also of André Charles Boulle, *ciseleur et doreur du roi*, and of Colbert, that admirable Minister of Finance, who knew so well how to second his royal master's taste for grandeur and magnificence. The Palace of Versailles bears throughout the stamp and impress of the majesty of *le Grand Monarque;* and the rich architectural ornament of the interior, with moulded, gilded and painted ceilings required the furnishing to be carried to an extent which had never been attempted previously.

Louis XIV. had judgment in his taste and he knew that to carry out his ideas of a royal palace he must not only select suitable artists capable of control, but he must centralise their efforts. In 1664 Colbert

CABINET.

By André Charles Boulle : Early Work.

Showing signs of period of transition, Louis XIII. to Louis XIV.

(Wallace Collection at Hertford House).

BOULLE ARMOIRE.

In the Jones Collection, Victoria and Albert Museum.

PERIOD: LOUIS XIV.

founded the Royal Academy of Painting, Architecture and Sculpture into which designs of furniture were admitted and it was here that the King collected together and suitably housed the different skilled producers of his furniture, placing them all under the control of his favourite artist, Lebrun, who was appointed director in 1667. The celebrated Gobelins tapestry factory was also established and the famous carpet manufactory of *La Savonnerie* with the tapestries of Beauvais also contributed to the sumptuous furnishing of the time.

ANDRÉ CHARLES BOULLE. — One of the most remarkable furniture artists of this time was André Charles Boulle, frequently spelt Buhl. He was born in 1642 and therefore was twenty-five years of age when Lebrun was appointed Art-director. He is generally supposed to have originated the method of ornamenting furniture which has since been associated with his name: this was to veneer his cabinets, pedestals, armoires, encoignures, clocks and brackets with tortoise-shell, into which a cutting of brass was laid, the latter being cut out from a design in which were harmoniously arranged scrolls, vases of flowers, satyrs, animals, cupids, swags of fruit and draperies. Fantastic compositions of a free Renaissance character constituted the panels to which bold scrolls in ormolu formed fitting frames; while handsome mouldings of the same material gave a finish to the extremities. These ormolu mountings were gilt by an old-fashioned process,* which left upon the metal a thick deposit of gold and they were cunningly chiselled by the skilful hands of the elder Caffieri and his contemporaries.

In an old inventory dated 1653 of Cardinal Mazarin's art treasures some furniture is described which is ornamented with brass tortoise-shell and copper, and there is a cabinet of this description in the Musée Cluny of an earlier date than Boulle's work. It is therefore probable that he revived and improved upon the work of some French *ébenistes* who preceded him by a few years.

Boulle subsequently learned to economise labour by adopting a similar process to that used by the marqueterie cutter; and by glueing together two sheets of brass or white metal and two of shell and placing over them his design, he was then able to pierce the four layers by one cut of the bandsaw; this gave four exact copies of the design. The same process would be repeated for the reverse side if, as with an armoire or a large cabinet, two panels, one for each door, right and left, were required; and then when the brass or white metal cutting was fitted into the shell so that the joins were imperceptible, he would have two right-hand and

* For description of method of gilding the mounts of French furniture, see Appendix.

two left-hand panels. These would be positive and negative: in the former pair the metal would represent the figured design with the shell as groundwork and the latter would have the shell as a design with a ground of metal. The terms positive and negative are the writer's, to explain the difference, but the technical terms are "first part" and "second part," or "Boulle" and "counter." The former would be selected for the best part

PEDESTAL CABINET.
By Boulle, formerly in Mr. Baring's Collection. Purchased by Mr. Jones for £3,000.
(*Jones bequest, Victoria and Albert Museum.*)

of the cabinet; for instance the panels of the front doors, while the latter would be used for the ends and sides. An illustration of this plan of using all four cuttings of one design occurs in the armoire in the Jones Collection, illustrated on page 214, and in a great many other excellent specimens. The brass or the white metal in the design was then carefully and most artistically engraved; and the beauty of the engraving of Boulle's finest productions is a great point of excellence giving as it does a character to the design, and emphasising its details. The mounting of the furniture in ormolu of a rich and highly finished character completed the design. The Musée du Louvre is rich in examples of Boulle's work; and there are some very good pieces in the Jones Collection, in Hertford House and Windsor Castle. It should be observed that the Boulle in the Wallace Collection although very good of its kind and in considerable quantity, is chiefly the work of makers of a much later date, who used the designs and patterns of the original Boulle. The majority of these pieces were made during the reign of Louis XVI. or later, and upon the descriptive labels attached to each piece for the guidance of the visitor there is information given by the authorities to this effect.

The fine cabinet supported by carved figures with term bases illustrated at the commencement of this chapter on page 213 is one of Boulle's earliest pieces of work and the design merits a careful examination by the student of French furniture. It shows that he used marqueterie in various woods, as well as brass and tortoise-shell, the drawer fronts and centre door in the upper part being panels of marqueterie.

The illustration on page 210 is of an armoire undoubtedly executed by Boulle from a design by Lebrun; it is one of a pair which was sold in 1882 at the Hamilton Palace sale by Messrs. Christie for £12,075. Another small cabinet in the same collection realised £2,310. The pedestal cabinet from the Jones Collection, illustrated on opposite page, is very similar to the latter and cost Mr. Jones £3,000. When specimens of the genuineness of which there is no doubt are offered for sale they are sure to realise very high prices. The armoire in the Jones Collection already alluded to on page 216, of which there is an illustration, cost Mr. Jones between £4,000 and £5,000.

In some of the best of Boulle's cabinets, as for instance in the Hamilton Palace armoire (illustrated), the bronze gilt ornaments stand out in bold relief from the groundwork. In the Louvre there is one which has a figure of *le Grand Monarque* clad in armour with a Roman toga and wearing the full-bottomed wig of the time, which scarcely accords with the costume of a Roman general. The absurd combination which characterises this affectation of the classic costume is also found in some portraits of our George II.

The masks, satyrs and rams' heads, the scrolls of the foliage, are also very bold in specimens of this class of Boulle's work; and the "sun" (that is, a mask with rays of light radiating from it) is a very favourite ornament of this period.

Boulle died in 1732; he had four sons who assisted and succeeded him, and notwithstanding the costly character of their work and their Royal patronage, father and sons all died in extreme poverty. There were also several pupils, among whom Levasseur, Montigny and Jacob all achieved distinction, and specimens of whose work can be seen in the Wallace Collection; they produced some excellent marqueterie furniture and did not confine themselves to the style of their former *maitre*. The school of decorative furniture founded by Boulle had its votaries and imitators. The word one frequently finds misspelt "Buhl" and the

A CONCERT DURING THE REIGN OF LOUIS XIV.
(From a Miniature dated 1696.)

term has come to represent any similar mode of decoration of furniture no matter how meretricious or common it may be.

Later in the reign of Louis XIV. as other influences were brought to bear upon the taste and fashion of the day, this style of furniture became more ornate and showy. Instead of the natural colour of the shell being shown, either vermilion or gold leaf was placed underneath the transparent shell; the gilt mounts became less severe and abounded with the curled endive ornament which afterwards became thoroughly characteristic of the fashion of the succeeding reign; and the forms of the furniture itself

DECORATION OF A SALON IN LOUIS XIV. STYLE.

followed the taste for a more free and flowing treatment; and it should be mentioned in justice to Lebrun that from the time of his death and the appointment of his successor, Mignard, a distinct decline in merit can be traced.

A contemporary of the elder Boulle who afterwards achieved great fame and of whom more will be said later was Jean François Oeben (1685-1765). There is an upright secretaire by him in the Jones bequest

BOUDOIR FURNISHED IN THE TASTE OF THE LOUIS XIV. PERIOD.
(From an Old Print.)

which represents his style of work; and in the Wallace Collection and the Louvre there are other examples. His treatment of marqueterie as a decorative effect was simpler and more dignified than that which was adopted by his successors while the mountings were in character with the furniture—handsome but free from excessive ornamentation

The great *tour de force* with which Oeben's name is associated is the magnificent *bureau du Roi* of which there is some description later in this chapter and a full-page illustration facing page 239. This famous bureau was completed by his pupil Riesener after Oeben's death.

Contemporary with Boulle's work were the richly mounted tables, having slabs of Egyptian porphyry or Florentine marble mosaic; and marqueterie cabinets with beautiful mouldings of ormolu or gilt bronze. Commodes and screens were ornamented with Chinese lacquer which had been imported by the Dutch and taken to Paris after the French invasion of the Netherlands.

DALKEITH PALACE.—In several of our great houses there are specimens of the stately and sumptuous furniture of the time and style identified

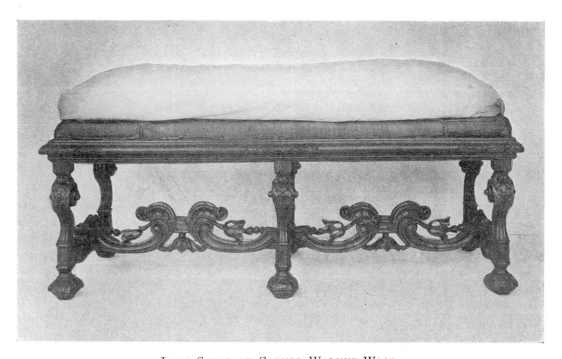

LONG STOOL OF CARVED WALNUT WOOD.
FRENCH: PERIOD LOUIS XIV.   (*Presence Chamber, Hardwick Hall.*)

with the reign of Louis Quatorze, but an exceptional interest is attached to some of the Boulle and marqueterie still to be seen in the Scottish home of the Buccleuch family. It was in 1663 that the handsome and fascinating James Duke of Monmouth married the Lady Anne Countess Buccleuch, and twenty-two years later, after the disastrous battle of Sedgemoor, he was beheaded for claiming the Crown of England. Dalkeith Palace was rebuilt and furnished by the Duke of Monmouth's widow, and some of the fine cabinets which it contains had been presented by the French monarch to King Charles the Second and given by him to his son long before his rebellion. A cabinet of ebony enriched with plaques of chased gold and two others of the marqueterie which one recognises as the early work of André Charles Boulle form a handsome and imposing set still known as the "Monmouth" cabinets. There are also two mirrors in the drawing room of the Palace which are ornamented with the coronet of the Duke and the initials of the Duchess, said to be wedding presents from Charles II. According to tradition much of this furniture was brought from Whitehall Palace. Dalkeith Palace contains many treasures of the seventeenth century and of later times and should be seen by everyone who is interested in our subject. It is only a short distance from Edinburgh and is shown to visitors.

Towards the end of the seventeenth century the resources of designers and makers of decorative furniture were reinforced by the

TWO STOOLS OF CARVED WALNUT WOOD.
FRENCH : PERIOD LOUIS XIV. (*Presence Chamber, Hardwick Hall.*)

introduction of glass in larger plates than had been possible previously. Mirrors of considerable size were first made in Venice; these were engraved with figures and scrolls and mounted in richly carved and gilt wood frames. Soon afterwards manufactories of mirrors and of glass in larger plates than before were set up in England, near Battersea, and in France at Tour la Ville, near Paris. This novelty not only gave a new departure to the design of suitable frames in carved wood (generally gilt) but also to that of Boulle work and marqueterie. It also led to a greater variety of the design for cabinets; and from this time we may date the first appearance of the "Vitrine" or cabinet with glass panels in the doors and sides for the display of smaller *objets d'art.*

The chairs and sofas of the latter half of the reign of Louis Quatorze are exceedingly grand and rich. The suite of furniture for the State apartment of a prince or wealthy nobleman comprised a *canapé* or sofa and six *fauteuils* or arm chairs the frames carved with much spirit, or with "feeling," as it is technically termed, and richly gilt. The backs and seats were upholstered and covered with the already famous tapestry of Gobelins or Beauvais. A short account of these factories is given in the Appendix. Some chairs of this period will be found illustrated in the "concert" shown on page 218.

In the presence chamber at Hardwick Hall there are some walnut wood carved stools of this period (illustrated on page 222) with the coverings much worn and which have apparently been in the house since the date of their first importation from France at the end of the seventeenth century. Sometimes this kind of stool was gilt and at others showed the natural colour of the wood, which was wax polished.

As an example of the change in both outline and detail which took place in design let the reader notice the form of the Louis Quatorze commode vignetted for the initial letter of this chapter, and then turn to the lighter and more fanciful cabinets of somewhat similar shape which will be found illustrated in the Louis Quinze section which follows overleaf. In the earlier Louis Quatorze cabinets the decorative effect so far as the woodwork is concerned was generally obtained first by the careful choice of suitable veneers and then by joining four pieces in a panel, so that the natural figure of the wood runs from the centre, and then a banding of a darker wood forms a frame. An instance of this will also be found in the above-mentioned vignette.

PERIOD OF THE REGENCY

When the old King died at the ripe age of seventy-seven the crown devolved on his great-grandson, then a child five years old; a Regency therefore became necessary; and this period of some eight years, until the death of Philip Duke of Orleans in 1723, when the King was declared to have attained his majority at the age of thirteen, is known as *l'Epoch de la Régence* and is a landmark in the history of furniture.

CHARLES CRESSENT.—A prominent name among the *ébenistes* of this short Regency period is that of Charles Cressent of whose work there are some fine examples in the Wallace Collection and also in the Jones bequest. One may say of his scheme of ornamentation, as compared with that of Caffieri, that there is a better method, somewhat less fancy and more moderation in the lines of his commodes, tables and cabinets. His fine scrolls and acanthus leaf ornaments are very spirited and this effect is obtained in a great measure by the varying depths of their relief; thus a flat-shaped scroll will have its head formed in high relief and this variation gives more play and effect to his designs. Cressent appears to have been better educated than the majority of his contemporary artists and he not only designed and carried out work for the Court but is said to have acted in the capacity of Art expert to the Regent.

COMMODE.
In Parqueterie, with massive mountings of Gilt Bronze, probably by Cressent.
LOUIS XV. PERIOD.
(*Formerly in the Hamilton Palace Collection.   Realised at Christie's £6,247 10s.*)

The later work of André Charles Boulle and the best of his sons' productions belong to the Regency period, which may be generally described as a continuation of the Louis Quatorze style upon a smaller scale and with more refinement. It is perhaps the best time of the whole period embraced by the reigns of the three Louis; for while we have the dignity of design under the influence of Berain and Lebrun there is a lack of that riotous superabundance of ornament which came to be the fashion in the later years of Louis XV.

For those of our readers who, when visiting Paris, desire to make a study of the best examples of the style of decoration which takes its name from *l'Epoch de la Régence* we may just name the beautiful Hotel Soubise, where are now housed the National Archives; also the present Bank of France, which was formerly the famous Hotel de Toulouse. The fine work of decoration effected by the carved wainscoting, or, as it is now termed the *boiserie*, or wood linings of the rooms, carved in the ornament of the period, with their appropriate panel paintings, cornices, ceilings and other details were the work of two celebrated artist-architects, Germain Boffrand and Robert de Cotte.

As a designer of furniture and many accessories of this time Jules Aurèle Meissonier was a celebrated artist. He was born in 1693 and died in 1750 and his work included not only many ornamental objects

BOULLE COMMODE.
Probably made during the period of the Regency.
(*Musée du Louvre*).

which appertained to furniture and decoration but those exquisite gold and enamelled snuff-boxes and articles of jewellery and personal adornment which represented the extravagant taste of the period. The later and more rococo designs in Chippendale's "Director" were no doubt influenced by drawings by this artist. In one of Chippendale's sofas the lines are nearly identical with those of a sofa by Meissonier.

THE LOUIS QUINZE PERIOD

There was a marked change about this period of French history in the social condition of the upper classes in France. The pomp and extravagance of the late monarch had emptied the coffers of the noblesse and in order to recruit their finances, marriages became common which a

FINE COMMODE.

By Charles Cressent.   French: Period of the Regency.

(In the Wallace Collection.)

BOULLE COMMODE. FRENCH: PERIOD OF THE REGENCY.

With fine Gilt Bronze Mounts. *(In the Wallace Collection.)*

FINE COMMODE.

By Jacques Caffieri.   FRENCH : PERIOD LOUIS XV.

(In the Wallace Collection.)

decade or two before that time would have hardly been thought possible. Nobles of ancient lineage married the daughters of bankers and speculators in order to supply themselves with the means of following the extravagant fashions of the day, and we find the wives of ministers of departments of State using their influence and power for the purpose of making money by gambling in stocks and accepting bribes for concessions and contracts.

PANEL FOR A SCREEN.
Painted by Watteau.   PERIOD OF THE REGENCY.

It was a time of corruption, extravagance, licentiousness and intrigue, and although one might ask what bearing this has upon the history of furniture a little reflection will show that the abandonment of the great State receptions of the late King and the pompous and gorgeous entertainments of his time gave way to a state of society in which the boudoir became of far more importance than the salon in the artistic furnishing of a fashionable house. Instead of the majestic grandeur of immense reception rooms and stately galleries we have the elegance and prettiness of the boudoir; and as the reign of the young King advances we find the structural enrichment of rooms more fanciful and busy with redundant ornament. The curved endive decoration so common in carved woodwork and its imitation in "compo." of this period is seen everywhere; in the architraves, in the panel mouldings, in the frame of an overdoor, in the design of a mirror frame; doves, wreaths, Arcadian fountains, flowing scrolls, cupids, and heads and busts of women terminating in foliage, are carved or moulded in relief on the walls, the doors and the alcoved recesses of the reception rooms, either gilded or painted white; and pictures by Watteau, Lancret or Boucher and their contemporaries are appropriate accompaniments.*

CONSOLE TABLE, CARVED AND GILT.
PERIOD: LOUIS XV.   *(Collection of M. Double, Paris.)*

The furniture was made to agree with this decorative treatment; couches and easy chairs were designed in more sweeping curves and on a smaller scale, the woodwork wholly or partially gilt and upholstered not only with the tapestry of Gobelins, Beauvais and Aubusson, but with soft coloured silk brocades and brocatelles; light occasional chairs were enriched with mother-of-pearl or marqueterie; screens were painted with love scenes and representations of ladies and gentlemen who look as if they passed their entire existence in the elaboration of their toilettes or the exchange of compliments; the stately cabinet is modified into the *bombé* fronted commode, the ends of which curve outwards with a graceful

* Watteau, 1684-1721.   Lancret, *b.* 1690, *d.* 1743.   Boucher, *b.* 1703, *d.* 1770.

sweep; and the bureau is made in a much smaller size, more highly decorated with marqueterie and more fancifully mounted to suit the smaller and more effeminate apartment. The elegant cabinet called *bonheur du jour* (a little cabinet mounted on a table); the small round occasional table called a *guéridon*, the *encoignure*, or corner cabinet; the *etagère*, or ornamental hanging cabinet with shelves; the three-fold screen, with each leaf a different height and with scroll-shaped top all date from this time. The *chaise à porteur* or Sedan chair on which so much work and taste were expended became more ornate so as to fall in with the prevailing fashion. Marqueterie became more fanciful.

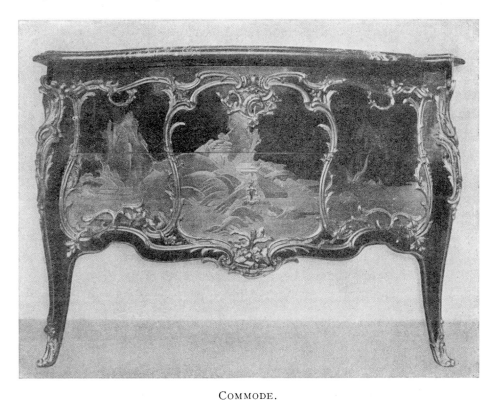

COMMODE.
With Chinese black and gold lacquer and fine mountings of gilt bronze.
PERIOD: EARLY LOUIS XV., OR REGENCY.   (*From "The Connoisseur," by permission.*)

The Louis Quinze cabinets were inlaid not only with natural woods but with veneers stained in different tints; and landscapes, interiors, baskets of flowers, birds, trophies, emblems of all kinds and quaint fanciful conceits were pressed into the service of marqueterie decoration.

LACQUERED FURNITURE

During the preceding reign the Chinese lacquer work then in use was imported from the East, the fashion for collecting this ware having set in ever since the Dutch had established a trade with China;

and subsequently as the demand arose for smaller pieces of *meubles de luxe*, collectors had these articles taken to pieces and the slabs of lacquer mounted in panels to decorate the table or cabinet in order to display the lacquer to advantage. *Ebenistes*, too, prepared such parts of woodwork as were intended to be ornamented in this manner and sent them to China to be coated with lacquer, a process which was at first only known to the Chinese; but the delay and expense quickened the inventive genius of the European craftsman and it was found that a preparation of gum and other ingredients applied again and again and each time carefully rubbed down, produced a surface which was almost as lustrous and suitable for decoration as the original material. A Dutchman named Huygens was the first successful inventor of this preparation; and owing to the adroitness of his work and of those who followed him and improved his process one can only detect European from Chinese lacquer by careful observation; the surface of the Chinese and Japanese lacquer is harder and more metallic in appearance and the decorations lack true Oriental character. In many cases these have been traced from Eastern original designs and the details filled in, but they are not as sharp or well defined as their models. The illustration on page 231 of a very fine commode in the Jones Collection is an excellent example of a piece which was sent out to Japan to be lacquered. In Chapters IV. and V. some remarks on Eastern lacquer can be referred to.

About 1740-4 the Martin family had three manufactories of this peculiar and fashionable work which became known as Vernis-Martin, or Martins' Varnish; and it is a singular coincidence that one of these was in the district of Paris then and now known as Faubourg Saint Martin. By a special decree a monopoly was granted in 1744 to Sieur Simon Etienne Martin the younger "To manufacture all sorts of work in relief and in the style of Japan and China." This was to last for twenty years; and we shall see that in the latter part of the reign of Louis XV., and in that of his successor, the decoration was not confined to the imitation of Chinese and Japanese subjects but the surface was painted in the style of the decorative artists of the day both in monochrome and in natural colours; such subjects as "Cupid Awakening Venus," "The Triumph of Galatea," "Nymphs and Goddesses," "Garden Scenes," and "Fêtes Champêtres" being represented in accordance with the taste of the period. It may be remarked in passing that lacquer work was also made previous to this time in England. Several cabinets of "Old" English lac were included in the Strawberry Hill sale catalogue; and these were richly mounted with ormolu in the French style. George Robins, so well known for his flowery descriptions, was the auctioneer, and the introduction to the catalogue was written by Harrison Ainsworth. This sale took place in 1842.

The gilt bronze mountings of the furniture of this time became less massive and much more elaborate; the curled endive ornament was very much in vogue; the acanthus foliage followed the curves of the commode; busts and heads of women, cupids, and satyrs terminating in foliage suited the design and decoration of the more fanciful shapes.

PART OF A SALON.
Decorated in the Louis Quinze style, showing the carved and gilt
Console Table and Mirror, with other enrichments, *en suite*.

THE CAFFIERIS.—The Caffieris, father and son, were great masters of the art of mounting in gilt bronze and some illustrations are given of commodes in the Wallace Collection and the Jones bequest which are recognised as their work. Jacques Caffieri the elder was employed in the decoration of Versailles as early as 1746-7 and there is at Hertford House a very fine chandelier of enormous proportions in his best manner signed and dated, " Caffieri à Paris, 1751." This is probably the most important single object made by him if we except the famous *pendule astronomique* at Versailles.

The tendency of Jacques Caffieri, and particularly of his son Phillipe, who assisted and succeeded his father, was to become extravagant in ornament and to forget that the bronze mountings should be subsidiary to the woodwork of the cabinet enriched. Instead of this we find in some of Caffieri's work the wood almost concealed by the elaborateness of the mountings. One looks for a sense of construction in the design of ornament, and one finds instead rather the play of fancy. Chinese dragons, mythical monsters, fantastic curves and scrolls are all introduced, the high excellence and spirit with which the designs are executed being some excuse for their extravagance.

There is an admirable example of Caffieri's style on a small scale in the clock which can be seen in the Jones bequest. An elephant is ridden by a monkey holding an umbrella and this may be quoted as an instance of quaintness of " motive " combined with excellent craftsmanship. Many pieces attributed to these famous mounters are stamped with a very minute C surmounted by a crown, the mark being so small that it must be diligently searched for just as we have to seek some of the small marks on foreign silver. In some cases, as in that of the elephant clock just referred to, there is a full signature *"fait par Caffiery."*

The amount of spirit imparted into the chasing of this ormolu is simply marvellous—it has never been equalled and could not be excelled. Time has now mellowed the colour of the woodwork it adorns; and the tint of the gold with which it is overlaid. The lights and shadows caused by the high relief of parts of the design and the consequent darkening of the parts depressed, together with the brightness of the more prominent ornaments which have been rubbed bright from time to time, all combine to produce an effect which is very rich and elegant. One cannot wonder that connoisseurs are prepared to pay such large sums for genuine specimens or that clever imitations are extremely costly to produce.

Illustrations are given from some of the more notable examples of decorative furniture of this period which were sold in 1882 at the celebrated Hamilton Palace sale together with the sums they realised; also of specimens in the Victoria and Albert Museum, the Jones Collection and from Hertford House.

We must also remember in considering the *meubles de luxe* of this time that in 1753 Louis XV. had made the Sèvres Porcelain Manufactory a State enterprise; and later, as that celebrated undertaking progressed, tables and cabinets were ornamented with plaques of the beautiful and

SMALL COMMODE.

Mounted by Jacques Caffieri.   Temp. Louis XV.

(*In the Wallace Collection.*)

choice *pâte tendre* the delicacy of which was admirably adapted to enrich the light and elegant furnishing of the dainty boudoir of a Madame du Barri or a Madame Pompadour. The frontispiece of this volume illustrates an excellent example of this combination of cabinet work mounting and Sèvres porcelain.

PIERRE GOUTHIÈRE.—Another famous artist in the delicate bronze mountings of the day was Pierre Gouthière. He commenced work some years later than Caffieri, being born in 1740; and like his senior fellow craftsman did not confine his attention to furniture but exercised his fertility of design and his passion for detail in mounting bowls and vases of jasper, of Sèvres and of Oriental porcelain. The character of his work is less forcible than that of Caffieri and comes nearer to what we shall presently recognise as the Louis Seize or Marie Antoinette style. In careful finish of minute details it resembles the fine goldsmith's work of the Renaissance.

Gouthière was employed extensively by Madame du Barri; and at her execution in 1793 he lost the enormous balance of 756,000 francs which was due to him but which debt the State repudiated and the unfortunate man died in extreme poverty, the inmate of an almshouse.

The Duc D'Aumont employed him extensively and at the sale of his collection no fewer than fifty specimens were sold which were guaranteed to be the work of this artist. There are several fine examples of his work in the Wallace Collection, not only in the mounting of cabinets but in clocks and candelabra and also the famous *belle coupe* which is considered to be one of his masterpieces.

TAPESTRY FURNITURE

The designs of the celebrated tapestry of Gobelins and of Beauvais used for upholstering the finest furniture of this time underwent a change; and instead of the representation of the chase, with a bold and vigorous rendering, we find shepherds and shepherdesses, nymphs and satyrs, the illustrations of a La Fontaine's fables, or renderings of Boucher's pictures. The arm chair, or *fauteuil*, with *upholstered* instead of *open* sides was introduced into the suite of tapestry furniture and the term by which it is known, "*chaise bergère*," seems to be a sign of the fashion of the day.

A suite of furniture of this description when considered by the experts to be perfectly genuine, that is, the woodwork, as to the carving and gilding, actually of the period, the tapestry of the best quality, woven in silk and of good design and having a rich ground colour, will command a price amounting to several thousand pounds and is really a great possession. There is at Chatsworth a remarkable one comprising two large sofas and eight *fauteuils,* or arm chairs, with a screen to match. These formerly were part of the State furniture of the Speaker's House at Westminster, and were sold by his wife Lady Canterbury to the sixth Duke of Devonshire. There is an interesting entry in a diary kept by the Duke and printed for private circulation in which he mentions

LOUIS XV, CARVED AND GILT " FAUTEUIL."
Upholstered with Beauvais tapestry.   Subject from La Fontaine's Fables.

this purchase, and also a legal question which was afterwards raised as to the lady's right to dispose of part of the contents of an official residence, though the point apparently was never settled. The enormous sum of forty thousand pounds is said to have been offered by a well-known London dealer for this furniture.

In the Wallace Collection there are several suites of furniture of Louis XV. and Louis XVI. period upholstered in Beauvais tapestry in which exotic birds, animals and scrolls are represented ; others of a series known as " Les Chasses " and also one with subjects from La Fontaine's fables. These are from the designs of Jean-Baptiste Oudry who from being a painter of portraits and of animals had been appointed director of the Royal Gobelins Works in 1736. Oudry exercised an important influence on the character of tapestry design in France and tapestries known to be from his drawings are worthy of attention so that they may be recognised. It will be observed that in many of the Wallace Collection examples the frames of the chairs and sofas are much later than the tapestry.

Without doubt the most important example of *meubles de luxe* of this reign is the famous " Bureau du Roi " made for Louis XV. in 1769 and which is fully described in the inventory of the " Garde Meuble " in the year 1775 under No. 2541. The description is in great detail and is fully quoted by M. Williamson in his valuable work " Les Meubles d'Art du Mobilier National," occupying in space no less than thirty-seven lines of printed matter. Its size is five and a half feet long and three feet deep ; the lines are the perfection of grace and symmetry ; the marqueterie is in Riesener's best manner ; the mountings are magnificent—reclining figures, foliage, laurel wreaths and swags chased with rare skill. The back of this famous bureau is as fully decorated as the front : it is signed " Riesener, f. e., 1769, á l'arsenal de Paris."

The order for this remarkable bureau of which we give a full-page illustration is said to have been given by the King in 1760 when Riesener was in the employment of Oeben as *contre-maitre* or foreman. We do not know the exact date of Oeben's death but there is still in existence the marriage contract of Riesener with his widow, dated 6th August, 1767, and even if the work was not commenced directly the order was given it probably took some seven or eight years to produce and although it bears the stamp of Riesener alone may be without doubt considered as the work of both Oeben and Riesener.

Some interesting particulars of the cost of this famous piece of furniture are quoted by Lady Dilke in her " French Furniture and Decoration of the XVIII. Century." They are taken from a document which in 1878 was in the possession of M. Leon Riesener, grandson of Jean Henri the famous *ébeniste*, and will serve to show that the production of such grand furniture was a very costly matter. This document contained a record of various sums spent in forwarding the work and the persons to whom they were paid. The list runs thus:—" Payé a M. Duplessis,

BUREAU DU ROI.

Made for Louis XV. by Oeben and Riesener. (See particulars on pages 220, 238 et seq.)

PERIOD: LOUIS XV. (In the Musée du Louvre)

modeleur, 1,500*l.*; au Sieur Winant, 1,000*l.*; pour les monteurs, 1,200*l.*; pour M. Hervieux, fondeur et ciseleur, 1,246*l.*; pour les mosaiques, 125*l.*; pour des rosettes, 16*l.*; pour la bâtis, 100*l.*; pour les differents bois de couleūr, 72*l.*" Of Duplessis, mentioned here as the modeller, we know that he was employed at the Royal Sèvres Porcelain Manufactory as modeller of vases for King Louis XV. and the work of Hervieux has been recognised in other finely chased mountings.

This celebrated *chef d'œuvre* was in the Tuileries in 1807 and was included in the inventory found in the cabinet of Napoleon I. It was moved by Napoleon III. to the Palace of St. Cloud and was only saved from capture by the Germans by its removal to its present home in the Louvre in August, 1870. It would probably realise if now offered for sale from twenty to twenty-five thousand pounds.

A similar bureau but differing in some of the details of ornamentation is in the Wallace Collection; it is also dated 1769. According to rumour this was made to the order of King Stanislaus of Poland.

Lady Dilke has been at some pains to trace this last-named bureau to its present home. She says that curiously enough it was omitted from the list of goods inherited by Oeben's widow which was made out when she married Riesener in 1767 but she quotes Baron Davillier's authority for it having been in the *mobilier de la Couronne de France* and sold in Holland together with other furniture from the same source; also that it was discovered by Sir Richard Wallace at Naples whither it had been taken by Sir William Hamilton. Another bureau of similar design but less handsomely mounted is at Buckingham Palace; another at the Bank of France; and there is also one in the possession of Mr. Alfred de Rothschild. Sir Richard Wallace had a copy of the famous *bureau du Roi* made by Dasson, one of the first *ébenistes* of Paris, who flourished in the latter part of the nineteenth century, and this can be seen at Hertford House and compared with the one made by Riesener.

LOUIS XVI. AND MARIE ANTOINETTE

It is probable that for some little time previous to the death of Louis XV. the influence of the beautiful daughter of Maria Theresa on the fashions of the day was manifested in furniture and its accessories. We know that Marie Antoinette disliked the pomp and ceremony of Court functions and preferred a simpler way of living at the favourite farm-house which was given to her husband as a residence on his marriage four years before his accession to the throne; and here she delighted to mix with the *bourgeoisie* on the terrace at Versailles or, donning a simple dress of white muslin, would busy herself in the

VIEW OF ONE END OF THE GALLERY IN THE RUE LAFITTE.

Paris Residence of the late Sir John Murray Scott, showing an arrangement of old Louis XVI. furniture.

(From "The Connoisseur," by permission.)

BUREAU.
With Oval Upper Part. In Marqueterie and Gilt Bronze.
Joint work of Riesener and Gouthière. (*Wallace Collection.*)
FRENCH: LATE PERIOD LOUIS XVI.

CONSOLE TABLE.
Carved Wood with Porphyry Slab. Gilt Bronze Mounts by Gouthière.
FRENCH: PERIOD LOUIS XVI.
(Wallace Collection.)

LOUIS SEIZE "FAUTEUIL."
Of White Enamelled Wood, upholstered with Beauvais Tapestry.
(*Lyne-Stephens Bequest, Victoria and Albert Museum.*)

garden or dairy. There was doubtless something of the affectation of a woman spoiled by admiration in thus playing the rustic : still one can understand that the best French society, weary of the domination of the late King's mistresses, with their intrigues, their extravagances and their creatures, looked forward at the death of Louis with hope and anticipation to the accession of his grandson and the beautiful young queen.

Gradually under the new *régime* architecture became more simple. Broken scrolls were replaced by straight lines, curves and arches were introduced when justified, and columns and pilasters reappeared in the ornamental façades of public buildings. Interior decoration necessarily followed suit : instead of the curled endive scrolls enclosing the irregular shaped panel and the superabundant foliage in ornament we find rectangular panels formed by simpler mouldings, with broken corners, having a patera or rosette in each corner and between the upright panels a pilaster of refined Renaissance design. In the oval medallions supported by cupids one finds a domestic scene by Fragonard or Chardin; and portraits of children by Greuze replaced the courting shepherds and mythological goddesses of Boucher and Lancret. Sculpture too became more refined and decorous in its representations.

As with architecture, decoration, painting and sculpture, so also with furniture. The designs became more simple but were relieved from severity by the amount of ornament which except in a few cases of over-elaboration was properly subordinate to the design and did not control it.

Mr. Hungerford Pollen attributes this revival of classic taste to the discoveries of ancient treasures in Herculaneum and Pompeii, but as these occurred in the former city so long before the time we are discussing as the year 1711 and in the latter as 1750 they can scarcely be the immediate cause; the reason most probably is that a return to simpler and purer lines came as a relief and reaction from the over-ornamentation of the previous period. There are not wanting however in some of the decorated ornaments of the time, distinct signs of the influence of these discoveries. Drawings and reproductions from frescoes found in these old Italian cities were in the possession of the draughtsmen and designers of the time; and an instance in point of their adaptation is to be seen in the small boudoir of the Marquise de Sérilly, one of the maids of honour to Marie Antoinette. The decorative woodwork of this boudoir is fitted up in the Victoria and Albert Museum.

This charming little specimen of French decorative art of this period should be carefully studied. It was designed by Rousseau de la Rottière, a young painter who was in favour with the Queen and who worked under Ledoux, an architect then high in court esteem. Mdlle. de Sérilly was married about 1780 and it was then in all probability that this work was carried out. Speaking of this boudoir Lady Dilke has observed in her valuable book on French furniture and decoration :—" The triumphant

MARQUETERIE CABINET.
With plaques of Sèvres China.
(*Jones Collection, Victoria and Albert Museum.*)

skill employed to get the most possible out of the proportions imposed by the restricted space at command may be placed to the account of the ingenious architect, but it must be admitted that his intentions have been abetted by Rousseau de la Rottière with rare intelligence and tact." It may be observed here that the beautiful Marie Antoinette Bedchamber at the Château of Compiègne and the music room at Fontainebleau were decorated by the same artist.

A notable feature in the ornament of woodwork and in metal mountings of this time is a fluted pilaster with quills or husks filling the flutings some distance from the base or starting from both base and top, and leaving an interval of the fluting plain and without ornament. An example of this will be seen in the woodcut opposite of a cabinet in the Jones Collection which has also the familiar " Louis Seize" riband surmounting the two oval Sèvres china plaques. When the flutings are in oak, in rich mahogany or painted white these husks are gilt and the effect is chaste and pleasing. Variation was introduced into the gilding of frames by mixing silver with some portion of the gold so as to produce two tints, red gold and green gold; the latter would be used for wreaths and accessories while the former, or ordinary gilding, was applied to the general surface. The legs of tables were generally fluted as noted above, tapering towards the feet, and were relieved from a stilted appearance by being connected by a stretcher.

There occurs in M. Williamson's valuable contribution to the literature of our subject (*"Les Meubles d'Art du Mobilier National"*), an interesting illustration of the gradual alterations which we are noticing as having taken place in the design of furniture about this time. This is a small writing table some 3ft. 6in. long made during the reign of Louis XV. but quite in the Marie Antoinette style, the legs tapering and fluted, the frieze having in the centre a plaque of *bronze doré,* the subject being a group of cupids, representing the triumph of Poetry, and having on each side a scroll with a head and foliage (the only ornament characteristic of Louis Quinze style) connecting leg and frieze. It was made for the Trianon and the date is just one year after Marie Antoinette's marriage. M. Williamson quotes verbatim the memorandum of which it was the subject :—" Memoire des ouvrages faits et livrés, par les ordres de Monsieur le Chevalier de Fontanieu, pour le garde meuble du Roy par Riesener, ébeniste a l'arsenal Paris, savoir Sept. 21, 1771 "; and then follows a fully detailed description of the table, with its price, which was 6,000 francs, or £240. An illustration of this table appears on page 248.

The maker of this piece of furniture was the same Riesener whose masterpiece is the magnificient *bureau du Roi* in the Louvre to which we have already alluded. This celebrated *ébeniste* continued to work for Marie Antoinette for about twenty years until she quitted Versailles and he probably lived quite to the end of the century, for during the Revolution we find that he served on the Special Commission appointed by the

WRITING TABLE.

Made by Riesener for Marie Antoinette. Collection "Mobilier National."

PERIOD: LATE LOUIS XV.

(From a pen and ink drawing by H. Evans.)

National Convention to decide which works of Art should be retained, and which should be sold out of the mass of treasure confiscated after the deposition and execution of the King.

Riesener's designs do not show much variety but his work is highly finished and elaborate. His method was generally to make the centre panel of a commode front, or the frieze of a table, a *tour de force*, the marqueterie picture being wonderfully delicate. The subject was generally a vase with fruit and flowers; the surface of the side panels was inlaid

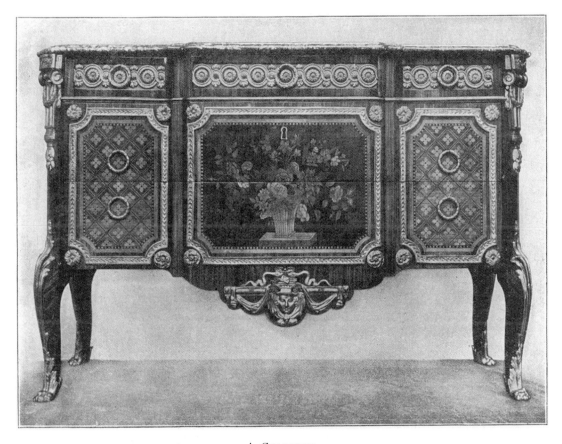

A COMMODE.
In Marqueterie, with gilt bronze mountings. Early Louis Seize.
Stamped R. V. L. C. (*supposed to be Robert Victor La Croix.*)
(*Victoria and Albert Museum.*)

with diamond-shaped lozenges, or a small diaper pattern in marqueterie; and then a framework of rich ormolu would separate the panels. The centre panel had sometimes a richer frame. His famous commode, made for the Château of Fontainebleau, which cost a million francs (£4,000) —an enormous sum in those days—is one of his *chefs d'œuvres* and is an excellent example of his style. A similar commode was sold in the Hamilton Palace sale for £4,305. An upright secretaire *en suite* with the

THE MARIE ANTOINETTE WRITING TABLE.

By Riesener and Gouthière.

(Formerly in the Hamilton Palace Collection.)

MARIE ANTOINETTE UPRIGHT SECRETAIRE.

By Riesener and Gouthière or Thomire.

(Formerly in the Hamilton Palace Collection.)

BEDSTEAD OF MARIE ANTOINETTE.

From Fontainebleau.   Collection "Mobilier National."

PERIOD: LOUIS XVI.

(From a pen and ink drawing by H. Evans.)

commode was also sold at the same time for £4,620 and the writing table for £6,000. There are illustrations of both table and secretaire on pages 250–51, but the details of this elaborate work and of Gouthière's skill in mounting are almost impossible to represent in woodcut. The table is described as follows in Christie's catalogue :

"Lot 303. An oblong writing table *en suite*, with drawer fitted with inkstand, writing slide and shelf beneath ; an oval medallion of a trophy and flowers on the top, and trophies with four medallions round the sides ; stamped J. H. Riesener and branded underneath with cypher of

CYLINDER SECRETAIRE.
In Marqueterie, with Bronze Gilt Mountings, by Gouthière.
PERIOD: LOUIS XVI.
(*Mr. Alfred de Rothschild's Collection.*)

Marie Antoinette, and *Garde Meuble de la Reine*." There is no date on the table but the secretaire is stamped 1790 and the commode 1791. If we assume that the table was produced in 1792 then these three specimens which have always been regarded as amongst the most beautiful work of the reign were almost the last which the unfortunate Queen lived to see completed.

The fine work of Riesener required to be mounted by artists of equal merit and in Gouthière and Thomire he was most fortunate. There is a famous clock case in the Wallace Collection fully signed "Gouthière, ciseleur et doreur du roi â Paris Quai Pelletier, á la Boucle d'or, 1771."

In the Louvre and also in the Wallace Collection are some beautiful examples of this co-operative work. In some of the cabinets, plaques of

ENCOIGNURE.
In the Louis XVI. style, showing the adoption of fine Japanese lacquer in combination with rich gilt bronze mountings to furniture of the period.
(*From "The Connoisseur," by permission.*)

very fine black and gold lacquer take the place of marqueterie; the centre panel being a finely chased oval medallion of Gouthière's gilt bronze while caryatides figures of the same material at the ends support the cornice.

In the Wallace Collection at Hertford House and also in the Jones bequest at South Kensington there are several charming examples of Louis Seize *meubles de luxe.* Some of these are enriched with plaques of Sèvres porcelain to which the jewel-like mounting of this time is better adapted than the rococo style which was in vogue during the preceding reign.

The upholstered furniture became simpler in design; the sofas and chairs have generally but not invariably straight fluted tapering legs which sometimes have the flutings spiral instead of perpendicular: the

ARM CHAIR OF LOUIS XVI. STYLE.

backs are either oval or rectangular and ornamented with a carved riband which is represented as tied at the top in a lover's knot. Gobelins, Beauvais and Aubusson tapestry are used for covering, the subjects being in harmony with the taste of the time. A sofa in this style, the frame elaborately carved with trophies of arrows and flowers in high relief and covered with fine old Gobelins tapestry was sold at the Hamilton Palace sale for £1,176. This was formerly at Versailles. Beautiful silks and brocades were also extensively used both for chairs and for the screens which at this period were varied in design and very decorative.

CARVED AND GILT CAUSEUSE OR SETTEE, AND FAUTEUIL OR ARM CHAIR.

Covered with Beauvais Tapestry. Collection " Mobilier National."

PERIOD: END OF LOUIS XVI.

(From a pen and ink drawing by H. Evans.)

Small two-tier tables of tulip wood with delicate mountings were quite the rage. The legs of small occasional pieces, like those of the chairs, are sometimes carved. An excellent example of a piece with cabriole legs is the charming little "Marie Antoinette" cylinder-fronted marqueterie escritoire in the Jones bequest (illustrated below).

DAVID RÖNTGEN.—This was the work of David Röntgen, formerly of Neuwied, near Coblentz, who was received into the corporation of Paris

MARQUETERIE ESCRITOIRE.
Said to have belonged to Marie Antoinette.   By David Röntgen.
(*Jones Bequest, Victoria and Albert Museum.*)

cabinet makers in 1780 and became *ébeniste mécanicien* to Queen Marie Antoinette. A specialité of this maker was to fit up the drawers of his cabinets and secretaires with numerous little compartments which opened and shut by cleverly contrived mechanical devices. The marqueterie of Röntgen, or of "David" as he has been so frequently called, was of a minute character and has been compared to marble mosaic work in

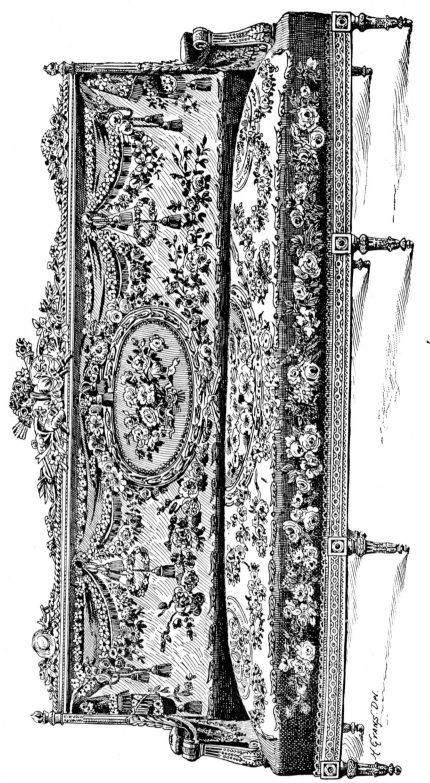

CARVED AND GILT CANAPÉ OR SOFA.

Covered with Beauvais Tapestry. Collection "Mobilier National."

PERIOD: END OF LOUIS XVI.

which the component parts of the picture are much smaller and therefore much more numerous than when the treatment of a subject in marqueterie is broader.

Röntgen travelled about Europe to sell his work and it is said that on more than one occasion he sold a whole collection of his furniture to the Empress Catherine in St. Petersburg.

The names of the more eminent French makers will be found in the list at the end of the book with notes for the reader's handy reference of their times and the kind of work for which they were noted.

Besides the older *ebenistes* such as Riesener, Carlin, the Sauniers and others who had worked for King Louis XV. and who had altered their style with the changes in fashion which had come about there were some fresh candidates for Royal favour as regards State furniture and several of these came from other countries to seek fortune in France. David Röntgen, already mentioned, was one of these ; among others were Charles Richter whose signature occurs on a beautiful cabinet in the Jones bequest ; G. Jansen, who has signed two tables in the same collection ; Adam Weisweiller and Schwerdfeger, two Germans, specimens of whose work are in the Wallace Collection : Benemann and many others. We find the names of several of these foreign craftsmen in the list of the members of the Incorporated Society of Paris Cabinet Makers, with the year of their admission; beyond that fact and their signatures upon some examples of their work in public and private collections we know scarcely anything about most of them.

There were several makers and mounters of fine furniture who lived through more than one reign—in some cases who carried on their business during three reigns—and as they naturally altered their style of work to accord with the fashion of the time it must be obvious that the identification of any particular kind of decorative treatment with the individual craftsmen becomes impossible except in certain cases where there are recognised peculiarities or characteristics. Another difficulty which confronts the expert in richly mounted French furniture is to decide between the work of "maker" and "mounter." In the case of Caffieri, Gouthière, Thomire, and some others we know that the metal work alone was designed and executed by them, but in the case of Charles Cressent, Martin Carlin, J. F. Leleu and many others who could be named, it is probable that the design was made by them and the mounting of the piece carried out under their direction. This was undoubtedly the case unless for some special order the cabinet, table or commode was entrusted to such a master of metal work (*fondeur et ciseleur*) as Gouthière or Thomire ; for more ordinary commissions the

Photo by Goupil et Cie.]

UPRIGHT SECRETAIRE.

By J. F. Leleu.

French: Executed at the close of the reign of Louis XV. in the Louis XVI. style.

(*Wallace Collection.*)   *See* page 262.

Photo by W. A. Mansell & Co.] **CABINET.**

In Mahogany, Mounted with Gilt Bronze.

Attributed to Martin Carlin, and representative of his style of work.

French : Period Louis XVI.

(Wallace Collection.) *See page* 262.

work would be entrusted to lesser men. We have seen how the magnificent *bureau du Roi* already described and illustrated in this chapter was the work of Oeben and Riesener in combination for the cabinet work, while Duplessis modelled the mounts, and Winant and Hervieux executed the metal work and yet the only signature stamped upon the finished piece is that of Riesener.

The wonderful Marie Antoinette furniture sold at the Hamilton Palace collection, also illustrated and described, is known to have been the result of co-operation between Riesener and Gouthière and there are many other instances in which a similar combination of the talents of maker and mounter can be traced; and we may take it that while the general lines of the piece were designed by Riesener the details of the mountings were thought out by Gouthière.

There are some remarkable examples such as the beautiful commodes by Cressent and by Caffieri in the Wallace Collection, illustrated on pages 226 and 228, in which the cabinet work as a decorative object is almost entirely covered by the mounts. In such examples the credit of the design must be given to the creator of those marvellous mounts which raise the manufacture of such French furniture to the highest level of the Industrial Art.

To return to some individual makers of Louis Seize furniture. Of several who deserve mention our space only admits the notice of a few whose work is known to us. In the two chief museums of furniture of this period accessible to every one—the Wallace Collection and the Jones bequest—some examples can be seen: there are also fine specimens at Windsor Castle, and if the reader visits Paris the *Musèe du Louvre* and the *Musèe du Garde Meuble* are available.

J. F. LELEU made furniture for the Garde Meuble and a very fine *cartonnière* table bearing his stamped signature was sold at the Hamilton Palace sale for £3,203. Two cabinets in the Wallace Collection bear his signature and one of these we are able to illustrate from which the reader can form an idea of the style he generally adopted. It will be observed that the fine panel of marqueterie in the flap of the secretaire is somewhat in the style of Riesener. The other specimen at Hertford House is a buffet of plain mahogany, enriched with finely executed gilt bronze mounts.

MARTIN CARLIN, another cabinet maker of this time, has six examples attributed to him in the Wallace Collection and we give a full-page illustration of a representative example of his style which is in every way typical of the period of Louis Seize.

There are one or two characteristics of his design which enable us to recognise his handiwork. One of these is a favourite method of introducing independent or detached balustrade columns, sometimes of wood and sometimes of gilt bronze or of the two materials combined, which support the friezes of his cabinets. An exceedingly handsome but somewhat overmounted cabinet of this kind with Sèvres china plaques let into the panels is at Windsor Castle and another is at Harewood House. Another peculiar and yet not quite satisfactory ornament of Carlin's design will be found in his later work. It consists of a fringe of drapery caught up with small tassels; there is a two-tier table in the Jones bequest thus ornamented.

CLAUDE CHARLES SAUNIER.—In the Wallace Collection is a pair of encoignures and also an upright secretaire which are admirable examples of the work of this famous *ébeniste*. The chief panel in the door of the secretaire is signed "Foulet," and the metal mounts are singularly handsome and massive. The style of Saunier's marqueterie resembles that of Oeben, but his time was later and although he was received into the corporation of Paris *ébenistes* in 1752 and therefore must have worked during the reign of Louis XV. we know that he was living in 1792 and the examples already referred to are of the style in vogue during the time of Louis XVI.

The secretaire is a remarkable specimen and is fairly represented in the photograph which we have been able to reproduce on page 265.

J. DUBOIS.—The work of Dubois belongs as much to the period of the Regency as to that of Louis XVI. There is a commode in the Victoria and Albert Museum bearing his stamp which forms part of the Lyne-Stephens bequest. It has mounts in which the terminals of the figures are twisted fish-tails, a form of ornament also favoured by Charles Cressent and already noticed in the earlier part of this chapter. An extraordinary commode of ultra-rich mountings is in the Wallace Collection, also signed by Dubois; this also bears the twisted mermaid appendages and is a "Regency" piece. Dubois lived and worked well into the reign of Louis XVI., to which time his later work only belongs.

JEAN PAFRAT.—A very charming little cabinet table or *bonheur du jour* in the Jones bequest bears the joint signatures of Carlin and Pafrat. The latter craftsman is said to have made a specialité of mounting panels of old lacquer into small pieces of furniture. He became a member of the corporation of Paris *ébenistes* in 1785 and therefore his work belongs to the time of Louis Seize.

WRITING TABLE.

Finished in Green Veneer in the style of Vernis Martin, with finely
executed gilt bronze mountings by Dubois.

FRENCH: PERIOD OF LOUIS XVI.

(Wallace Collection)

UPRIGHT SECRETAIRE.

By Claude Charles Saunier.   The principal panel of marqueterie is signed " Foulet."
FRENCH : TRANSITIONAL PERIOD, LOUIS XV. TO LOUIS XVI.

(Wallace Collection.)

SECRETAIRE WITH SÈVRES PORCELAIN PLAQUE.
Probably by Martin Carlin.   FRENCH: PERIOD LOUIS XVI.
(*Wallace Collection.*)

BENEMANN.—This *ébéniste* was one of a number of German crafts-men who found patronage and employment in the Court of Queen Marie Antoinette. His style is somewhat ponderous, and lacks the grace and delicacy of Oeben or Riesener in combination with Gouthière. He generally used mahogany for the construction of his *grands pièces* and overmounted them with gilt bronze. Lady Sackville has a fine commode made by Benemann for Marie Antoinette which formerly belonged to Sir John Murray Scott, the friend and private secretary of Sir Richard Wallace. The cabinet work is almost covered by elaborated mounts with a gilt bronze medallion in the centre of the design. Benemann became a member of the Paris corporation of *ébénistes* in 1785. There is an illustration of a copy of one of this maker's cabinets in Chapter IX.

WEISWEILLER.—Adam Weisweiller was another German *ébéniste* who found favour with Marie Antoinette as is evidenced by the fine cabinet, illustrated on page 268, in the Wallace Collection. It will be seen that the mounts of gilt bronze with terminal figures at the sides are some-what similar to the designs of Dubois. The two plaques of Sèvres porcelain in the panels of the doors are hard paste and of a very late period of the factory, while the monogram of the queen which ornaments the small plaque in the stretcher which connects the legs of the cabinet-stand, indicates that it was made to her order. The cabinet is typical of the Marie Antoinette taste and period, and the mounts which are very finely executed are attributed to Gouthière.

FAMILY OF PETIT.—The stamp of "Petit" occurs upon many pieces of furniture of varying excellence, and this is accounted for by the fact of there being no fewer than five members of the family who were members of the Paris corporation of cabinet makers. Lady Dilke has given us their names and dates of reception into this guild of workers. Gilles Petit, 1752; Jean Marie, 1777; Nicholas, 1761 and 1765; Nicholas-Gilles, 1774; Richard Alexandre, 1777. Of these the first-named was the most famous and the fine table in the Jones bequest stamped "Petit" is attributed to him and is one of the best specimens of its period which was some twenty-five years anterior to the time which we are now considering. The work of the other members of the Petit family may be said to come within the time of Louis Seize and Marie Antoinette, and the majority of pieces which we have seen stamped "Petit" are of that style and period.

DE LA FOSSE.—The celebrated mounter of this name was with Gouthière a pupil of Jean Martincourt and his work became so noted

CABINET OF THUJA WOOD.

DECORATED WITH PLAQUES OF SÈVRES PORCELAIN.

On the small plaque in the centre of the supports which connect
the legs at their base is the monogram of Marie Antoinette.

By Adam Weisweiller. FRENCH: PERIOD OF LOUIS XVI.

(Wallace Collection.)

that it is not uncommon to see tables, clocks and cabinets described as in "le style de De la Fosse" in some French catalogues. There is a cartel clock in the Wallace Collection attributed to him with a vase on the top from which hang swags of drapery and pendant husks. This has been very freely copied by modern makers. The furniture which we recognise as mounted by him is very decorative; satyrs' heads, female masks, and scrolls with the feet representing lions' claws, all beautifully chased and gilt, are favourite ornaments. A fine table mounted in this rather exuberant manner was sold at Christie's for 1,600 guineas: the table in the Wallace Collection known as the "Abercorn table" is undoubtedly his work.

THOMIRE.—Another great artist in gilt bronze mountings of furniture and other *objets d'art* was Thomire; and as his name is less familiar to the public than that of Gouthière much of his work is ascribed to

ENCOIGNURE OF AMBOYNA WOOD AND MAHOGANY.
With Bronze Mountings attributed to Thomire. Cabinet work by J. H. Riesener (stamped).
FRENCH: LOUIS XVI. PERIOD. (*Wallace Collection.*)

the latter. Thomire was a pupil of Houdon; he was born in 1751 and lived until 1843, so that only his earlier work was contemporary with that of Gouthière.

In the Wallace Collection there are two encoignures and an upright secretaire of amboyna wood and mahogany inlaid with stained woods, made by Riesener, the mounts of which had been ascribed to Gouthière until M. Molinier in his work "Le Musée Wallace" gave reasons for attributing the metal work to Thomire. It is exceedingly difficult to decide when the work of both artists is so similar both in style and in excellence. There are at Hertford House no fewer than fourteen examples of mounting attributed to Gouthière and five to Thomire. The reader has therefore ready to hand the opportunity of carefully studying and comparing the work and forming an opinion. The writer feels inclined to give to Gouthière the credit for mounts where wreaths of flowers and scrolls are the chief features of the design, and to ascribe to Thomire the designs in which the oval plaques of figures in slight relief are introduced into the enrichment of the furniture. There is also in the Wallace Collection a fine Sèvres vase mounted by Thomire, the date of which is about 1790. The length of Thomire's career has caused his name to be more generally associated with the time of the first Empire and of the period of the Directory which preceded it than with his earlier work.

Some of the best sculptor modellers who prepared the original designs for the *fondeur et ciseleur* were Martin, Boizot and de Hauré. The latter was appointed by the Crown to make agreements with those who executed or repaired State furniture or *meubles de la Couronne de France.*

Nearly all the bronzes made by Gouthière for Madame du Barri at Luciennes were designed by a noted architect of the time, Le Doux.

GAUDREAUX.—This maker of costly furniture was more lavish in decorative gilt bronze than Benemann, and his pieces are representative of the *style rocaille* which marked the latter part of the time of Louis XV. It is redundant in ornament, and only the fine finish of the metal work redeems it from vulgarity. A striking example of his work in the Bibliothèque Nationale in Paris is a massive commode in which he introduces some oval medallions with gilt bronze reliefs standing out on a ground of blue enamel. He is said to have worked from designs by the brothers Slodtz.

FRENCH INFLUENCE ON OTHER COUNTRIES

The influence exercised by the splendour of the Court of Louis Quatorze and by the bringing together of artists and skilled handicraftsmen for the adornment of the palaces of France which we have seen took place during the latter half of the seventeenth century was not without its effect upon the Industrial Arts of other countries. Macaulay mentions the "bales of tapestry" and other accessories which were sent to Holland to fit up the camp quarters of Louis le Grand when he went there to take the command of his army against William III. and he also tells us of the sumptuous furnishing of the apartments at St. Germains when James II. during his exile was the guest of Louis. The grandeur of the French King impressed itself upon his contemporaries, and war with Germany as well as with Holland and England helped to spread this influence. We have noticed how Wren designed the additions to Hampton Court Palace in imitation of Versailles; and in the chapter which follows this it will be seen that the later designs of Chippendale were reproductions of French furniture of the time of Louis Quinze.

As an instance of the influence of French taste upon the Courts of Europe we may mention that in 1716 a numerous company of artists, sculptors, mounters and makers of furniture and of artistic accessories had the especial leave of the French King to visit St. Petersburg at the request of the Empress Catherine, where they carried out the work of decorating and furnishing her palaces under the direction of some of the best talent from Paris.

The King of Sweden, Charles XII., "the Madman of the North" as he was called, imitated his great French contemporary and in the palace at Stockholm there are still to be seen traces of the Louis Quatorze style in decoration and in furniture: such adornments being quite out of keeping with the simplicity of the habits of the present Royal family of Sweden.

A Bourbon Prince too succeeded to the throne of Spain in 1700 and there are still in the palaces and picture galleries of Madrid some fine specimens of French furniture of the three reigns which have just been discussed. It may be taken therefore that for a period dating from the latter part of the seventeenth century the dominant influence upon the design of decorative furniture in Europe was of French origin.

The collector will often be puzzled to attribute correctly some good commodes of Louis XV. design veneered with tulip-wood or partly with king-wood and tulip, sometimes enriched with panels of marqueterie of floral design; such appear to be undoubtedly genuine work of the time, say from the middle to the latter half of the eighteenth century and yet there is a coarseness of finish both in the cabinet work and also in the metal mounts which does not seem to warrant their being considered to be the production of the highly skilled craftsmen who made such furniture for the Court and nobility of France. The gilt bronze or lacquered handles are not highly chased and the "knee" and "toe" ornaments as well as those on the corners of the commode are of poor quality. Such pieces may generally be ascribed to the Dutch makers of the time who copied the furniture made in Paris; and though very desirable as genuine old decorative work should not be confounded with the Paris-made articles.

Having described somewhat in detail the styles which prevailed and some of the changes which occurred in France from the time of Louis XIV. until the Revolution it is unnecessary for the purposes of this sketch to do more than briefly refer to the work of those countries which may be said to have adopted to a greater or less extent French designs. For reasons already stated an exception is made in the case of our own country; and the following chapter will be devoted to the furniture designed and made by some of the English craftsmen of the latter half of the eighteenth century. Of Italy it may be observed generally that the Renaissance of Raffaelle, Leonardo da Vinci and Michael Angelo which we have seen became degenerate towards the end of the sixteenth century relapsed still further during the period

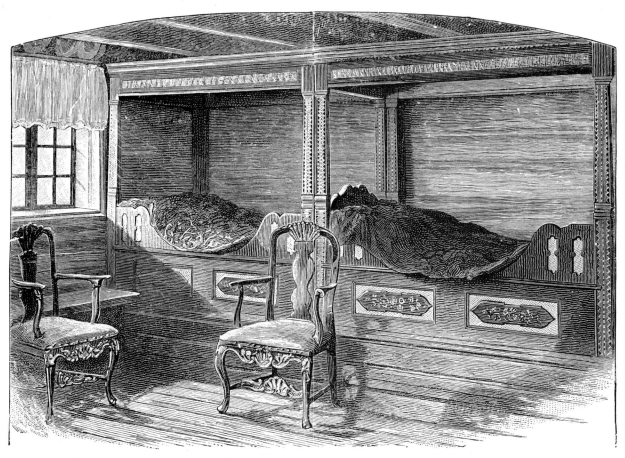

A Norse Interior, Showing Chairs of Dutch Design
Early XVIII. Century.

which we have just been discussing; and although the freedom and grace of the Italian carving and the elaboration of inlaid arabesques must always have some technical merit, the work of the seventeenth and eighteenth centuries in Italy compares very unfavourably with that of the earlier period of the Renaissance.

There are many other museum specimens which might be referred to to prove the influence of French design of the seventeenth and eighteenth centuries on that of other countries. The illustration on this page of a

Norse interior shows that this influence penetrated as far as Scandinavia; the old-fashioned box-like bedsteads which the Norwegians had retained from early times and which in a ruder form are still to be found in the cottages of many Scottish counties, especially of those where the Scandinavian connection existed, are characteristic of the country. The design of the chairs in the illustration is an evidence of the innovations which had been made upon native fashions. These chairs are in style

SECRETAIRE.
In King and Tulip Wood with Sèvres Plaques and Ormolu Mountings.
PERIOD: EARLY LOUIS XVI.
(*Jones Bequest, Victoria and Albert Museum.*)

thoroughly Dutch of about the end of the seventeenth or early in the eighteenth century; the cabriole legs and shell ornaments were probably the direct result of the influence of the French on the Dutch. The woodcut is from a drawing of an old house in Norway.

In some of the press criticisms on the earlier editions of this work it was said that in dealing with French furniture of the period considered in this chapter such *pieces de luxe* as had been described were quite beyond the attainment of ordinary persons and it was a fault laid to the author's account that the more ordinary furniture was not given its due share of attention. The answer to this criticism is that the lines and general design of such furniture during the latter part of the reign of Louis Quatorze and during the two succeeding reigns were almost precisely the same as those of such cabinets, chairs and tables as have been described and illustrated. The chief difference lies either in the absence of mounting or in the poverty and coarseness of the mounts where

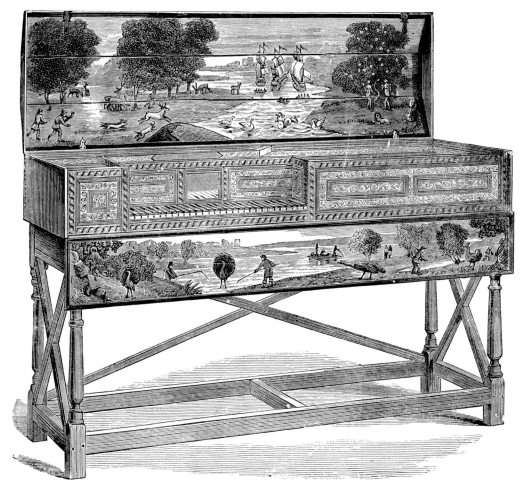

HARPSICHORD.
DATE ABOUT 1750.   *See* Appendix.
(*Victoria and Albert Museum*)

mounting was used. If decorative and expensive veneers and artistic marqueterie were not employed the simpler designs of the furniture, either plain or carved more or less carefully, still followed the lines and contour of the more costly furniture and when the tapestries of Gobelins, Beauvais or Aubusson were omitted cheaper coverings were used such as a mixture of silk and cotton or other suitable materials.

As an instance of this similarity of general design in both the ordinary *meubles de commerce* and in *meubles de luxe* one may state that some of the greatest and most ingenious impositions have been made on collectors by the unscrupulous dealer or "faker" who obtains an ordinary piece of furniture *actually of the period* and then by veneering, inlaying, and richly mounting this "Cinderella," glorifies and transforms it into a museum specimen. Some of these "rehabilitated" examples are difficult to detect when the decorative work has been carried out with knowledge and skill and a generous disregard of cost. It is only the enormous and almost fabulous prices which rich collectors are willing to give for furniture which they believe to have been once in the possession of princes and nobles of the *ancien régime* that render it profitable to expend so much money upon these made up specimens.

The really genuine work of the eminent craftsmen discussed in this chapter merits on the part of anyone interested in the study of furniture the most careful attention. In the finer and more elaborate examples there is a sumptuousness of decorative work, a richness of design, and a marvellous skill in execution that are simply extraordinary. A great deal of the exquisite metal mounting by Gouthière seems more applicable to jewellery than to cabinet work, and some of the finest marqueterie of the best masters is quite worthy of being framed as pictures of *tours de force* in mosaic woodwork.

When the generous bequest of the John Jones Collection was made to the nation a writer in the *Times* alluded to the historic and artistic value of some of these gems of French workmanship in an article which seemed so appropriate to its subject that we beg leave to conclude this chapter with an extract:—"As the visitor passes by the cases where these curious objects are displayed he asks himself what is to be said on behalf of the art of which they are such notable examples. Tables, chairs, commodes, secretaires, wardrobes, porcelain vases, marble statuettes, they represent in a singularly complete way the mind and the work of the *ancien régime*. Like Eisen's vignettes or the *contes* of innumerable story-tellers they bring back to us the grace, the luxury, the prettiness, the frivolity of that Court which believed itself till the rude awakening came, to contain all that was precious in the life of France. A piece of furniture like the little Sèvres inlaid writing table of Marie Antoinette is, to employ a figure of Balzac's, a document which reveals as much to the social historian as the skeleton of an ichthyosaurus reveals to the palæontologist. It sums up an epoch. A whole world can be inferred from it. Pretty, elegant, irrational and entirely useless, this exquisite and costly toy might stand as a symbol for the life which the Revolution swept away."

THE CORONATION CHAIR OF GEORGE III.
Attributed to Chippendale. The property of the Duke of Devonshire.
See pages 310-11.
(Photo by Keene, of Derby, taken especially for this work.)

CHAPTER VII

The Georgian Period

Chippendale and his Contemporaries

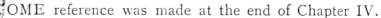

SOME reference was made at the end of Chapter IV. to the dominating influence of Dutch taste on the design of English woodwork and furniture about the end of the seventeenth century with the accession of William and Mary. Before we consider the work of our notable designers and makers who form the subject matter of this chapter it seems necessary to glance at the prevailing taste of the period from which the new departure was made.

About the time of the accession of George I. we find that a heavy and ponderous style of building and consequently of furnishing was general and pronounced. Public buildings and mansions were designed in imitation of Greek and Roman temples as regards exterior, while the interior decoration was stiff and formal. Rooms, halls and staircases were lined with plain panels of a larger surface than previously, and the carved enrichments such as architraves, chimney-pieces, picture and mirror frames, followed their French models but with heavier treatment; fluted columns supported a heavily moulded cornice and the whole was painted white in imitation of the French fashion. As a contrast to these architectural features in white, the massive and rather clumsy furniture of rich Spanish mahogany which succeeded the age of oak and walnut produced a good effect, and the Spanish mahogany doors of the time, designed with panels framed with carved egg and tongue mouldings showed to advantage in their white setting.

Mahogany may be said to have come into general use subsequent to 1720 and an interesting story is told of the first attempt to use it. Dr. Gibbon of King Street, Covent Garden, had some planks sent him by his brother, a West Indian captain, and these had lain by in his garden for some time. His wife wanted a candle box, an article of common domestic use of the time, and the Doctor asked a joiner to use a part of the wood; it was found too tough and hard for the tools of the period, but the Doctor was not to be thwarted and insisted on harder-tempered tools being found; when the task was completed the result was the production of a candle box which was admired by everyone. He then ordered a bureau of the same material and when it was finished he invited his friends to see the new work; amongst others the Duchess of Buckingham begged a small piece of the precious wood and it soon became the fashion. On account of its toughness and peculiarity of grain it was capable of treatment impossible with oak, and the high polish it took by bees-wax and rubbing (not French polish, a later invention) caused it to come into great request.

The removal of the duty on imported timber by Sir Robert Walpole in 1733 no doubt encouraged the use of mahogany which was imported from the West Indies.

The firm of Gillows of which the reader will find some interesting particulars a few pages later on, was chiefly responsible for the handsome and solid but rather heavy mahogany furniture of this period. There was also a strong partiality for gilt furniture of a ponderous character on the lines of the Louis Quatorze period but lacking the spirit and grace of their French originals. At Hampton Court Palace, Chatsworth and many other old English country houses one can still find these examples of Georgian furniture in console tables, pier glasses, chairs and couches; and although strictly speaking the reigns of the Georges extended all through the period of Chippendale, Sheraton and their contemporaries it is to this early massive and stiff period that the term " Georgian " is now often restricted.

WILLIAM KENT.—As a designer of English mahogany furniture of this time the name of William Kent comes first. Born in 1684 and a coach painter by trade, he was fortunate in obtaining the patronage of Lord Burlington, by whose assistance he travelled in Italy where he adopted the designs of such architects as the renowned Palladio, built Chiswick House for his patron, and designed the furniture for it. He also designed the furniture for Houghton, Holkam and Raynham, all in Norfolk. The Horse Guards and Devonshire House also stand to his credit. At Holkam Hall the furniture is still in the apartments for which it was designed.

Chiswick House passed into the possession of the Cavendish family by the marriage in 1748 of Lord Burlington's surviving daughter with the Marquis of Hartington. The furniture was moved to Devonshire House a hundred years later when the iron gates were also transferred, but since the sale of Devonshire House as a building site in 1920, these gates have been

CARVED AND GILT MIRROR FRAME.
Designed by William Kent for the Prince
of Wales. Date 1743.
(*Victoria and Albert Museum.*)
(*From "The Connoisseur," by permission.*)

CARVED AND GILT MIRROR FRAME.
Designed by William Kent. Date 1735-40. The property
of the Duke of Devonshire.
(*From "The Connoisseur," by permission.*)

removed to the opposite side of Piccadilly. When Devonshire House was dismantled a good deal of Kent's furniture was loaned to the Victoria and Albert Museum and our illustrations are taken from this exhibition. Kent's style was somewhat heavy and cumbersome, designed for the furnishing of great houses and stately apartments, and he introduced a Venetian character from types which he had studied during his travels. His designs suffer by comparison with those of Thomas Chippendale, which are more delicate and refined. Kent is interesting as an historical link between the period of Queen Anne and that of the middle of the eighteenth century. His console tables, generally gilt, were designed with the heavy scrolls and swags of fruit and flowers, the scrolls not infrequently terminating with eagles' heads. His furniture which was not gilt was almost exclusively made of mahogany. It is more than probable that a great deal of this furniture was made by Gillow. Kent died in 1748. The illustration on next page of the card table with the lions' masks and pendant rings would be attributed by some experts to Chippendale, as one of the type sometimes termed " Lion Chippendale," but the writer is of opinion that it should be more correctly credited to Kent.

When the second half of the eighteenth century set in, during the latter days of the second George and the early part of his successor's long reign a distinct change is apparent in the design of English decorative furniture.

CARVED AND GILT CONSOLE TABLE.
Designed by William Kent, Formerly in Devonshire House.
(From " The Connoisseur," by permission.)

Sir WILLIAM CHAMBERS, R.A. (1726-96) an architect who has left us Somerset House as a lasting monument of his talent appears to have been the first to impart to the interior decoration of houses what was termed " the Chinese style " as the result of his visit to China, to which there is a reference in the chapter on Eastern furniture; and as he was considered an " oracle of taste " about this time his influence was very powerful. Chair backs consequently have the irregular lattice work which is a peculiar feature of Chinese fretwork, while pagodas, Chinamen and monsters occur in his designs for cabinets. The overmantel which had hitherto been designed with some architectural pretension now gave way to the use of mirrors which were introduced owing to the improved manufacture of plate glass. During his travels in Italy Chambers found some Italian sculptors and brought them to England to carve in marble his designs for chimney-pieces; these were generally of a free Italian character with scrolls of foliage and figure ornaments: but as they were in marble and stone and not in wood, they scarcely belong to our subject save to indicate the change in fashion under Chambers' influence.

CARD TABLE OF MAHOGANY.
With the carved lion head ornament in favour about 1730.
Probably one of William Kent's designs.
(*From "The Connoisseur," by permission.*)

THE ADAM BROTHERS.—The influence of the brothers Adam upon the architecture, decoration and furniture of the latter half of the eighteenth century was very marked. Robert was the most distinguished of the four brothers whose father was an architect established in Edinburgh. The period of the Adams' exceedingly active and versatile work in England would appear to be from about 1762 to about 1785 and during those years we have to credit them with not only a great many public and private buildings in London, Edinburgh and Dublin, but with the designs of the interior decorative work, the furniture, even the fire-grates and many minor accessories of domestic equipment. James Adam was Robert's colleague in some of the published works on ornament of which there are no less than thirty volumes (three of which deal with furniture) in the Soane Museum in Lincoln's Inn Fields. One of these books contains two hundred and twenty-four designs of tables, slabs, sofas, commodes, terms (or pedestals), bookcases, chairs, screens, presses, cabinets, grates, cornices, chimney-pieces, besides counterpanes and carpets. Another volume is devoted to musical instruments, brackets, plate and brasswork, while the third deals with frames for mirrors and girandoles, containing over two hundred various designs. Robert Adam held the appointment of architect to the King and Queen in 1762, was elected member of Parliament for Kinross-shire in 1768, died in 1792 and was buried in Westminster Abbey.

There is a close resemblance between the Adam style and that of the Directoire Period which followed somewhat later, and this is to be accounted for by the fact that the old Greek and Roman Art was the inspiration in both cases. The sphinxes, griffins and festooned husks are prevalent in both styles. It is worthy of remark that Robert Adam seems to have been so little affected by the rococo style which was prevalent in France when he was a young man and travelling in that country. With few exceptions he and his brother were loyal to a neo-classic style in all their designs. " Rich but neat, refined but not effeminate, chaste but not severe," is an epigrammatic description of their style for which we are indebted to a writer in the " Dictionary of National Biography."

Harewood House, about half-way between Leeds and Harrogate, the stately home of the Earl of Harewood, is a notable example of a country mansion, the interior decoration and furnishing of which was entrusted to Robert Adam. To the student of our national style of decorative treatment during the latter half of the eighteenth century nothing can be more instructive. The stucco enrichments of the panels of walls and ceilings, with reproductions of antique Greek cameos framed by scrolls with rams' heads, husks, and festooned drapery, and the panel paintings by Angelica Kauffmann and Zucchi, provide a fitting background or setting for the furniture made from Robert Adam's drawings and present us with a charming picture of the interior of a house furnished at the time.

Miss Constance Simon in " English Furniture Designers of the Eighteenth Century " has contributed to the literature of our subject by much useful research and she quotes some of the original documents and bills of cost which are in the possession of the present Earl. From these interesting papers it is evident that Thomas Chippendale actually made a good deal

Facsimile of Original Drawings by Robert Adam (reduced).

DINING ROOM FURNITURE.   Designed by ROBERT ADAM.

At Harewood House.

(*By permission of Miss Constance Simon, from "English Furniture Designers of the Eighteenth Century". Published by A. H. Bullen.*)

of the furniture at Harewood, but as so few pieces are in the rococo taste which we generally identify with him we must conclude that he was content to modify his style in accordance with the desire of his patrons and that under Adam he executed the classic designs of console tables and mirrors which accord so well with the general treatment of the chief reception rooms. In the drawing room there are some curious valances of blue drapery festooned and tied with gilt cords and tassels. At first sight these would certainly be taken to be composed of a soft material such as rep or silk but they are *tours de force* of wood carving and, upon the authority of an old guide book to Harewood written so far back as 1817, are said to have been carved by Chippendale himself. Some of the drawings of Robert Adam preserved in the Soane Museum are almost identical with the decoration of the rooms at Harewood; and the dates of these correspond with the time when we know the work was executed (1765-71).

The illustration which we are able to give of a beautiful sideboard and two of the chairs in the dining room is an excellent example of the more ornate furniture of this class when one of a pair of pedestals stood at each end of the sideboard and these were surmounted by two graceful vases of the kind which contained sometimes knives and forks and sometimes a basin for washing them. In the case of the Harewood dining room the vases were apparently for ornament only, as on either side of the fireplace there are two special tables evidently intended to act in the dual capacity of knife boxes and conveniences for washing, as there is a lead-lined basin attached to each table. The wood of this elegant furniture is carefully selected mahogany rather pale in colour and enriched by gilt metal mountings of festoons of husks. The wine cooler is particularly graceful and has a cover of boldly gadrooned pattern.

The chairs were almost certainly made by Chippendale as they have the curved or "dip" seats often found on chairs of this period and the "splats" which are characteristic of him. They afford another interesting example of Adam and Chippendale working together.

We know that about this time there was a fashion for painting and graining white wood to represent different coloured marbles and also some of the rarer woods, and there is more of this painted furniture than one would expect to find in such a house as Harewood. Some of the sets of chairs which appear to be of mahogany or of walnut are upon close inspection found to be of white wood and some term-shaped pedestals on the landing which are ornamented with characteristic Adam enrichment are painted to represent porphyry and Sienna marble. One cannot help regretting that the good name of Robert Adam should be associated with work of this kind. There are numerous pieces of eighteenth century English furniture at Harewood which deserve description, but as the owner is considerate enough to allow the public to see the chief reception rooms if permission is first obtained, it should be sufficient to remind our readers of this great privilege and let them take an opportunity of seeing this most interesting house.

CYLINDER-TOP DESK IN SATIN-WOOD.
Designed by Robert Adam for Syon House. The property of the Duke of Northumberland.
(*From "The Connoisseur," by permission.*)

Another typical example of Robert Adam's treatment of interior decoration and furniture is Syon House, the Brentford residence of the Dukes of Northumberland. The first Duke gave him a free hand in 1762 and the decoration and furniture of this great mansion show lavish expenditure.

The illustration of the Syon House desk is an example of his treatment of marqueterie. The drawing and dining rooms also contain carved and gilt console tables designed by him, some of which are surmounted by inlaid marble slabs of Italian marble.

There is a peculiar interest attaching to No. 25 Portland Place because this was the house built, decorated and furnished by Robert Adam for his own residence, and fortunately the chief reception rooms remain to show the style then in vogue. To sum up, the brothers Adam introduced into England the application of composition ornaments to woodwork in their decoration of rooms, and this work is characterised by festoons of drapery, wreaths of flowers caught up with rams' heads, or swags of husks tied with a knot of riband, and with oval paeræ to mark divisions in a frieze or to emphasise a break in the design. Furniture was designed to harmonise with such decoration. The sideboard had a straight or not infrequently a serpentine-shaped front, with square tapering legs surmounted by a pair of urn-shaped knife cases, the wood used being almost invariably mahogany with the inlay generally of plain flutings relieved by fans or oval paeræ in satin-wood.

Piranesi, Cipriani and Pergolesi, Zucchi and his wife Angelica Kauffmann, had been attracted to England by the promise of lucrative employment and not only decorated the panels of ceilings and walls which were enriched by the Adam "*compo.*" (in reality a revival of the old Italian gesso-work) but also painted the ornamental cabinets, occasional tables and chairs of the time, many of which were made of satin-wood. The method of Pergolesi's decoration of furniture differed somewhat from that of Kauffmann, Zucchi and Cipriani. He generally worked on hard wood which he first painted entirely with a "flat" colour as a ground, and then decorated this ground colour, generally a pale green but sometimes yellow, with scrolls and figures. In my book "*Antiques genuine and spurious*" (Bell and Son, 1921) I have devoted a special chapter to painted satin-wood furniture which may interest those who collect this kind of decorative woodwork, and shall refer to its introduction in a later paragraph.

JEAN BAPTISTE PIRANESI—This designer deserves rather more notice than a mere passing mention. The author has a large folio book of designs of chimney-pieces, clocks, candelabra, console tables and other decorative objects which Piranesi published in 1769. The title page is printed in English, Italian and French and runs thus: "Divers manners of ornamenting chimneys and all other parts of houses, taken from the Egyptian, Tuscan and Grecian architecture, with an apologetic essay in defence of the Egyptian and Tuscan architecture."

The illustration given of one of these copper-plates will serve to show the kind of ornamentation affected and it is somewhat curious

DESIGNS OF COMMODE AND SEDAN CHAIRS.

Reproduced from Jean Baptiste Piranesi's folio work, published in 1769.

that although a good deal of this kind of work must have been carried out for wealthy people of the time very few specimens seem to have survived. The plates are all signed "Cavalieri Piranesi inv. ed inc."

SATIN-WOOD FURNITURE

Towards the end of the century satin-wood was introduced into England from the West Indies and became very fashionable. It was used as a favourite ground-work for decoration, figure subjects, such as cupids and wood nymphs, painted on medallions or panels of darker coloured woods, forming an effective relief to the yellow satin-wood. Sometimes the cabinet, writing table or spindle-legged occasional piece was made entirely of this wood having no other decoration

HALF-ROUND SATIN-WOOD CABINET.
With panels painted by Angelica Kauffmann. ENGLISH: End of Eighteenth century.
(*From "The Connoisseur," by permission.*)

beyond the beautiful marking of carefully chosen veneers; sometimes it was branded with tulip-wood or harewood (a name given to sycamore artificially stained) and at other times painted as just described. A very beautiful example of this last-named treatment is the dressing table in the Victoria and Albert Museum, an illustration of which is given on page 346.

Besides Chambers and the Adams there were several other architects now almost forgotten who designed furniture about this time. Abraham Swan, some of whose designs for wooden chimney-pieces in the quasi-classic style are known, flourished about 1758; John Carter, who published " Specimens of Ancient Sculpture and Painting "; Nicholas Revitt and

Scale of [scale bar] 4 feet

CHIMNEY-PIECE AND OVERMANTEL.

Designed by W. Thomas, Architect, 1783,

Very similar to Robert Adam's work,

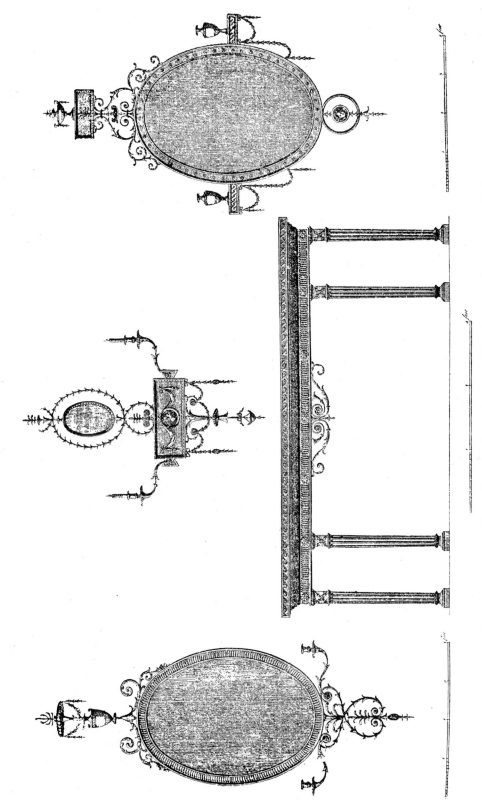

GIRANDOLES AND PIER TABLE, DESIGNED BY W. THOMAS. ARCHITECT, 1783.

Reproduced by Photography from an old Print in the Author's possession.

James Stewart, who jointly published "Antiquities of Athens" in 1762; J. C. Kraft, who designed in Robert Adam's style; W. Thomas, F.S.A., and others have left us many drawings of interior decorations, chiefly chimney-pieces and architraves of doors, all of them having the ornament in low relief and of a classical character as was the fashion towards the end of the eighteenth century.

Josiah Wedgwood, the famous potter, turned his attention to the production of plaques in relief for adaptation to chimney-pieces of this character. In a letter written from London to Mr. Bentley, his partner, at the works, he deplores the lack of encouragement in this direction which he received from the architects of his day; he however persevered and by the aid of Flaxman's inimitable artistic skill as a modeller produced suitable plaques of his beautiful jasper ware which were let in to the friezes of chimney-pieces and also into other woodwork. There can be seen in the Victoria and Albert Museum a pair of pedestals of this period (1770-90) so ornamented.

We now come to the work of a group of English cabinet makers who not only produced much excellent furniture but who also published a large number of designs drawn with extreme care and a considerable degree of artistic skill.

THOMAS CHIPPENDALE.—It is singular that we have comparatively little information of a personal character about a man who must have been so well known during a long business career as Thomas Chippendale; but since the first edition of this book was published, some new facts have come to light. The first Thomas Chippendale with whom we are concerned was a carver and picture frame maker who after carrying on business in Worcestershire came to London. The exact date of this migration is not known but Miss Constance Simon who has gleaned much interesting information says that it was previous to 1727. His son, also named Thomas, was born in Worcestershire in 1709 and appears to have assisted his father. In 1749 he took a shop in Conduit Street, Long Acre, and carried on a business as joiner, cabinet maker and carver. Four years later he moved to larger premises at 60 St. Martin's Lane where he became the widely known and famous designer and manufacturer of furniture of a certain character with which his name is closely associated. Mr. F. S. Robinson, a diligent student of the history of English furniture designers, has quoted from J. T. Smith, in "Nollekins and his Times" in 1829, who mentions the extensive premises, No. 60 St. Martin's Lane, "now occupied by Mr. Stutely, the builder," as formerly held by Chippendale, "the most famous upholsterer and cabinet maker of his day." The same writer, J. T. Smith, also makes a forecast of the future which has been singularly verified. He writes:—"As most fashions come round again I should not wonder notwithstanding the beautifully classic change brought in by Thomas Hope, Esq., if we were to see the unmeaning scroll and shell work with which the furniture of the reign of Louis Quatorze was so profusely encumbered revive, *when Chippendale's will again be sought after with redoubled avidity; and as many of the copies (of his book) must have been sold as waste paper, the few remaining will probably bear rather a high price.*"

The exact date of the second Thomas Chippendale starting in business on his own account is presumably 1749, but we may assume that for a good many years previously he was the master mind in his father's designing room, and was producing some of the furniture which we now recognise as early Chippendale. There is an entry in the Parish Register of St. George's Chapel, Mayfair, of the marriage of a Thomas Chippendale with Catherine Redshaw, of St. Martin's-in-the-Fields, and Miss Simon quotes an appeal that he made in 1755 against his rates. The *Gentleman's Magazine* of April 5th, 1755, gives an account of a fire which broke out in his workshop "and consumed the same, wherein were the chests of twenty-two workmen." Again she tells us of the death of his partner, one James Rannie, a Scotsman, in 1766, and an advertisement which gave notice of the dissolution of the partnership owing to his decease and requesting all claims upon his estate to be sent to a Mr. Thomas Haig, who subsequently became a partner in the firm about 1770. This partnership will be commented on later in connection with an old bill of Haig and Chippendale's of which we give an extract in facsimile on page 315. The Nostell Priory accounts for furniture supplied are dated from 1766 to 1770 and bear the name of Thomas Chippendale only.

The date of Chippendale's death taken from the burial register of St. Martin's Church is "*1779, November 13, Thomas Chippendale*"—and in December letters of administration were granted to his widow. Some lengthy Chancery proceedings which afterwards took place with regard to a debt due to Chippendale's firm are of some interest and an account of them will be found in Miss Simon's book.

Chippendale (II.) published "The Gentleman and Cabinet Maker's Director," not as stated in the introduction to the catalogue to the Victoria and Albert Museum in 1769 but some years previously, as is testified by a copy of the "third edition" of the work which is in the writer's possession and bears date 1762, the first edition having appeared in 1754. The title page of this edition is reproduced in *facsimile* overleaf.

THE

GENTLEMAN and CABINET-MAKER's
DIRECTOR:

Being a large COLLECTION of the

Moſt ELEGANT and USEFUL DESIGNS

OF

HOUSEHOLD FURNITURE,

In the Moſt FASHIONABLE TASTE.

Including a great VARIETY of

CHAIRS, SOFAS, BEDS, and COUCHES; CHINA-TABLES, DRESSING-TABLES, SHAVING-TABLES, BASON-STANDS, and TEAKETTLE-STANDS; FRAMES for MARBLE-SLABS, BUREAU-DRESSING-TABLES, and COMMODES; WRITING-TABLES, and LIBRARY-TABLES; LIBRARY-BOOK-CASES, ORGAN-CASES for private Rooms, or Churches, DESKS, and BOOK-CASES; DRESSING and WRITING-TABLES with BOOK-CASES, TOILETS, CABINETS, and CLOATHS-PRESSES; CHINA-CASES, CHINA-SHELVES, and BOOK-SHELVES; CANDLE-STANDS, TERMS for BUSTS, STANDS for CHINA JARS, and PEDESTALS; CISTERNS for WATER, LANTHORNS, and CHANDELIERS; FIRE-SCREENS, BRACKETS, and CLOCK-CASES; PIER-GLASSES, and TABLE-FRAMES; GIRANDOLES, CHIMNEY-PIECES, and PICTURE-FRAMES; STOVE-GRATES, BOARDERS, FRETS, CHINESE-RAILING, and BRASS-WORK, for Furniture.

AND OTHER

ORNAMENTS.

TO WHICH IS PREFIXED,

A Short EXPLANATION of the Five ORDERS of ARCHITECTURE;

WITH

Proper DIRECTIONS for executing the moſt difficult Pieces, the Mouldings being exhibited at large, and the Dimenſions of each DESIGN ſpecified.

The Whole comprehended in TWO HUNDRED COPPER-PLATES, neatly engraved.

Calculated to improve and refine the preſent TASTE, and ſuited to the Fancy and Circumſtances of Perſons in all Degrees of Life.

By THOMAS CHIPPENDALE,

CABINET-MAKER and UPHOLSTERER, in St. Martin's Lane, London.

THE THIRD EDITION.

LONDON:

Printed for the AUTHOR, and ſold at his Houſe, in St. Martin's Lane; Also by T. BECKET and P. A. DE HONDT, in the Strand.

MDCCLXII.

Facsimile of the Title-Page of Chippendale's " Director."

(Reduced by Photography). The original is folio size.

Two Bookcases.

J. Chippendale invt. et delint.

J. Taylor Sculp.

Published according to Act of Parliament 1759.

FACSIMILE OF A PAGE IN CHIPPENDALE'S "DIRECTOR."

(The original is folio size.)

This valuable work of reference contains over two hundred copper-plate engravings of chairs, sofas, bedsteads, mirror frames, girandoles, torchères or lamp stands, dressing tables, cabinets, chimney-pieces, organs, jardiniéres, console tables, brackets and other useful and decorative articles of which a great many examples are reproduced in these pages. It will be observed that these designs of Chippendale are very different from those popularly ascribed to him. Indeed it would appear that this maker has become better known than any other from the fact of the designs in his book having been recently republished in various forms; his popularity has thus been revived while the names of many of his

CHAIRS.
With ornament in the Chinese (lattice) style, by Thomas Chippendale.

contemporaries are forgotten. For the last twenty or thirty years therefore, during which time the fashion has obtained of collecting the furniture of a bygone century, almost every cabinet, table or mirror frame presumably of English manufacture which is slightly removed from the ordinary type of domestic furniture has been for want of a better title called " Chippendale." As a matter of fact he appears to have adopted from Chambers the fanciful Chinese ornament and later the rococo style of his time which gradually gave way to the quiet and more classic designs of Adam and his contemporaries.

In the chapter on Louis XV. and Louis XVI. furniture it has been shown how French fashion went through a similar change about this same period. In Chippendale's chairs and console tables, in his State bedsteads and his lamp stands, one can recognise the broken scrolls and curved lines so familiar in the bronze mountings of Caffieri. The change which had occurred in France during the Louis Seize period is equally evident in this country, and later received an impulse from the migration into England of skilled workmen from France during the troubles of the Revolution at the end of the century. Some of Chippendale's designs bear such titles as " French chairs " or a " bombé-fronted commode." These might have appeared as illustrations in a contemporary book on French furniture, so identical are they in every detail with the carved woodwork of Pineau of Cauvet or of Nilson who designed the flamboyant frames of the time of Louis XV. Other designs have more individuality. In his mirror frames he introduced a peculiar bird with a long snipe-like

TEA CADDY.
Carved in the French style.   (From Chippendale's " Director.")

beak and rather impossible wings, an imitation of rockwork and dripping water, Chinese figures with pagodas and umbrellas; and sometimes the illustration of Æsop's fables interspersed with scrolls and flowers. By dividing the glass unequally, by the introduction into his design of bevelled pillars with carved capitals and bases, he produced a quaint and pleasing effect very suitable to the rather effeminate fashion of his day and in harmony with three-cornered hats, wigs and patches, embroidered waistcoats, knee breeches, silk stockings, and enamelled snuff-boxes. In some of the designs there is a fanciful Gothic to which he makes special allusion in his preface as likely to be considered by his critics impracticable but which he undertakes to produce if desired—

"Though some of the profeſſion have been diligent enough to repreſent them (eſpeſcially those after the Gothick and Chinese manner) as ſo many ſpecious drawings impoſſible to be worked off by any mechanick whatſoever. I will not ſcruple to attribute this to Malice,

A Design for a State Bed.

T. Chippendale inv.t & delin.   Published according to Act of Parliament D. 1761.   J. Taylor sculp

FACSIMILE OF A PAGE IN CHIPPENDALE'S "DIRECTOR."

(The original is folio size).

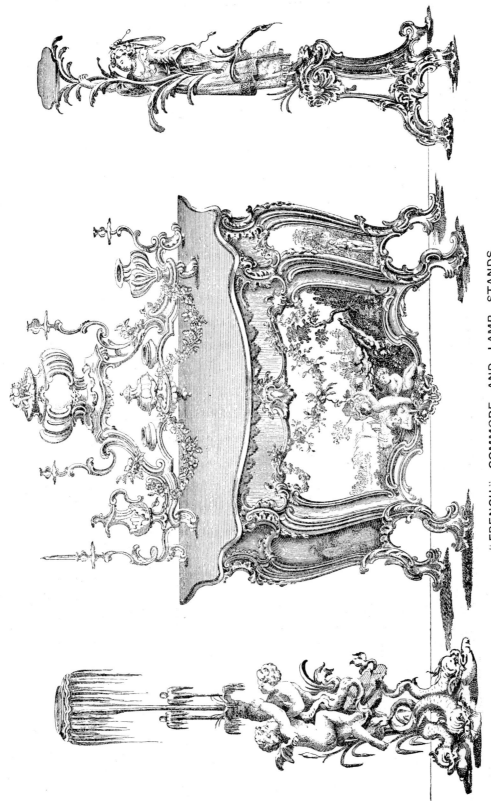

"FRENCH" COMMODE AND LAMP STANDS.

Designed by T. Chippendale, and published in his "Director."

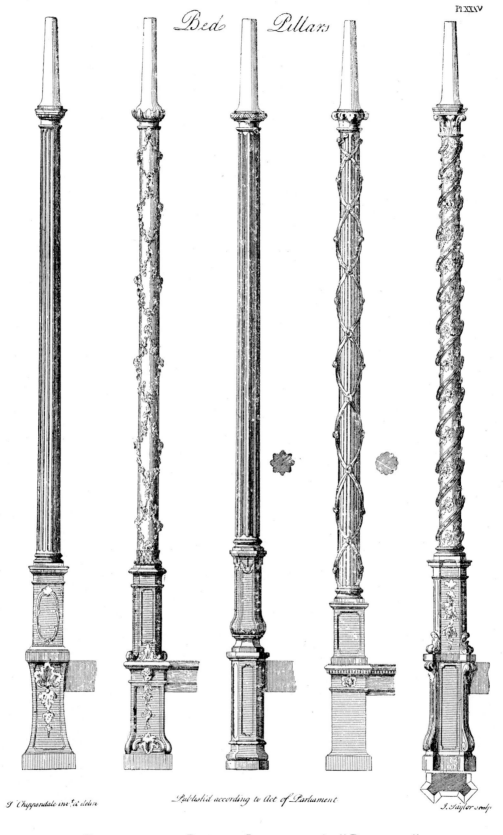

Pl XXXV

Bed Pillars

J. Chippendale inv.t & delin.   Publish'd according to Act of Parliament   J. Taylor sculp.

FACSIMILE OF A PAGE IN CHIPPENDALE'S "DIRECTOR."
(The original is folio size).

CHIMNEY-PIECE AND MIRROR.

Designed by T. Chippendale, and published in his "Director."

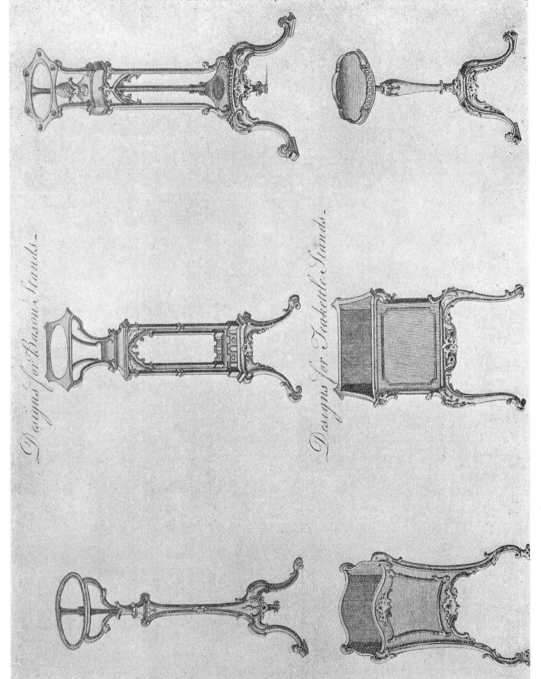

Designs for Basons Stands.

Designs for Teakettle Stands.

DESIGNS REPRODUCED FROM CHIPPENDALE'S "DIRECTOR."

Designs for Pedestals.

DESIGNS REPRODUCED FROM CHIPPENDALE'S "DIRECTOR."

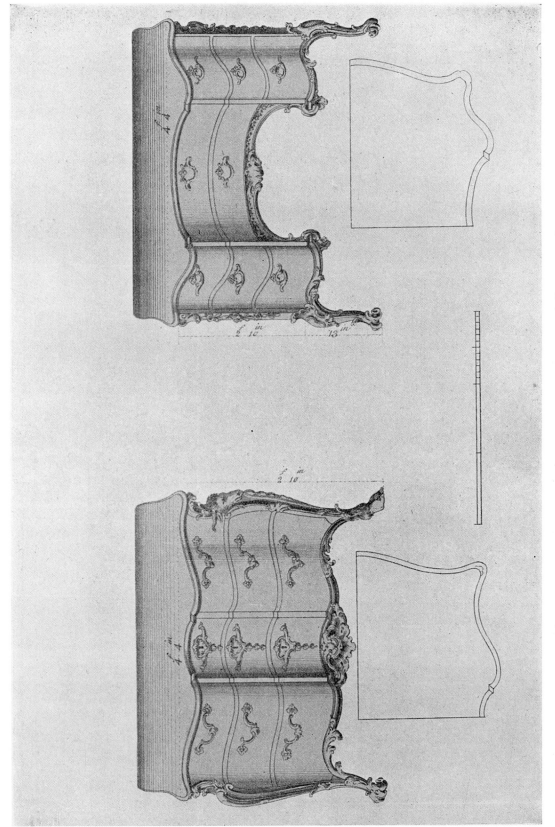

DESIGNS REPRODUCED FROM CHIPPENDALE'S "DIRECTOR."

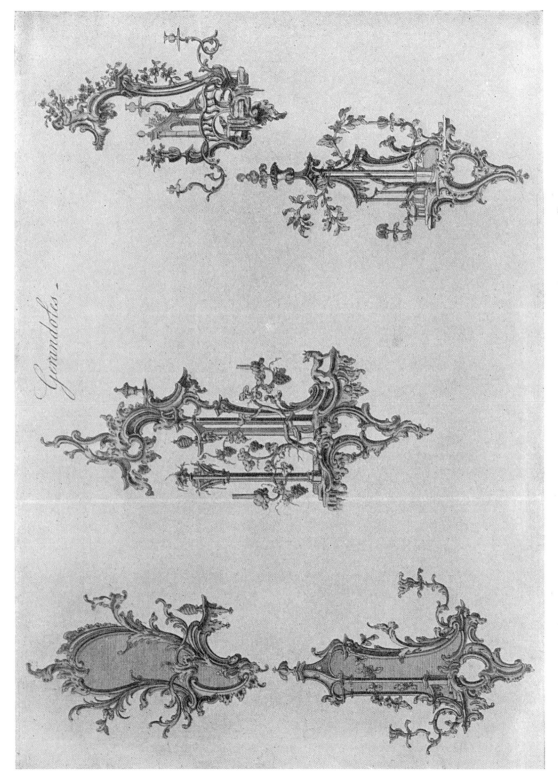

Girandoles.

DESIGNS REPRODUCED FROM CHIPPENDALE'S "DIRECTOR."

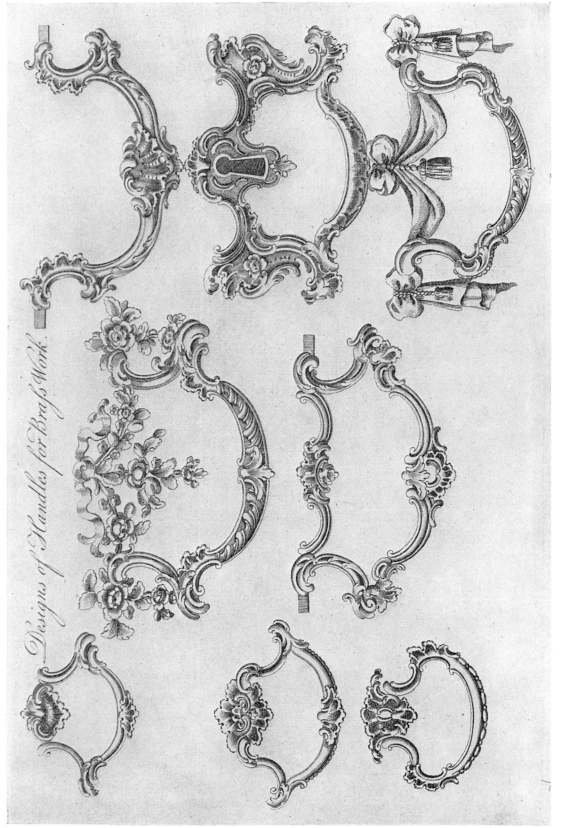

Designs of Handles for Brass Work.

DESIGNS REPRODUCED FROM CHIPPENDALE'S "DIRECTOR."

CARVED MAHOGANY ARM CHAIR.

By Thomas Chippendale. Early Work in 1730-40.

In Sir John Soane's Museum, Lincoln's Inn Fields.

(From a photo taken especially for this work.)

the reader for close examination, as it is in the Soane Museum in Lincoln's Inn Fields. The original bill of Thomas Chippendale for the price of this chair was formerly amongst the records in the Museum but has unfortunately been lost. The general lines of the back seat and legs are similar to the Dutch chairs of the end of the seventeenth century but the eagles' heads and husks which ornament the upright support of the back and in fact all the carved ornament is thoroughly English in character. The rich colouring of the mahogany and the spirit which is the charm of the carving of this chair render it one of the best examples of Chippendale's early period of work, probably from 1730-40.

A great deal of Chippendale furniture appears to have been made about this time for some of the best houses in Ireland. In these pieces the foliage ornament is generally carved boldly and masks of heads of men and animals (lions for preference) are introduced into the carved enrichments and have been called "Irish Chippendale." Many of these specimens were copied in Dublin from existing pieces or made from Chippendale's designs.

We give a reproduction on opposite page of one of a set of eight single chairs the backs of which are upholstered with old seventeenth century *petit point* needlework, and the fret-work ornament on the front and sides of the seats is carved out of the *solid* mahogany, thus producing a far more satisfactory effect than the applied fret-cut veneer which is so common. These chairs were sold at Christies' rooms on May 18th, 1906, and realised the large price of £1,344 or an average of nearly £170 each.

It is evident from a careful study of Chippendale's designs, from his own comments on them, and from examples of work attributed to him, that he was an adapter of prevailing fashions rather than an original designer. His early work was as we have seen somewhat similar to the Dutch chair introduced into this country at the time of William III.'s accession; then came the Chinese style to which reference has been made and later the adaptation of the cursive and more flowing and ornate scrolls of French character.

We have given many examples taken from his "Director" and also some from other sources showing the different influences under which he produced his chairs, mirror frames and other articles of furniture. There is a famous pair of chairs and footstools which we are permitted to add to these illustrations by the courtesy of the Duke of Devonshire. These were used at the coronation of King George III. and Queen Charlotte and are part of the famous treasures at Chatsworth. When the writer visited Chatsworth in 1905 for the purpose of making a catalogue of its contents he had an opportunity of very closely examining these chairs. There is no documentary evidence to prove them of Chippendale's make but the character and spirit of the carving leaves no doubt in the writer's mind that they were made by him and the date of their production just coincides with the best period of Chippendale's work when he was carrying on an extensive and high-class business in St. Martin's Lane. Both chairs are identical save for the cypher in the oval shield at the

CHAIR, ATTRIBUTED TO CHIPPENDALE (one of a set of eight.)
Upholstered in seventeenth century *petit point* needlework.
(*Sold at Christies', May, 1906, for £1,344*).

top, one of these having " G. R." and the other " C." The illustration will be found on page 276.

Apart from the several books of design noticed in this chapter there were published two editions of a work undated containing many of the drawings found in Chippendale's book. This book was entitled " Upwards of One Hundred New and Genteel Designs, being all the most approved patterns of household furniture in the French taste. By a Society of Upholders and Cabinet makers." It is almost certain that Chippendale was a member of this Society and that some of the designs were his, but that he severed himself from it and published his own book, preferring to advance his individual reputation. The "sideboard" which one so generally hears called "Chippendale" scarcely existed in his time. If it did it must have been quite at the end of his career. There were side tables, sometimes called "Side-Boards," but they contained neither cellaret nor cupboard; only a drawer for table linen.

DESIGN FOR A CLOCK CASE.
(From Chippendale's "Director.")

In considering the work of this undoubtedly great craftsman there are some items of interest which have not been noticed in the foregoing brief sketch.

We have seen that William Kent designed mahogany furniture from about 1720-40 and therefore Thomas Chippendale was a contemporary starting work some ten years later than Kent, but quite twenty years before the publication in 1754 of his first edition of the "Director." He did not originate the claw-and-ball foot which is to be seen in Dutch chairs of an earlier date, and were adapted probably from the Chinese who had used the claws of dragons holding balls in the designs of porcelain and bronze of a much earlier period. As the fashion inclined to a lighter treatment in the lines of chairs and sofas, and later still of commodes, clock cases, pier tables and mirrors, Chippendale, followed the vogue and his designs become more rococo as regards scrolls and foliage just as in France we have seen the dignified and stately furniture of Louis XIV. give way to the more frivolous design of the time of Louis XV. and Madame Pompadour.

Towards the end of his career we have evidence in some bills for furniture made for Nostell Priory and quoted by Mr. Percy Macquoid, that he worked in satin-wood and also in marqueterie within a few years of the first importation of satin-wood into England.

The extract from the *Gentleman's Magazine* of April 5th, 1755, mentions that Chippendale's staff of workmen consisted of twenty-two. This must give us pause when we contemplate the enormous amount of so-called "Chippendale" furniture which we are asked to accept as made under his direction. Even if after careful examination the expert decides that the piece is of Chippendale's time, it must be evident that the term must be taken as what is known as a *genre* term rather than absolute proof that it originated in his workshop. It must be remembered that he gave his designs to the public when he issued his "Director" and it was open to any skilled workman to copy them.

There are two illustrations of chairs on page 314 which will convey to the reader the difficulty if not the impossibility of deciding the authorship of some of the furniture which was made during Chippendale's lifetime or within some few years of his death. In the Freemasons' Lodge of St. John the Baptist in Exeter are three chairs, one the Master's and two the Wardens', which can be attributed to their makers by documentary evidence for which we are indebted to the antiquarian research of Miss Constance Simon. Written in faded ink under the Master's chair is "Daniel Simpson, Sculpsit, 1769." As regards the two Wardens' chairs there is the following "minute" in the Lodge books of December 2nd, 1774: "That the plan of the Wardens' chairs now produced by Messrs. Stowey and Jones be carried into execution so as the expense does not exceed twelve guineas." Miss Simon tells us that between the years 1769 and 1774 Daniel Simpson had become insolvent and in all probability Messrs. Stowey and Jones were his successors in business. The chairs are of good sound Spanish mahogany, they have the cabriole legs with carved foliage on the knees, and the Wardens' chairs have claw-and-ball feet. The carving of riband designs and the Bible set in conventionalised clouds and other details are all worthy of Chippendale, and but for the evidence to the contrary these chairs would be assigned to him.

After the death of Thomas Chippendale the Second the style of the firm became Haig and Chippendale and by the courtesy of Captain Terry who possesses an old bill of this firm for furnishing the London house of his great-uncle, Sir Richard Frederick, Bart., the writer is enabled to reproduce the first and last folios of this interesting document.

TWO CHAIRS.
Similar to Chippendale's, from the Freemasons' Lodge of St. John the Baptist, Exeter.
Under the Master's chair (left) is written in ink " Daniel Simpson, Sculpsit."
(Reproduced by permission from " The Queen.")

It will be seen that the bill, which consists of many folios, begins in 1790, and was receipted in 1796 by Thomas Chippendale. This, the third of the name, was the famous cabinet maker's son who had taken Haig into partnership. The style of the firm appears in old London directories as Haig and Chippendale, " upholders and cabinet makers," of 60 St. Martin's Lane, up to 1798, when the name of Thomas Chippendale appears alone, from which it is evident that the partnership had been dissolved either by death or consent.

The articles charged for in the bill referred to are in many cases of the most ordinary household description and only in a few cases are there chairs or tables of an unusual character or price. The following quotation will serve to show the amount charged for a set of dining-room chairs of ordinary description suitable for a gentleman's town house:—

> " Twelve neat carv'd Mahogany square back Parlor Chairs, the seats stuffed and covered with the finest Green Morocco Leather, and finished with double rows of best gilt nails, 48/- each - - - - - - - - - - - - £28 16 0
>
> " Six ditto Arm'd Chairs, stuffed and covered in the same manner, 58/- each - - - - - - - - - - £17 8 0."

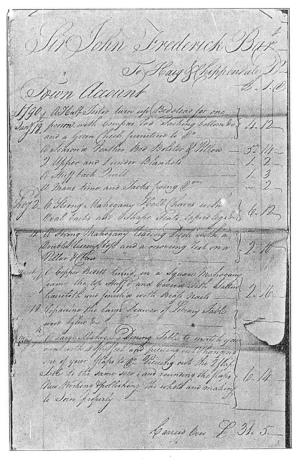 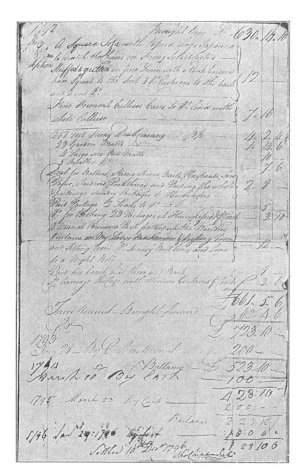

FIRST AND LAST PAGES OF AN OLD BILL.

There are several items in the bill in which "tapered" legs are mentioned, from which it is evident that Haig and Chippendale, like all other manufacturers of furniture, had conformed to the more sedate and sober lines which had succeeded the rococo curves and scrolls of the previous fashion.

In the Victoria and Albert Museum we have another interesting example of the work of this firm and as there is also exhibited the original bill of its cost, no doubt exists as to its origin. It is a suite of bedroom furniture made to the order of David Garrick for his villa at Hampton of

no great beauty either in design or execution, but very interesting because
it shows that this firm made furniture of an entirely different character
from that which is usually associated with the name of Chippendale. This
David Garrick suite is of a buff coloured lacquer and but for evidence of its
origin would certainly not be attributed to Chippendale.

The bill of Haig and Chippendale which is to be seen at the Victoria and
Albert Museum is for the furnishing of Garrick's house in the Adelphi, and is

CORNER CUPBOARD OF LACQUER.
Made by Haig and Chippendale for David Garrick.   (Victoria and Albert Museum.)
(From " The Connoisseur," by permission.)

dated 1771 and 1772, and a letter in the possession of Mr. H. E. Trevor, who
presented the bedstead of the Hampton villa bedroom suite to the Museum,
written by Garrick about the hangings of this bedstead which were sent to
him from Calcutta, bears the date 1775, so that the whole suite must have
been supplied about that time. The writer is indebted to Mr. H. Clifford
Smith, the Assistant Keeper of the Victoria and Albert Museum (Furniture
and Woodwork Department) for this information.

ROBERT MANWARING.—The name of Robert Manwaring ranks high as one of Chippendale's contemporaries. He published "The Chairmakers' Guide" in 1766 which included "upwards of two hundred new and genteel designs both decorative and plain of all the most approved patterns for burjairs, toillets, cornishes and lanthorns, etc."

The patterns of his chair-backs are very similar to those of his contemporaries and four of his designs only differ in slight details from some of those illustrated here as the work of Ince and Mayhew.

The introduction of a small ornamental bracket connecting the front legs of the chair with its frame is said to be one of the distinctive signs of a Manwaring design. From a reference which he makes to Chippendale in the preface of one of his published books one sees that he looked upon Thomas Chippendale as his friend and master, and his designs are generally speaking not distinguishable from those of the more celebrated maker. Manwaring also designed china cabinets, fenders, balconies and other decorative items and he is believed to have been a leading member of the Society of Upholders and Cabinet Makers already mentioned.

INCE AND MAYHEW.—Two other designers and makers of mahogany ornamental furniture who also deserve special mention in the discussion of eighteenth century English furniture are W. Ince and J. Mayhew who were partners in business in Broad Street, Golden Square, and contemporary with Chippendale. They also published a book of designs with the rather extravagant title of "The Universal System of Household Furniture," three hundred designs on ninety-five plates. This large folio work was published about 1770 and evidently was intended to appeal to foreign as well as English customers, for the description of the plates appeared in both French and English, though the letterpress is extravagant and unworthy of the excellent designs: Sheraton in his drawing book severely criticises the work of Ince and Mayhew. Several reproductions from the book of these makers are given, from which it is evident that without any distinguishing brand or without the identification of any particular piece of furniture with one of their designs it is difficult to distinguish between their work and that of Chippendale and other contemporary makers.

It is however noticeable after careful comparison of the work of Chippendale with that of Ince and Mayhew that the furniture designed and made by the latter firm has many of the characteristic details and ornaments which are now generally looked upon as denoting the work of Chippendale; for instance the fretwork ornaments finished by the carver and then applied to the plain mahogany; the open-worked scroll shaped

THREE CHINA SHELVES, DESIGNED BY W. INCE.

Reproduced by Photography from an old Print in the Author's possession.

Parlour Chairs, Designed by W. Ince.

LADIES' SECRETAIRES, DESIGNED BY W. INCE.

Reproduced by Photography from an old Print in the Author's possession.

DESK AND BOOKCASE, DESIGNED BY W. INCE.

Reproduced by Photography from an old Print in the Author's possession.

CHINA CABINET, DESIGNED BY J. MAYHEW.

Reproduced from an old Print in the Author's possession.

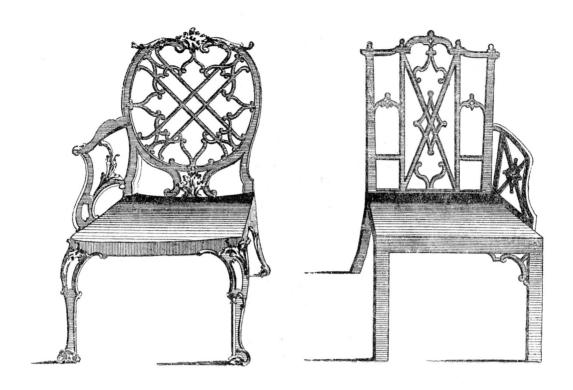

"Dressing Chairs," Designed by J. Mayhew.

These show the influence of Sir W. Chambers' Chinese style.

backs to encoignures or china shelves; and the carved Chinaman with the pagoda. Some of the frames of chimney glasses made by Ince and Mayhew are almost identical with those attributed to Chippendale, and as our illustrations show, some of the chairs are very similar.

HEPPELWHITE* AND CO.—A copy of Heppelwhite's Book in the author's possession (published in 1789) contains 300 designs " of every article of household furniture in the newest and most approved taste" and it is worth while to quote from the preface to illustrate the high esteem in which English cabinet work was held at this time:

INLAID TEA CADDY AND TOPS OF PIER TABLES.
From Heppelwhite's "Guide."

"English taste and workmanship have of late years been much sought for by surrounding nations; and the mutability of all things, but more especially of fashions, has rendered the labours of our predecessors in this line of little use; nay in this day can only tend to mislead those foreigners who seek a knowledge of English taste in the various articles of household furniture."

It is amusing to think how soon the "mutabilities of fashion" did for a time supersede many of these designs.

A selection of drawings from Heppelwhite's book is given and it will be instructive to compare them with those of other contemporary makers. From such a comparison it will be seen that in the progress from the

* This name is generally spelt Hepplewhite, but in the edition referred to of " The Cabinet Maker and Upholsterer's Guide," the spelling is as given in the text. A first edition, containing only 125 plates, was published in 1788, and a third in 1794.

rococo of Chippendale to the more severe lines of Sheraton, Heppelwhite forms a connecting link between the two.

The names given to some of these designs appear curious; for instance:

"Rudd's table or reflecting dressing table," so called from the first one having been designed for a popular character of that time.

"Knife cases," for the reception of the knives which were kept in them and used to "garnish" the sideboards.

"Cabriole chair," implying a stuffed back and not having reference as it does now to the curved form of the leg.

"Bar backed sofa," being what we should now term a three or four chair settee, *i.e.*, like so many chairs joined and having an arm at either end.

"Library case" instead of Bookcase.

"Confidante" and "Duchesse," which were sofas of the time.

"Gouty stool," a stool having an adjustable top.

"Tea chest," "Urn stand," and other names which have now disappeared from ordinary use in describing similar articles.

Since the earlier editions of this book were published some further particulars of Heppelwhite have become known. George Heppelwhite, who was probably the founder of the firm, was an apprentice to Gillow of Lancaster and afterwards established himself in London where he died in 1786. The business was carried on by his widow Alice under the style and title of A. Heppelwhite and Co. and this is the name which appears on the title page of the "Guide" already referred to and quoted from. Whether all the designs contained in the book are by George Heppelwhite or whether they are from drawings made by artists employed by Mrs. Heppelwhite and those who assisted her we do not know. It is singular that the London Directory of this time contains no reference to Heppelwhite although the firm of "Haig and Chippendale, cabinet makers and upholders," of 60 St. Martin's Lane, is mentioned in the Directories of 1790-98. In the list of cabinet makers and designers of furniture published by Sheraton in 1803 the name of Heppelwhite is not included.

A great many reproductions from the "Guide" have been given in order that these designs may be more easily identified. In many works on English furniture published within the past few years the authors appear to have depended very much upon their own personal opinions as to a piece of furniture being the work of any individual designer and many of Heppelwhite's designs have been erroneously attributed. This cannot be the case when the plates from the book published by a particular firm are reproduced in facsimile for the reader's comparison.

Heppelwhite had a "*specialité*" to which he alludes in his firm's book and of which there are several designs. This was the japanned or painted furniture. The wood was coated with a preparation after the manner of Chinese or Japanese lacquer and then decorated, generally with gold on a black ground, the designs being in fruits and flowers: and also medallions painted in the style of Cipriani and Angelica Kauffmann. Subsequently furniture of this character instead of being japanned was only painted white. It is probable that many of the chairs of this time made of wood of inferior quality and with scarcely any ornament, were originally decorated in the manner just described and therefore the

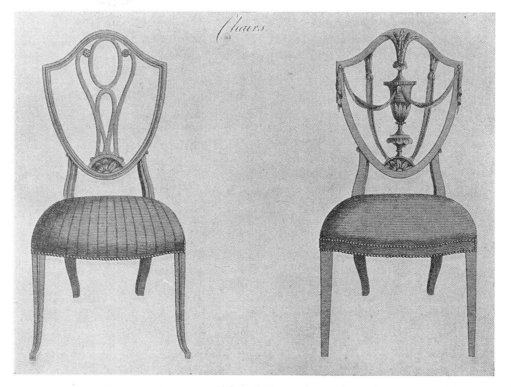

DESIGNS FOR CHAIRS.
Reproduced from Heppelwhite's "Guide."

carving of details would have been superfluous. Injury to the enamelling by wear and tear was most likely the cause of their being stripped of their rubbed and partly obliterated decorations and they were then stained and polished, presenting an appearance which does not do justice to the designer and manufacturer.

In some of Heppelwhite's chairs, too, as in those of Sheraton, there is a reminiscence of the squabbles of two fashionable factions of this time, "the Court party" and the "Prince's party." The latter is represented by having the Prince of Wales' plumes very prominent, some-

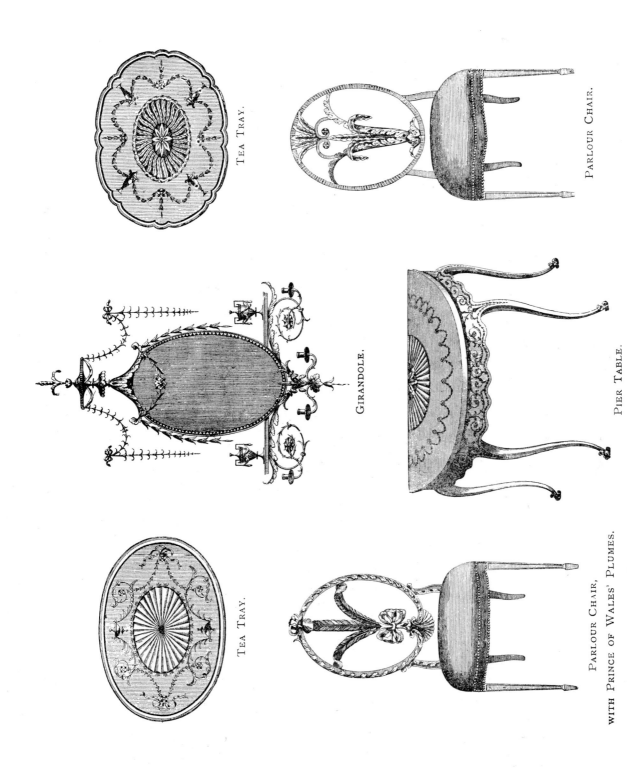

TEA TRAY.

PARLOUR CHAIR.

GIRANDOLE.

PIER TABLE.

TEA TRAY.

PARLOUR CHAIR,
WITH PRINCE OF WALES' PLUMES.

DESIGNS OF FURNITURE.

FROM HEPPELWHITE'S "GUIDE," PUBLISHED 1789.

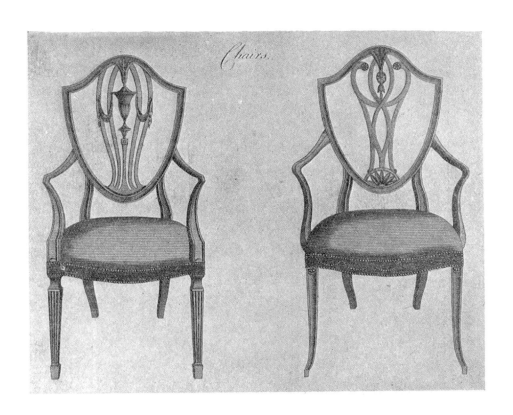

DESIGNS FOR CHAIRS.

Reproduced from Heppelwhite's "Guide."

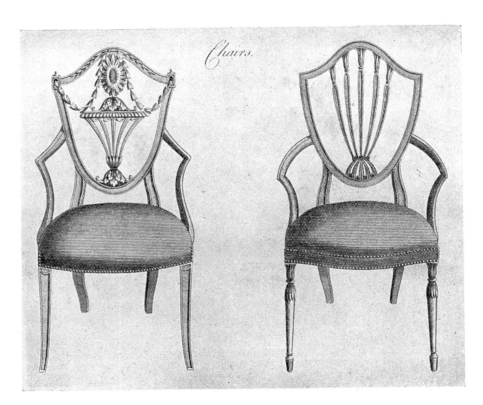

DESIGNS FOR CHAIRS.

Reproduced from Heppelwhite's "Guide."

DESIGN FOR A WINDOW SEAT.

Reproduced from Heppelwhite's "Guide."

DESIGN FOR A WINDOW SEAT.
Reproduced from Heppelwhite's "Guide."

DESIGN FOR A SOFA ("CONFIDANTE").
Reproduced from Heppelwhite's "Guide."

DESIGN FOR A COUCH (" DUCHESSE ").

Reproduced from Heppelwhite's " Guide."

DESIGN FOR A SIDEBOARD.

Reproduced from Heppelwhite's " Guide."

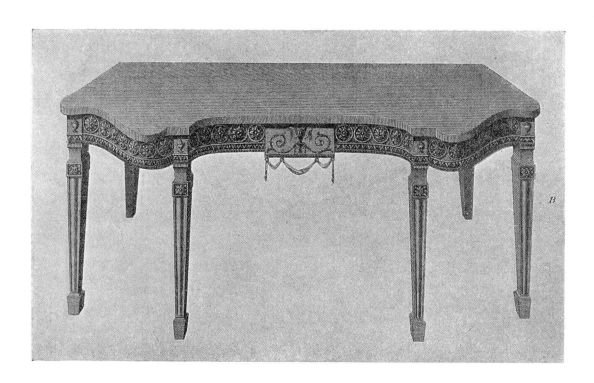

DESIGNS FOR SIDEBOARDS.

Reproduced from Heppelwhite's "Guide."

DESIGNS FOR PEDESTALS AND VASES.

Reproduced from Heppelwhite's "Guide."

Pier Glasses.

DESIGNS FOR PIER GLASSES.

Reproduced from Heppelwhite's "Guide."

times forming the ornamental support of the back of the chair, and at others being part of the enrichment. Another noticeable feature is the carving of wheat ears on the shield shape backs of the chairs.

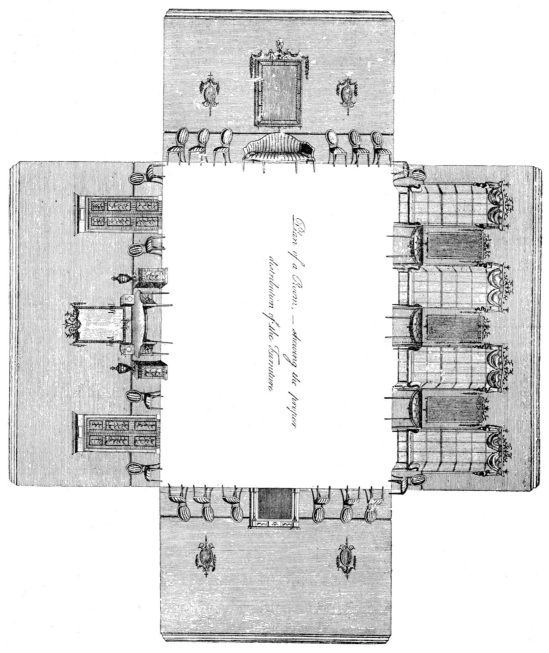

FACSIMILE OF PAGE IN HEPPELWHITE'S "CABINET MAKER'S GUIDE."

To convey an idea of the fashion of the day "the plan of a room showing the proper distribution of the furniture" is given here. It is evident from the large looking-glasses which overhang the sideboard and sofa that the fashion had now set in to use such mirrors.

The methods of grinding and polishing plate glass were gradually improved and larger plates became available for the designers of mirrors. There are some very large mirrors in the drawing room at Harewood House, near Leeds, which it is said were there when the house was furnished (1765-70) and Mr. Lenygon quotes a bill of Chippendale's for "a very large pier glass £290" charged to Mr. Lascelles in 1773, also "a very fine looking-glass, 91in. by 57½in., £160," also for Harewood House.

There are some large mirrors at Chatsworth with the frames as well as the centres made of glass ornamented with engraving and bevelling; also some at Hampton Court Palace which are almost certainly the production of our Vauxhall and Lambeth glass works of the early part of the eighteenth century. These works were closed in 1780.

Another side-light upon the mirrors of this time is thrown by "The Plate Glass Book" published in 1773 with list of sizes and prices of plate glass, the largest piece of which was 66in. high. The earlier Vauxhall plates did not exceed 40in. to 50in. in length and the edges were bevelled.

THOMAS SHERATON.—The name which, next to that of Chippendale, is the best known to those who are interested in the furniture of our own country, made during the latter part of the eighteenth century, is that of Thomas Sheraton and owing to much more information being now available than when this book was first published it is possible to give some particulars about him. He was born at Stockton-on-Tees in 1751 and is said to have taught himself the art of geometrical drawing. He was a zealous Baptist, and the first literary work of which we have any knowledge are some pamphlets and tracts in connection with his religious belief. In 1782 he published a book on the doctrine of regeneration in which it is interesting to find that the author describes himself as " Thomas Sheraton, junior, a mechanic." His first work, containing designs for furniture, consisted of eighty-four large folio plates, and is not dated.

The book with which his name is more generally associated is " The Cabinet Maker and Upholsterer's Drawing Book," a thick quarto volume, the first edition of which appeared in 1791 and was followed by a second in 1793 and a third in 1802. The last contains 122 plates, but several of the designs are strongly affected by the fashion for copying the neo-classic style at its worst and stiffest. These properly belong to the following chapter and are by no means a credit to Sheraton since they represent a deterioration in his methods of design.

In the memoirs of Adam Black, the publisher, there is a passage descriptive of Sheraton which is worth quoting:—"This many-sided, worn-out encyclopædist and preacher is an interesting character. . . . He is a man of talent, and, I believe, of genuine piety. He understands the cabinet business; I believe was bred to it. He is a scholar, writes well, and, in my opinion, draws masterly; is author, bookseller, and teacher. I believe his abilities and resources are his ruin in this respect; by attempting to do everything he does nothing."

The last sentence probably only refers to the writer's sense of doing nothing in the way of making a commercial success of his business attainments. Sheraton's excellent designs and drawings must ever remain as testimony to his ability and industry but it will probably be somewhat of a shock to many who have bought furniture supposed to have been made by him that he was evidently never in a position to carry on the business of a manufacturer, though his careful working drawings were

Kneehole Table, Designed by Sheraton.

freely used by other craftsmen. As proof of the writer's statement that Sheraton's designs were carried out by cabinet makers of his time we are able, by the courtesy of Messrs. Waring and Gillow, to give an extract from their books in the form of a record of the manufacture by Gillow during the reign of George III., of a "Carleton House Table," which is one of the designs in Sheraton's book. The extract is reproduced in facsimile (reduced in size for convenience) and the reader will be interested to see the details of cost of materials and cabinet maker's time (351 working hours) which were employed in its production. In the "Drawing Book" there are some directions for the furnishing of the different rooms in a gentleman's house, also some didactic criticisms on his contemporaries' work, some of which by the light of recent events in the sale rooms of Messrs. Christie are amusing reading. For instance, writing of Chippendale's book after criticising the absence of perspective in his drawings, he goes on to observe:

"*and as for the designs themselves, they are now wholly antiquated and laid aside though possessed of great merit, according to the times in which they were executed.*"

The numerous selections made from his book for reproduction in these pages render descriptions unnecessary. It will be readily observed that the fashion had now changed; instead of the rococo—literally, rock work and shell (*rocquaille et coquaille*)—ornaments which had gone out, a simpler and more severe taste had come in.   In Sheraton's cabinets,

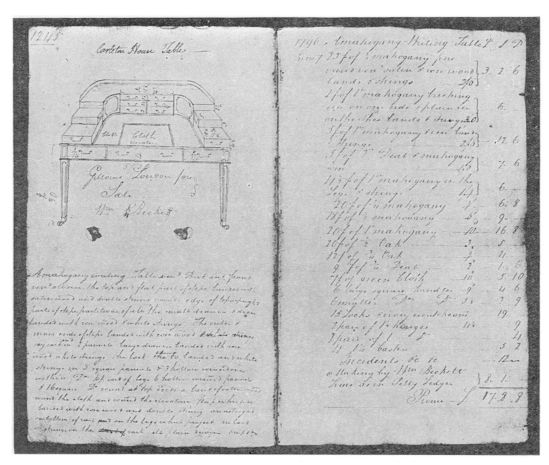

EXTRACT FROM THE OLD BOOK OF RICHARD GILLOW.
(*By permission of Messrs. Waring and Gillow.*)

chairs, writing tables and occasional pieces we have therefore no longer the cabriole leg or the carved ornament; but, as in the case of the brothers Adam and the furniture designed by them for such houses as those in Portland Place, we have now square tapering legs, severe lines and quiet ornament.   Sheraton trusted chiefly for decoration to his marqueterie, but he used inlaid brass as an ornament of his later work.   He introduced occasionally into his scrolls animals with foliated extremities and he also affected trophies of musical instruments, but as a rule the decoration was in wreaths of flowers, husks, or drapery. A characteristic feature of his cabinets was the swan-necked pediment sur-

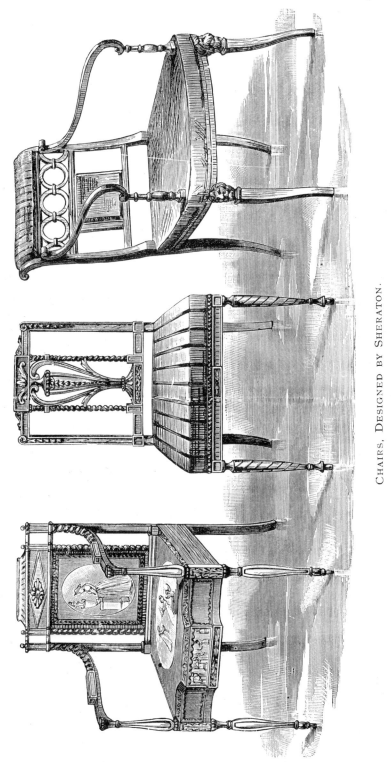

CHAIRS, DESIGNED BY SHERATON.

mounting the cornice, a revival of an ornament fashionable during Queen Anne's reign, although the work then was chiefly carried out in stone, marble or cut brickwork. We give from his book a reproduction of a page of these pediments and cornices.

Sheraton may be said to have excelled all his contemporary designers in the comparative simplicity of outline and his recognition of the proper subordination of ornament to construction. He was especially happy in the design of those charming bijou pieces of furniture, such as screen tables, work tables, miniature writing cabinets, and such smaller and dainty little pieces of cabinet work, which found appropriate interpretation in

A CHINA CABINET AND A BOOKCASE WITH SECRETAIRE.
Designed by T. Sheraton, and published in his "Cabinet Maker and Upholsterer's Drawing Book," 1793.

the newly introduced satin-wood. Some of his bedroom furniture was designed for the purpose of concealing its particular purpose, so that the room could be utilised for receptions, as was the custom of the day. It was with this idea that certain examples more or less familiar to collectors were designed. Commodes were made with serpentine fronts, and the top drawer fitted with numerous box-like receptacles for toilet requisites and with a mirror made to rise or fall on a sliding rack; there was also a smaller dressing table, with two flaps which open for use, and which when closed conceal the washing basin.

There is a great deal of careful and highly skilled workmanship in these delicate little pieces and when such come into the market and are recognised as genuine old specimens their price is very high.

A peculiarity in the design of his chair backs and also those of Heppelwhite will be observed in which they differ from Chippendale and other makers. The ornamental part of the chair back almost invariably is built on a rail which is an inch or two above the back of the seat. The backs of Chippendale's chairs and also those of Ince and Mayhew are made to come right down to the seat. This peculiarity will be observed if the illustrations of the chairs, taken from his book, are compared with the designs of Chippendale and Ince.

The last work of Sheraton—he did not live to complete it—was termed the " Cabinet Maker and Artist's Encyclopædia " and was to be

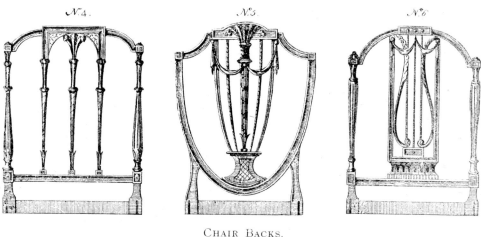

CHAIR BACKS.

From Sheraton's " Cabinet Maker."

published in one hundred and twenty-five parts, of which he only lived to see thirty in print. It is sad to relate that he died in mean lodgings in 1806 in great poverty.

SEDDON, SONS AND SHAKLETON.—The name of this firm has received scant attention from writers on the subject of English furniture and these notes should prove that a great deal of the so-called Sheraton furniture should be placed to their credit. In my book, *"Antiques genuine and spurious,"* published in 1921, there is an illustration of a very important satin-wood cabinet with paintings attributed to W. Hamilton, R.A., which was made to the order of King Charles IV. of Spain by this firm, and signed by their chief cabinet maker with the date of completion, "James Newham, June 28th, 1793." An illustration of this with full description was also given by Mr. Frederick S. Robinson in his " English Furniture." The cabinet was seen by me many years ago, and its decorative treatment resembled in every way the painted satin-wood dressing table in the Victoria and Albert Museum which is illustrated on page 346. This piece has been generally attributed to Sheraton, but the writer has no doubt that it was made by Seddon. In Chapter VIII., when considering some of the furniture manufacturers of the early part of the nineteenth century, the reader will notice that the descendants of

ARM CHAIR OF SHERATON DESIGN.
In Sir John Soane's Museum, Lincoln's Inn Fields.
(*From a Photo especially taken for this work.*)

the older Seddon had a very large account for furnishing and decorating Windsor Castle for King George IV., and it is quite clear that the firm was one of high standing. Another side-light on this firm's position is thrown by an extract from the *Annual Register* of 1768 :—" A dreadful fire burnt down London House, formerly the residence of the Bishops of London, now occupied by Mr. Seddon, one of the most eminent of the cabinet makers of London. The damage is computed at £20,000." This large sum when we consider the difference in money value one hundred and fifty years ago, indicates a business of great importance.

In the History of Furniture of this period the names of Chippendale, Sheraton and Heppelwhite loom large, but this prominence is mainly due to the fact that they published books of design, and that these designs were widely known and much used by cabinet makers as is evident from the list

TRIPOD FIRE-SCREENS.
Reproduced from Sheraton's " Cabinet Maker."

of subscribers to Sheraton's book which included, besides his aristocratic patrons, a large number of firms engaged in the furniture trade. To many of these is due the credit of sound craftsmanship, adaptability in execution and high finish which is characteristic of the work of this period. As they ignored the art of advertisement and in nearly all cases failed to adopt any trade mark of identification, their names are mostly forgotten, but it is possible to rescue a few from oblivion. Among the trade subscribers, to the number of four hundred and fifty, may be mentioned—France, Cabinet

DESIGNS OF CORNICES AND PEDIMENTS.

Reproduced from Sheraton's ''Cabinet Maker,''

Maker to His Majesty, St. Martin's Lane; Charles Elliott, Upholder to His Majesty and Cabinet Maker to the Duke of York, Bond Street: Campbell and Sons, Cabinet Makers to the Prince of Wales, Marylebone Street, London. Besides those who held Royal appointments there were other manufacturers of decorative furniture—Thomas Johnson, Copeland, Robert Davy, George Atkinson, and William Somerville, mentioned in Shearer's book, a French carver named Nicholas Collett, who settled in England and many others.

Of the above we know very little. Thomas Johnson, a carver, also published some designs for girandoles. Copeland was sometime partner with Matthias Lock, who appears to have been in a considerable way of business, and is said to be the only chair-maker of his time who introduced the lathe-

SMALL DRESSING TABLE AND GLASS IN SATIN-WOOD.
Sheraton Style.   ENGLISH: LATE EIGHTEENTH CENTURY.

turned leg. The name of Dowbiggin does not figure among Sheraton's subscribers, but he was an apprentice to Richard Gillow, and the founder of the well-known firm of Holland and Sons.

Gillows have already been referred to and as a very old established firm continued their high-class work through several generations of designers.

SOME MINOR DESIGNERS OF THE EIGHTEENTH CENTURY

The names of a few other publishers of designs for furniture may be given, but little is known of them nor is there any information available as to the firms by whom their designs were executed.

William Jones, a contemporary of Kent, published in 1739 "*The Gentleman and Builders' Companion,*" and several of his designs are reproduced

ENGLISH SATIN-WOOD DRESSING TABLE.

With Painted Decoration.   Probably by Seddon and Shakleton.

END OF XVIII. CENTURY.

(Victoria and Albert Museum.)

in Mr. Lenygon's book; from which it will be seen that the mirrors are somewhat architectural in character, less ornate than Kent's and the ornament is restrained and in good taste.

Batty Langley was evidently a fashionable designer of his time, and in a letter written by Horace Walpole in 1755, his designs are very severely criticised as "Bastard Gothic." He published "The Workman's Treasury of Designs" in 1739, with a second edition in 1745.

Matthias Darley published a book of designs about 1769, which are very similar to Chippendale's. Matthias Lock, whose work has already been mentioned, published a "New Book of Pier Frames, Ovals, Girandoles, Tables, etc." about the same time, many of the drawings being in the Adams style. He was for a time in partnership with Copeland, whose drawings of chairs may be classed as debased Chippendale.

Another designer of much excellent furniture of this time was Shearer. In an old book of designs in the author's possession the wording "Shearer delin." and "published according to Act of Parliament, 1788," appears underneath the representations of sideboards, tables, bookcases, and dressing tables which are very similar in every way to those of Sheraton his contemporary. Shearer also published "The Cabinet Maker's London Book of Prices," which ran through some three or four editions and contained the actual prices paid for material and labour used in the manufacture of furniture. It is evident that he must have been a man of some mark in the "trade" of his time, say from 1788 to 1805, the date of his last edition. George Richardson, Isaac Ware, W. Casement Halfpenny, Thomas Cranden, Michael Angelo Pergolesi, J. Wyatt, N. Wallis, should also be mentioned as designers of furniture and decorative details of this time, several of whom published books of drawings.

DEVELOPMENT OF THE SIDEBOARD

No account of English furniture of the eighteenth century would be complete without a short history of the development of the sideboard. The various changes in form and fashion of this important article of domestic furniture are interesting, and to explain them a slight retrospect is necessary. The word "buffet," has been sometimes translated "sideboard" in descriptions of Continental pieces of furniture of the fifteenth and sixteenth centuries, but the sideboard we know is different. It seems to have been introduced during the reign of William III. and there is a fair specimen in the Victoria and Albert Museum of one of this period; an illustration of which has been given in the chapter dealing with that time.

The term certainly occurs in earlier writers, as Milton's "Paradise Regained" speaks of the "stately sideboard," and Dryden when contrasting

the furniture of the classical period with that of his own time had the
following line :—

"No sideboards then with gilded plate were dressed."

Early in the eighteenth century in many old houses especially in
the neighbourhood of Portland Place and in the Palaces of St. James's
and of Kensington we find a fashion for making the doors of a room

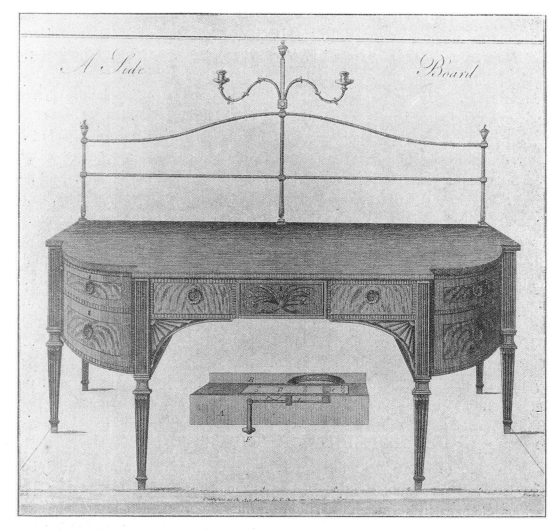

A SIDEBOARD.

Reproduced from Sheraton's "Cabinet Maker."

symmetrical. This entails one of the doors being false and these were used
as cupboards for the storage of glass, crockery and reserve wine. After
the middle of the eighteenth century however these extra doors gradually
disappeared, and the mahogany side table came into fashion. Cupboard
room was still required and this was supplied by separate pedestal
cupboards placed on either side of the table. A pair of urn-shaped

A SIDEBOARD IN MAHOGANY WITH INLAY OF SATIN-WOOD.

Designed by Robert Adam.

mahogany vases stood on the pedestals and these generally contained receptacles for hot water for washing the knives and forks and the ice for cooling the wine. The reader will find two sets of these pedestals and vases illustrated among the Heppelwhite designs and there is also an excellent example already noticed in the sideboard with pedestals and cellaret at Harewood House. This has been fully described and illustrated in the earlier pages of this chapter when noticing the work of Robert Adam.

A brass rail with ornamented pillars and branches for candles was added to the back of the sideboard and gave it a handsome finish. We can thus trace the gradual development of the modern sideboard from a combination of side table, pedestals and cellaret.

Before we dismiss the furniture of the dining room of this period it may interest some of our readers to know that until the first edition of "Johnson's Dictionary" was published in 1755 the term "dining room" was not to be found in the vocabulary. In Barrat's "Alvearic" published in 1580, "parloir" or "parler" was described as "a place to sup in," and later Minsheu's "Guide unto Tongues" in 1617 gave it as "an inner room to dine or to suppe in," but Johnson's definition is "a room in houses on the first floor, elegantly furnished for reception or entertainment."

THE DINING TABLE

We now come to the gradual development of our modern dining table. The "pillar and claw" table came into fashion towards the end of the eighteenth century, and consisted of a round or square top supported by an upright cylinder which rested on a stand which carried three or sometimes four feet carved as claws. In order to extend these tables for a large party, several of these were placed side by side and bolted together. When apart they served as pier or side tables and some of these—the two end ones being semi-circular—may still be found in some of our old hotels and country houses.*

It was not until the year 1800 that Richard Gillow, of the well-known firm in Oxford Street, invented and patented the convenient telescopic contrivance which with slight improvements has given us the table of the present day. The term still used by auctioneers in describing a modern extending table as a "set of dining tables" is probably a survival of the older method of providing for a dinner party. Gillow's patent is described as "an improvement in the method of constructing dining and other tables calculated to reduce the number of legs, pillars and claws and to facilitate and render easy their enlargement and reduction."

* The Court room of the Stationers' Hall contains an excellent set of tables of this kind.

As an interesting link between the present and the past it seems opportune to introduce here a slight notice of this old and well-known firm of furniture manufacturers, for which the writer is indebted to Mr. Clarke, one of the partners in Gillows, now with other firms absorbed in Waring and Gillow:—"We have an unbroken record of books dating from 1724, but we existed long anterior to this: the house originated in Lancaster, which was then the chief port in the north, before Liverpool came into existence, and Gillows exported furniture largely to the West Indies, importing rum as payment, for which privilege they held a special charter. The house opened their branch in London in 1765, and for some time the Lancaster books bore the heading and inscription, 'Adventure to London.' On the architect's plans for the premises in Oxford Street occur these words: 'This is the way to Uxbridge.'" Mr. Clarke's information may be supplemented by adding that Dr. Gillow,

URN STAND.　　　　　TOILET GLASS.　　　　　URN STAND.

whom the writer had the pleasure of meeting many years ago, and who was the thirteenth child of the Richard Gillow before mentioned, told him that this same Richard Gillow retired in 1830 and died as lately as 1866 at the age of ninety.

URN STANDS AND TEA-POYS

To the latter part of the eighteenth century belong the quaint little "urn stands" which were made to hold the urn with boiling water, while the teapot was placed on a little slide which is drawn out from underneath the top. In those days tea was an expensive luxury and was served with some state, so we find these urn stands elaborately inlaid. These together with the old mahogany or marqueterie tea-poys which were sometimes the object of considerable skill and care are dainty relics of the past. One of these designed by Chippendale and another by

Heppelwhite will be found amongst the illustrations taken from their books of patterns. They were fitted with receptacles to hold the black and green teas with a glass basin for sugar.

WINE TABLES

The "wine table" of this time deserves a word. These are now somewhat rare and are only to be found in a few old houses and in some of the Colleges at Oxford and Cambridge. Some are fitted with revolving tops, and some were shaped like a half moon. These latter were for placing in front of the fire when the outer side of the table formed a convivial circle, round which men gathered after they had left the dinner table. One of these old tables is still to be seen in the Hall of Gray's Inn. They are generally of good rich mahogany and have legs more or less ornamental.

The writer remembers that in the Master's room at Trinity Hall, Cambridge, there is still a half-circular wine table which is so arranged that when the decanters have been passed round the convex side at which the guests sit, there is a "railway" which takes them along the straight side of the table which is next the fire and saves the trouble of "passing the bottle" back. The date of this wine table is about the end of the eighteenth century.

A distinguishing feature of English furniture of the eighteenth century was the partiality for secret drawers and contrivances for hiding away papers or valued articles; and in old secretaires and writing tables we find a great many ingenious designs which remind us of the days when there were but few banks and people kept money and deeds in their own custody.

CARVED JARDINIERE, BY CHIPPENDALE.

CHAPTER VIII

First Half of the Nineteenth Century

The French Revolution—Period of the Directory and the First Empire—Influence on design of Napoleon's Campaigns—The Cabinet presented to Marie Louise—Dutch Furniture of the time—English Furniture—Sheraton's later work—Thomas Hope, architect—George Smith's designs—Fashion during the Regency—Gothic Revival—Seddon's Furniture—Other makers—Influence on design of the Restoration in France—Furniture of William IV., and early part of Queen Victoria's reign—Baroque and Rococo styles—The panelling of rooms, dado and skirting—The Art Union—The Society of Arts—Sir Charles Barry and the New Palace of Westminster—Pugin's designs—Auction prices of Furniture—Christie's—The London Club Houses—Steam power—Exhibitions in France and England—Harry Rogers' work—Queen Victoria's Cradle—State of Art in England—Continental designs—Italian carving—Cabinet work in Antwerp, Liége, Brussels and Vienna—General remarks.

EMPIRE FURNITURE

THE movement towards classicalism in the designs of French furniture was noticed in a previous chapter, during what may be termed the Marie Antoinette period, and we have also seen that it found an echo in the work of some English designers.

The French Revolution which brought ruin on the Court and old aristocracy, the patrons of French Art, had the effect of dislocating everything connected with the work of the Industrial Arts, but that all interest in Art was not lost during the worst years of anarchy and disorder of this terrible time in France is shown by the fact that the National Convention appointed a Commission composed of competent men in different branches of Art to determine what State property in artistic objects should be sold and what was of sufficient historical interest to be retained as a national possession. Riesener, the celebrated *ébeniste*, and David, the famous painter of the time, both served on this Commission, of which they must have been valuable members.

There is a passage in an article on "Art" by a democratic French writer as early as 1790—when the great storm-cloud was already threatening to burst—which is quoted by Mr. C. Perkins, the American translator of Dr. Falke's German work, "Kunst im Hause," and gives us the keynote to the great change which took place in the fashion of furniture at this time :—" We have changed everything; freedom, now consolidated in France, has restored the pure taste for the antique! Farewell to your marqueterie and Boulle, your ribbons, festoons and rosettes of gilded bronze; the hour has come when objects must be made to harmonise with circumstances."

THE DIRECTORY

After the abolition of the Revolutionary tribunal the Directory was established in 1795 and lasted until its deposition some four years later, and although generally speaking the term "Empire furniture" is taken to include that produced during these four years, it is more correct to consider the *Directoire* style as ante-Empire before the Napoleonic stamp gave a distinguishing character to the furniture which was made in the early years of the nineteenth century. We find in furniture of this period the reproduction of ancient Greek forms for chairs and couches; ladies' work tables too are fashioned somewhat after the old drawings of sacrificial altars; and the classical tripod is a favourite support. The mountings represent antique Roman fasces with an axe in the centre; trophies of lances surmounted by a Phrygian cap of liberty; winged figures emblematic of freedom; and antique heads of helmeted warriors arranged like cameo medallions.

These classical ornaments in the mounts of furniture and on the marble clocks and candelabra of this period are frequently found in combination with the scrolls, rosettes and many ornamental details which were in fashion during the Marie Antoinette period. Doubtless the same craftsmen were employed and they used some of the older patterns which harmonised with the new style.

THE FIRST EMPIRE

The rise of Bonaparte after his successful campaigns in Italy and that in Egypt gave a more definite and somewhat narrower direction to the classical movement. When we look at the portrait of the great soldier represented with the crown of bay leaves and other attributes of the old Roman imperialism, we realise that the Cæsars were his models and that his mind was set on reviving with all its splendour the old idea of a world-wide Empire upon which he would be able to stamp his own individuality and mould it as he wished.

The cabinet which was designed and made for Marie Louise on his marriage with her in 1810 is an excellent example of the Napoleonic furniture. The wood used for this style of furniture was almost invariably rich mahogany, the colour of which made a good ground for the bronze

CABINET IN MAHOGANY WITH BRONZE GILT MOUNTINGS.

Presented by Napoleon I. to Marie Louise on his Marriage with her in 1810.

PERIOD: NAPOLEON I.

gilt mounts which were applied. The full-page illustration shows these mountings, which are all classical in character; and though there is no particular grace in the outline or form of the cabinet there is a certain dignity and solemnity, relieved from oppressiveness by the fine chasing and gilding of the metal enrichments and the excellent colour and markings of the rich Spanish mahogany used. This cabinet and several other more or less ornate pieces of Napoleonic furniture may still be seen in the Château of Fontainebleau.

On secretaires and tables a common ornament of this description of furniture is a column of mahogany with a capital and base of bronze (either gilt, part gilt or green) in the form of the head of a sphinx—no doubt suggested by his Egyptian campaign—with the foot of an animal; console tables are supported by sphinxes, griffins and chimeras; and candelabra and wall brackets for candles have winged figures of females, stiff in modelling and constrained in attitude, but almost invariably of good material with careful finish.

A Paris *ébeniste* named Georges Jacob and his son Jacob Desmaller made a great deal of this Empire furniture: he was probably a grandson of the Georges Jacob admitted into the Corporation of Paris Cabinet Makers in 1765. In an Exhibition of Empire furniture given at the Burlington Fine Arts Club in 1918, there were some important pieces which had been made for Napoleon and branded with the Imperial N, signed Jacob frères. There were also pieces of the same kind and date signed R. Meslee.

The bas-reliefs in metal which ornament the panels of the fronts of cabinets or the marble bases of clocks are either reproductions of mythological subjects from old Italian gems and seals, or represent the battles of the Emperor, in which Napoleon is portrayed as a Roman general. Owing to the demand which had arisen among the new men of the Empire a vast quantity of decorative furniture was made during the few years which elapsed before the disaster of Waterloo caused the disappearance of Napoleon's meteoric career.

One of the best authorities on Empire furniture is the book of designs published in 1812 by the architects Percier and Fontaine.* It is the more valuable as a work of reference from the fact that every design represented was actually carried out and is not a mere exercise of fancy as is the case with many such drawings. In the preface the authors modestly state that they are entirely indebted to the antique for the reproduction of the different designs; and the originals, from which came

---

* Recueil de décorations interiereures comprenant tout ce qui a rapport à l'ameublement composé par C. Percier et P. F. L. Fontaine.

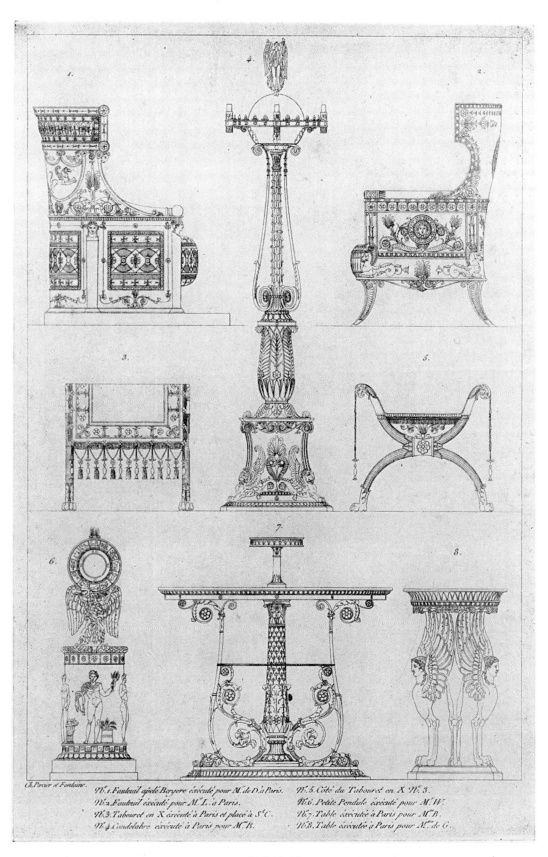

DESIGNS.

By Percier and Fontaine.

Reduced to about quarter size, from their folio work on "Empire Furniture."

the inspiration in marble stone and bronze, can still be seen in a fragmentary form in the Museum of the Vatican.

While this kind of furniture is not free from the stiffness and constraint inseparable from classic designs the rich colour of the mahogany, the high finish and good gilding of the bronze mounts and the costly silk with which it is generally covered render it attractive and gives it an artistic value of its own.

The reproduction which we give of one of the finely executed copper plates of MM. Percier and Fontaine's book of designs will serve to show the reader the careful and minute detail of their work as well as to convey an idea of the best kind of this Empire furniture. Amongst the designs are several which were carried out for the Emperor for the Palace of the Tuileries, the Château of Saint Cloud, the Musée Napoleon; also for Malmaison, when he was First Consul, and for St. Petersburg and Sweden. In some instances it is stated that the design has been made for execution in the country for which it was ordered.

The "Table Explicative" is worth quoting, which describes Plate XXXIX, which has been selected for reproduction :—" Candélabre en cuivre doré, disposé de manière àporter quatre lampes à courant d'air. Table à thé soutenue sur une colonne en bronze et sur des enroulemens de rinceaux légers. Table ou chiffonnière portée sur des pieds de chimères ailées. Petite pendule dont le cadran est porté sur les ailes d'un aigle ; les saisons sont representées en bas-reliefs sur son piédestal. Grand fauteuil et bergère recouverts en panneaux d'étoffe de velours brodé, et tabouret ou pliant dans la forme d'un X. On doit remarquer que l'on a cherché à subordonner en tous points les decorations de ces différens meubles d'usage ordinaire aux conditions exigées par leur utile."

The more ordinary furniture however of the same style, but without these decorative accessories, is stiff, ungainly and uncomfortable, and seems to remind us of a period in the history of France when political and social disturbance deprived the artistic and pleasure-loving Frenchman of his peace of mind, distracting his attention from the careful consideration of his work. It may be mentioned here that in order to supply a demand which has lately arisen, chiefly in New York but also to some extent in England, for the best Empire furniture, the French dealers have bought up some of the old undecorated pieces and by ornamenting them with gilt bronze mounts cast from good patterns have sold them as original examples of the *meubles de luxe* of the period.

In Dutch furniture of this time the Napoleonic fashion was closely followed. Many marqueterie secretaires, tables, chairs, and similar articles are mounted with the heads and feet of animals, with lions' heads and

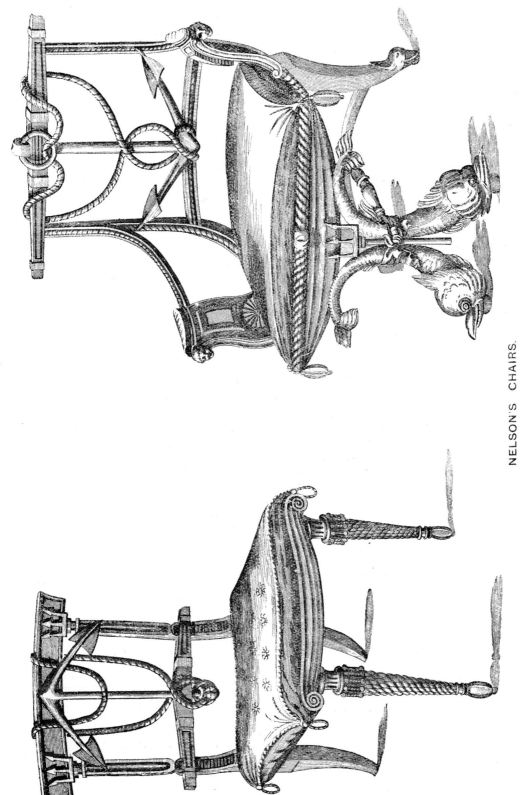

NELSON'S CHAIRS.

Designs published by T. Sheraton, October, 1806.

Showing the deterioration of design from his earlier period.

sphinxes, designs which could have been derived from no other source; and the general design of the furniture loses its bombé form and becomes rectangular and severe. Whatever difficulty there may be in sometimes deciding between the designs of the Louis XIV. period, towards its close, and those of Louis XV., there can be no mistake about *l'epoch de la Directoire* and *le style de l'Empire*. These are marked and branded with the Egyptian expedition and the Syrian campaign as legibly as if they

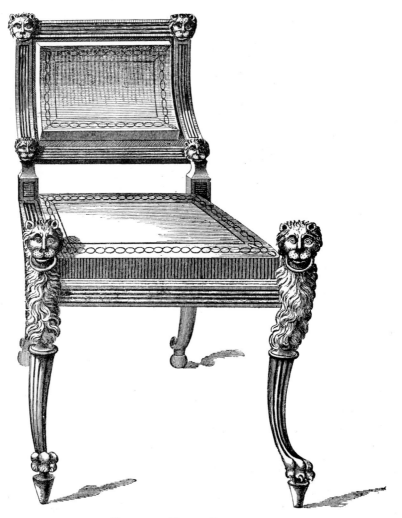

DRAWING ROOM CHAIR.
Design published by T. Sheraton, April, 1804.

all bore the familiar plain Roman N surrounded by a laurel wreath, or the Imperial eagle which had so often led the French legions to victory.

It is curious to notice how England, though so bitterly opposed to Napoleon, caught the infection of the dominant features of design which were prevalent in France about this time. Thus if we refer to Sheraton's later drawings which are dated about 1804 to 1806 we see the constrained figures and heads and feet of animals all brought into the designs as shown in the drawing room chair illustrated. These show unmistakable signs of the French Empire influence, the chief difference between the French and English work being that, whereas in French Empire furniture the excellence of the metal work redeems it from heaviness or ugliness such merit was wanting in England, where bronze work was not a strong point and the ornament was generally carved in wood, either gilt or coloured bronze-green. When metal was used it was brass, cast and fairly finished by the chaser, but much more clumsy than the French work. Therefore the English furniture of the first years of the nineteenth century is stiff, massive and heavy, equally with its French contemporary wanting in gracefulness but without the compensating attractions of fine mounting or the originality and individuality which must always add an interest to Napoleonic furniture.

There is at the Admiralty House, Whitehall, a suite of this Empire furniture carved and gilt, the ornaments being naval emblems in honour of Lord Nelson. It was the gift of a Mr. John Fish and is signed by the maker, William Collins, fecit A.D. 1813. The gilt bronze mountings are by Thomire, the French mounter, whose work has already been mentioned.

There was however made about this time by Gillow, to whose earlier work reference has been made in the previous chapter, some excellent furniture which, while to some extent following the fashion of the day, did so more reasonably. The rosewood and mahogany tables, chairs, cabinets and sideboards of his make, inlaid with scrolls and lines of flat brass and mounted with handles and feet of brass, generally representing the heads and claws of lions, do great credit to the English work of this time. The sofa table and sideboard illustrated on page 364 are of this class and show that Sheraton, too, designed furniture of a less pronounced character, as well as the heavier kind to which reference has been made.

A very favourable example of the craze in England for classic design in furniture and decoration is shown in the reproduction on page 367 of a drawing by Thomas Hope (known as "Anastasius Hope"), in 1807, a well-known architect of the time, in which it will be observed that the forms and fashions of some of the chairs and tables described and illustrated in the chapter on "Ancient Furniture" have been taken as models. Another designer of furniture of this type was John Papworth, architect, sculptor and decorator artist, who contributed to a monthly review published by Ackerman between the years 1808 and 1829. These designs can be referred to in "Ackerman's Repository of Arts" and they will be found

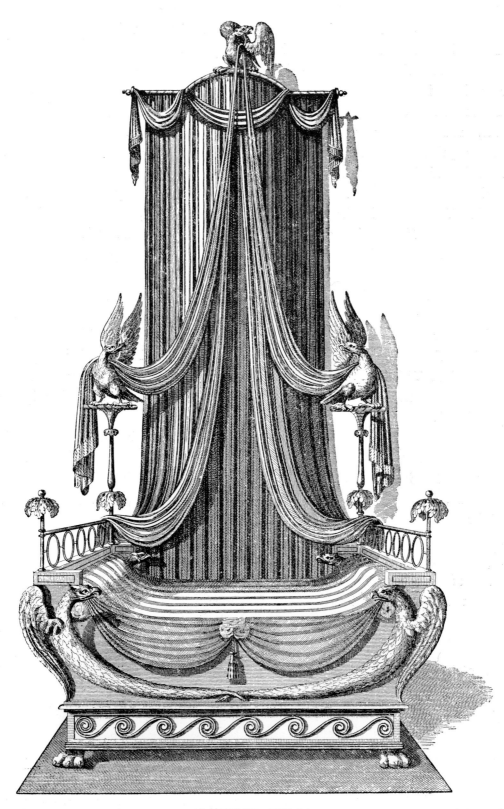

"CANOPY BED."

Design published by T. Sheraton, November 9th, 1803.

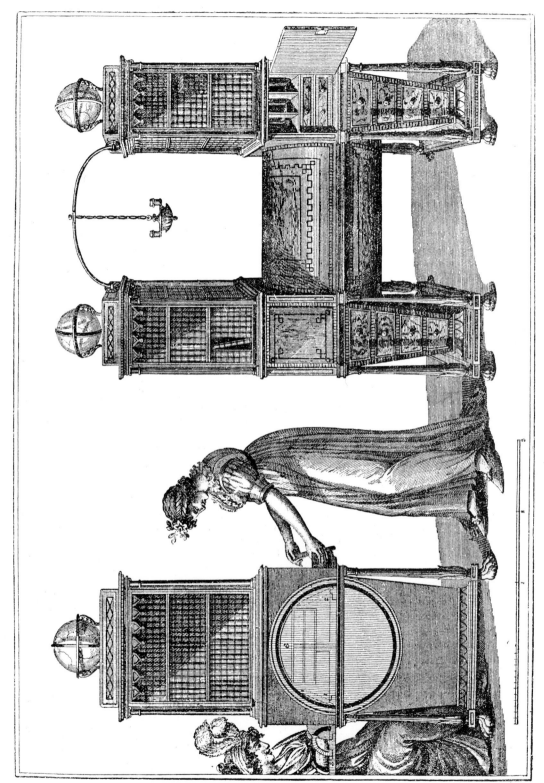

"SISTERS' CYLINDER BOOKCASE."

Designed by T. Sheraton, 1802.

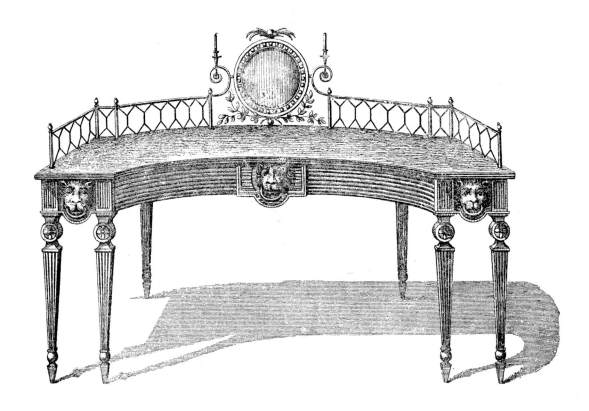

SIDEBOARD.

In Mahogany, with Brass Rail and Convex Mirror at back.

Design published by T. Sheraton, 1802.

SOFA TABLE.

Design published by T. Sheraton, 1804.

BOOKCASE.

Design published by T. Sheraton, June 12th, 1806.

NOTE.—Very similar bookcases are in the London Mansion House.

of the classic character which we recognise as "Empire." Papworth designed furniture for buildings in New York and Philadelphia; he was born in 1775 and died in 1847 at Papworth Hall, a house which he had designed in 1806.

The work of the brothers Adam, which is more fully described in Chapter VII., also included designs for furniture in the classical style. There is a handsome carved and gilt suite of furniture at Syon House, Brentford, which was made for the first Duke of Northumberland from their designs, and also some fine furniture of this kind in Windsor Castle, particularly a throne chair in which the two sides are composed of winged chimerical figures, the wings forming the elbows of the chair, while the back is an adaptation of an ancient Greek design. Sir John Soane's Museum in Lincoln's Inn Fields contains some representative specimens.

The fashion for this kind of furniture was very prevalent at the time of the Regency and continued during the reign of George IV. This is evident in the buildings that were erected about this period, such as the Regent Street Quadrant in London and such ranges of houses as Brunswick Terrace in Brighton. It has been said that our acquisition of the Elgin marbles which were placed in the British Museum in 1816 increased the popular taste for designs after antique Greek models, and the literature of the period abounds in references to Classic research.

There were several makers of first-class furniture, some of whose names still survive in the "style and title" of firms of the present day, who are their successors, while those of others have been forgotten save by some of our older manufacturers and auctioneers who at the request of the writer have been good enough to look up old records and revive the memories of sixty or seventy years ago. Of these the best known was Thomas Seddon who came from Manchester and settled in Aldersgate Street. We have the late Sir Guy Laking's authority for stating that in the year 1830 the large sum of £179,300 was spent in furnishing and decorating Windsor Castle and the Seddons firm had the greater part of the contract. At the King's death their account was disputed and £30,000 was struck off, a loss which necessitated an arrangement with their creditors. Shortly after this however they took the Barracks of the London Light Horse Volunteers in the Gray's Inn Road (now the Hospital) and carried on there for a time a very extensive business. Seddon's work ranked with Gillow's and he carried out many of the best orders for furniture. Some of the carved and gilt suites of furniture in Windsor Castle, upholstered with fine Aubusson and Beauvais tapestry in the Louis Seize style, are known to have been made by the

Design of a Room in the Classic Style, by Thomas Hope, Architect, in 1807.

Seddons firm, although upon a cursory examination they might pass for old French work. Some of the cabinets in the French style were also made by them. The title of the firm mentioned by Sir Guy Laking, who had access to the Windsor Castle accounts, was Morel and Seddon. The work of the founder of the firm has already been noticed in the preceding chapter.

Thomas Seddon, painter of Oriental subjects, who died in 1856, and P. Seddon, a well-known architect, were grandsons of the original founder of the firm. On the death of the elder brother, Thomas, the younger one then transferred his connection to the firm of Johnstone and Jeanes in Bond Street, another old house which until recently carried on business as "Johnstone and Norman," and who some few years ago executed a very extravagant order for an American millionaire. This was a reproduction of Byzantine designs in furniture of cedar, ebony, ivory, and pearl, made from drawings by the late Sir Alma Tadema, R.A.

Snell, of Albemarle Street, was established early in the nineteenth century and had obtained an excellent reputation; his specialité was well-made birch bedroom suites, but he also made furniture of a general description. The predecessor of the present firm of Howard and Son, who commenced business in Whitechapel as early as 1800, and the first Morant, founder of the firm of Morant, Boyd and Morant, may all be mentioned as manufacturers in the first quarter of the last century.

Somewhat later, Trollope, of Parliament Street; Holland, who had succeeded Dowbiggin (Gillow's apprentice), first in Great Pulteney Street and subsequently at the firm's present address; Wilkinson, of Ludgate Hill, founder of the present firm of upholsterers until recently in Bond Street; Aspinwall, of Grosvenor Street; the second Morant, of whom the great Duke of Wellington made a personal friend; and Crace, a prominent decorator of great taste, who carried out many of Pugin's Gothic designs, were all makers of good reputation. Miles and Edwards, of Oxford Street, whom Hindleys succeeded, were also well known for furniture of a high class. These are some of the best known manufacturers of the first half of the last century and though until after the Great Exhibition there was as a rule little in the designs to render their productions remarkable, the work of those named will be found sound in construction and free from the faults which accompany the cheap and showy reproductions of more pretentious styles, which mark so much of the furniture of the present day. With regard to this, more will be said in the next chapter.

There was then a very limited market for any but the most commonplace furniture. Our wealthy people bought the productions of French cabinet makers, either made in Paris or by Frenchmen who came over to England, and the middle classes were content with the most ordinary and useful articles. If they had possessed the means they certainly had neither the taste nor the education to furnish more ambitiously. The great extent of suburbs which now surround the Metropolis and which include such numbers of expensive and extravagantly fitted residences of merchants and tradesmen did not then exist. The latter lived over their shops or warehouses and the former only aspired to a dull house in Bloomsbury, or like David Copperfield's father-in-law, Mr. Spenlow, a villa at Norwood, or perhaps a country residence at Hampstead or Highgate, Mitcham or Epsom.

In 1808 a designer and maker of furniture, George Smith by name, who held the appointment of "Upholder extraordinary to H.R.H. the

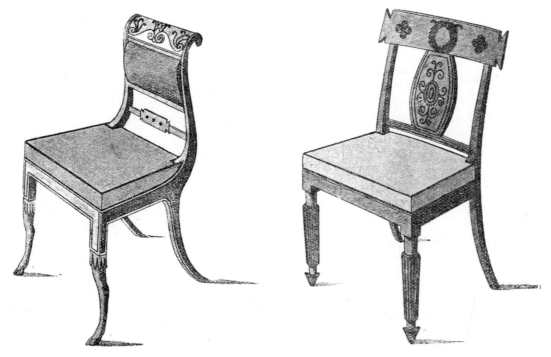

"PARLOR CHAIRS."
Showing the inlay of brass referred to. From Smith's Book of Designs, published in 1808.

Prince of Wales," and carried on business at "Princess" Street, Cavendish Square, produced a book of designs one hundred and fifty-eight in number published by "Wm. Taylor," of Holborn. These include cornices, window drapery, bedsteads, tables, chairs, bookcases, commodes and other furniture, the titles of some of which occur for about the first time in our vocabularies, having been adapted from the French. "Escritoire, jardinière, dejunè-tables, chiffoniers" (the spelling copied from Smith's book) all bear the impress of the pseudo-classic taste; and his designs, some of which are here reproduced, show the fashion of our so-called artistic furniture in England at the time of the Regency. Mr. Smith, in the "Preliminary Remarks" prefacing his illustrations gives us an idea of the prevailing taste which it is instructive to peruse as a reminiscence of a hundred

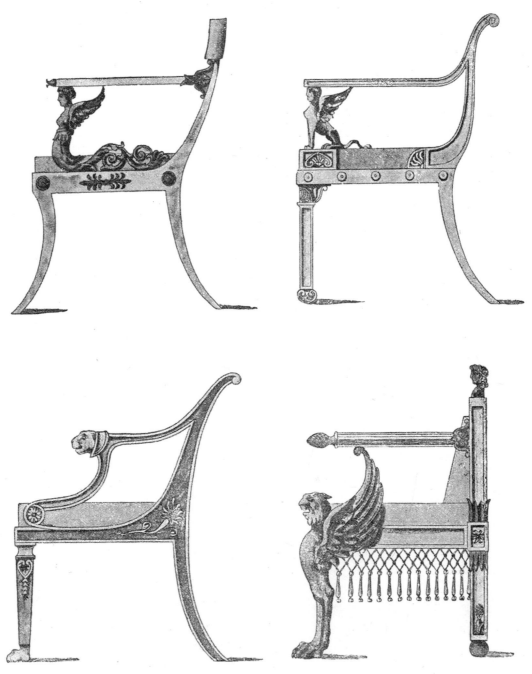

"Drawing Room Chairs in Profile."
From G. Smith's Book, published in 1808.

years ago:—"The following practical observations on the various woods employed in cabinet work may be useful. Mahogany, when used in houses of consequence, should be confined to the parlour and the bedchamber floors. In furniture for these apartments the less inlay of other woods, the more chaste will be the style of work. If the wood be of a fine, compact and bright quality, the ornaments may be carved clean in the mahogany. Where it may be requisite to make out panelling by an inlay of lines, let those lines be of brass or ebony. In drawing-rooms, boudoirs, ante-rooms, East and West India satin-woods, rosewood, tulip-wood and the other varieties of woods brought from the East may be used; with satin and light coloured woods the decorations may be of ebony or rosewood; with rosewood let the decorations be ormolu, and the inlay of brass. Bronze metal, though sometimes used with satin-wood, has a cold and poor effect: it suits better on gilt work, and will answer well enough on mahogany."

Amongst the designs published by him are some few of a subdued Gothic character; these are generally carved in light oak, or painted light stone colour and have in some cases heraldic shields with crests and coats-of-arms picked out in colour. There are window seats painted to imitate marble, with the Roman or Greco-Roman ornaments painted green to represent bronze. The least objectionable are those of mahogany with bronze green ornaments.

Of the furniture of this period there are several pieces in the Mansion House, in the City of London, which apparently was partly refurnished about the commencement of the century.

In the Court room of the Skinners' Company there are tables which are now fitted with extensions, so as to form a horseshoe table for committee meetings. They are good examples of the heavy and solid carving in mahogany early in the century before the fashion of representing the heads and feet of animals in the designs of furniture had gone out. These tables have massive legs, with lions' heads and claws, carved with great skill and showing much spirit, the wood being of the best quality and rich in colour.

The name of a French immigrant who made furniture somewhat in the style of Boulle has escaped the notice of many writers on English furniture. Constantin Louis le Gaigneur used brass and tortoise-shell in combination with pewter and copper for the marqueterie with which he veneered the surface of his cabinets and tables.

In the Wallace Collection there is a library table of this description, signed " Louis le Gaigneur, fecit "; the design of which somewhat recalls the fantastic decoration which originated with Berain who designed for André Charles Boulle. In Sir Guy Laking's catalogue of the King's furniture at Windsor Castle there is mention of two pieces by this maker and in an article contributed to the *Burlington Magazine,* of December, 1915, by

CORONATION CHAIR OF GEORGE IV.

The property of the Duke of Devonshire.

Mr. Alfred Jones, there is a record of a bill for two library tables made to the order of the Prince Regent in 1815 and 1816 for £250 each. Le Gaigneur carried on business at "The Buhl" Manufactory, 19 Queen Street, Edgware Road.

EARLY VICTORIAN

In the work of the manufacturers just enumerated may be traced the influence of the " Empire " style. With the restoration however of the Monarchy in France came the inevitable change in fashions and *" Le style de l'Empire "* was condemned. In its place came a revival of the Louis Quinze scrolls and curves, but with less character and even less restraint. Ornament of a florid and incongruous character was lavished on decorative furniture, and the style is now known as " baroque,"* or debased " rococo."

It has been our English custom for some long period to take our fashions from France and therefore about the time of William IV. and during the early part of Queen Victoria's reign, the furniture for our best houses was designed and made in the French style although there is generally something in the character of the work which conveys to the mind of an expert its British workmanship. The massively carved gilt chairs which were used at the coronation of King George IV., and also of William IV. and Queen Adelaide, are very good examples of this. They are still to be seen at Chatsworth, having been the perquisite of the sixth Duke of Devonshire in his official capacity of Chamberlain; and by the courtesy of the present Duke we are enabled to give a reproduction from a photograph taken expressly for the writer's use. The design of this chair should be carefully compared with that of the chairs used at the coronation of King George III., which are attributed to Chippendale (see page 276), and a very good idea will be obtained of the decadence which had taken place in taste since 1760.

The old fashion of lining rooms with oak panelling which has been noticed in an earlier chapter had undergone a change worth recording. If the illustration of the Elizabethan oak panelling, as given in the English section of Chapter III., be referred to, it will be seen that the oak lining reaches from the floor to within about two or three feet of the cornice. Subsequently this panelling was divided into an upper and lower part, the former commencing about three feet from the floor, with a moulding which formed a sort of cap to the lower part. Pictures

---

* The word baroque, which became a generic term, was derived from the Portuguese "barrocco," meaning a large irregular-shaped pearl. At first a jeweller's technical term, it came later, like "rococo," to be used to describe the kind of ornament which prevailed in design of the nineteenth century after the disappearance of the classic.

were let into the panelling; and presently the upper part disappeared and the lower wainscoting was termed the Dado,* an architectural member which we have seen revived both in wood and in various decorative materials of the present day. During the period we are now discussing this arrangement lost favour in the eyes of our grandfathers and the lowest member, or base, of the Dado only was retained and is now termed the " skirting board."

As we approach nearer our own time it is very interesting to turn over the leaves of the back numbers of such magazines and newspapers as treated of the Industrial Arts. The *Art Union*, which changed its title to the *Art Journal* in 1849, had then been in existence for about ten years and had done good work in promoting the encouragement of Art and manufactures. The " Society of Arts " had been formed in London as long ago as 1756 and had given prizes for designs and methods of improving different processes of manufacture. Exhibitions of the specimens sent in for competitions for the awards were, and are still, held at their house in Adelphi Buildings. Old volumes of " Transactions of the Society " are quaint works of reference with regard to these exhibitions.

About 1840, Mr. (afterwards Sir) Charles Barry, R.A., had designed and commenced the present, or as it was then called, the New Palace of Westminster, and following the Gothic character of the building the furniture and fittings were naturally of a design to harmonise with what was then quite a departure from the heavy architectural taste of the day. Mr. Barry was the first in the last century to leave the beaten track, although the Reform and Travellers' Clubs had already been designed by him on more classic lines. The Speaker's chair in the House of Commons is evidently designed after one of the fifteenth century " canopied seats," which have been noticed and illustrated in the second chapter ; and the " linen scroll pattern " panels can be counted by the thousand in the Houses of Parliament and the different official residences which form part of the Palace. The character of the work is subdued and not flamboyant, excellent in design and workmanship and it is highly creditable when we take into consideration the very low state of Art in England at that time.

This want of taste was very much discussed in the periodicals of the day and yielding to public opinion Government had in 1840-1 appointed a Select Committee to take into consideration the promotion of the Fine Arts in the country. Mr. Charles Barry, Mr. Eastlake, and Sir Martin

---

* Mr. Parker defines Dado as " The solid block, or cube, forming the body of a pedestal in classical architecture, between the base mouldings and the cornice : an architectural arrangement of mouldings, etc., round the lower parts of the wall of a room, resembling a continuous pedestal."

Shee, R.A., were amongst the witnesses examined. The report of this Committee in 1841 contained the opinion "that such an important and National work as the erection of the two Houses of Parliament affords an opportunity which ought not to be neglected of encouraging not only the higher but every subordinate branch of Fine Art in this country."

Mr. Augustus Welby Pugin was a well-known designer of the Gothic style of furniture of this time. Born in 1811, he had published in 1835

PRIE-DIEU.
In Carved Oak, enriched with Painting and Gilding.
Designed by Mr. Pugin and manufactured by Mr. Crace, London.

his "Designs for Gothic Furniture" and subsequently his "Glossary of Ecclesiastical Ornament and Costume"; and by skilful application of his knowledge to the decorations of the different ecclesiastical buildings he designed, his reputation became established. One of his designs is here reproduced. Pugin's work and reputation have survived notwithstanding the furious opposition he met with at the time. In a review of one of his books in the *Art Union* of 1839 the following sentence concludes the criticism :—" As it is a common occurrence in life to find genius mistaken for madness, so does it sometimes happen that a madman is mistaken for a genius. Mr. Welby Pugin has oftentimes appeared to us to be a case in point."

The anxiety as to the state of the Fine Arts generally, which resulted in the Select Committee of 1840, does not appear to have extended to household furniture. There are but few allusions to the design of decora-

SECRETAIRE AND BOOKCASE.
In Carved Oak, in style of German Gothic.
(From a Drawing by Professor Heideloff. Published in the "Art Union," 1846.)

tive woodwork in the periodicals of the day; and the auctioneers' advertisements—with a few notable exceptions like that of the Strawberry Hill Collection of Horace Walpole—gave no descriptions; no particular interest in the subject appears to have been manifested save by a very limited number of the dilettanti, who collected the curios and cabinets of former days.

York House was redecorated and furnished about this time and as it is described as " excelling any other dwelling of its own class in regal magnificence and vieing with the Royal Palaces of Europe," we may take note of an account of its re-equipment written in 1841 for the *Art Union*. This notice speaks little for the taste of the period and less for the knowledge and grasp of the subject by the writer of an Art critique of the day :—" The furniture generally is of no particular style but on the whole there is to be found a mingling of everything in the best manner of the best epochs of taste." Writing farther on of the ottoman couches, *causeuses*, etc., the critic describes an alteration in fashion which had evidently just taken place thus :—" Some of them, in place of plain or carved rosewood or mahogany, are ornamented in white enamel, with classic subjects in bas-relief of perfect execution."

Towards the close of the period embraced in the limits of this chapter the eminent firm of Jackson and Graham was making headway. A French designer named Prignot was of considerable assistance in establishing their reputation for taste ; and in the Exhibition which was soon to take place this firm took a very prominent position. Collinson and Lock,* who afterwards acquired this firm's premises and business, were both brought up in the house as young men and left for Herrings, of Fleet Street, whom they succeeded about 1870.

Another well-known decorator who designed and manufactured furniture of good quality was Leonard William Collmann, first of Bouverie Street and later of George Street, Portman Square. He was a pupil of Sydney Smirke, R.A. (who designed and built the Carlton and the Conservative Clubs), an excellent draughtsman who carried out the decoration and furnishing of many public buildings, London Clubs, and large private houses. His son was some years ago director of decorations to Queen Victoria at Windsor Castle. Collmann's designs were occasionally Gothic but generally classic.

There is evidence of the want of interest in the subject of furniture in the auctioneers' catalogues of the day. By the courtesy of Messrs. Christie Manson and Woods, the writer has had access to the records of this old firm and two or three instances of sales of furniture may be given. While the catalogues of the Picture sales of 1830-40 were printed on paper of quarto size and the subjects described at length those of "Furniture" are of the old-fashioned small octavo size resembling the catalogue of a small country auctioneer of the present day, and the printed descriptions rarely exceed a single line. The prices seldom amounted to more than £10; the whole proceeds of the day's sale were often less than £100 and sometimes did not reach £50. At the sale of Rosslyn House, Hampstead, in 1830 a mansion of considerable im-

---

* Collinson and Lock amalgamated with Warings in 1897.

portance, the highest priced article was "A capital mahogany pedestal sideboard, with hot closet, cellaret, two plate drawers, and fluted legs," which brought £32. At the sale of the property of "A Man of Fashion," a marqueterie cabinet, inlaid with trophies, the panels of Sèvres china, mounted in ormolu, sold for twenty guineas; and a "Reisener (*sic*) table, beautifully inlaid with flowers and drawers," which appears to have been reserved at nine guineas, was bought in at eight-and-a-half guineas. Frequenters of Christie's of the present day who have seen such a table as is here described realise more than a thousand pounds will appreciate the enormously increased value of really good old French furniture.

Perhaps the most noticeable comparison between the present day and that of some seventy years ago may be made in reading through the prices given at the great sale at Stowe House in 1848 which lasted thirty-seven days and realised upwards of £71,000, of which the proceeds of the furniture amounted to only £27,152. We have seen in the notice of French furniture that armoires by Boulle have during the past few years brought from £4,000 to £6,000 each under the hammer and the want of appreciation of this work, probably the most artistic ever produced by designer and craftsman, is sufficiently exemplified by the statement that at the Stowe sale two of Boulle's famous armoires, of similar proportions to those in the Hamilton Palace and Jones Collections, were sold for £21 and £19 8s. 6d. respectively.

We are accustomed now to see the bids at Christie's advance by guineas, by fives, tens and fifties; and it is amusing to read in these old catalogues of marqueterie tables, satin-wood cabinets, rosewood pier tables, and other articles of "ornamental furniture," as it was termed, being knocked down to Town and Emanuel, Webb, Morant, Hitchcock, Baldcock, Forrest, Redfearn, Litchfield (the writer's father), and others who were the buyers and regular attendants at "Christie's" (afterwards Christie and Manson) of 1830 to 1845, for such sums as 6s., 15s., and occasionally £10 or £15.

A single quotation is given, but many such are to be found :—

Sale on February 25th and 26th, 1841. Lot 31. "A small oval table, with a piece of Sèvres porcelain painted with flowers. 6s."

It is pleasant to remember as some exception to this general want of interest in the subject that in 1843 there was held at Gore House, Kensington, then the fashionable residence of Lady Blessington, an exhibition of old furniture, when a series of lectures was given by Mr. (afterwards Sir) J. C. Robinson. The Venetian State chair illustrated on page 74 was amongst the examples lent by Queen Victoria on that occasion. Specimens of Boulle's work and some good pieces of Italian

Renaissance were also exhibited. The idea of the present Victoria and Albert Museum may be said to have dated from this exhibition.

A great many of the older Club Houses of London were built and furnished between 1813 and 1851, the Guards' being of the earlier date, and the Army and Navy of the latter; and during the intervening thirty odd years the United Service, Travellers' Union, United University, Athenæum, Oriental, Wyndham, Oxford and Cambridge, Reform, Carlton, Garrick, Conservative, and some others were erected and fitted up. Many of these still retain much of the furniture of Gillows, Seddons, and some of the other manufacturers of the time whose work has been alluded to and these are favourable examples of the best kind of cabinet work done

CRADLE.

In Boxwood, for H.M. Queen Victoria.   Designed and Carved by H. Rogers, London.

in England during the reign of George IV., William IV., and that of the early part of Queen Victoria. It should be remembered that during this period steam power which had been first applied to machinery about 1815 came into more general use in the manufacture of furniture. With its adoption there seems to have been a gradual abandonment of the apprenticeship system in the factories and workshops of our country; and the present "piece-work" arrangement which had obtained more or less since the English cabinet makers had brought out their "Book of Prices" some years previously became generally the custom of the trade in place of the older "day work" of a former generation.

In France the success of national exhibitions had become assured, the exhibitors having increased from only one hundred and ten when the first experiment was tried in 1798 until at the eleventh exhibition in 1849 the number rose to four thousand four hundred and ninety-four. The *Art Journal* of that year gives us a good illustrated notice of some of the exhibits, and devotes an article to pointing out the advantages to be gained by something of the kind taking place in England.

From 1827 onwards we had established local exhibitions in Dublin, Leeds and Manchester. The first time a special building was devoted to the exhibition of manufactures was at Birmingham in 1849; and from the illustrated review of this in the *Art Journal* it is apparent that there was a desire on the part of our designers and manufacturers to strike out in new directions and make progress.

We are able to reproduce some of the designs of furniture of this period; and in the cradle designed and carved in Turkey-boxwood for Queen Victoria by Mr. Harry Rogers we have a fine piece of work which would not have disgraced the latter period of the Renaissance. Indeed, Mr. Rogers was a very notable designer and carver of this time; he had introduced his famous boxwood carving about seven years previously.

This cradle was by Queen Victoria's command sent to the Exhibition of 1851 and it may be worth while quoting the artist's description of the carving:—" In making the design for the cradle it was my intention that the entire object should symbolize the union of the Royal House of England with that of Saxe-Coburg and Gotha and with this view I arranged that one end should exhibit the arms and national motto of England and the other those of H.R.H. Prince Albert. The inscription, 'Anno, 1850,' was placed between the dolphins by Her Majesty's special command."

In a criticism of this excellent specimen of work the *Art Journal* of the time said:—" We believe the cradle to be one of the most important examples of the art of wood carving ever executed in this country."

Rogers was also a writer of considerable ability on the styles of ornament: and there are several contributions from his pen to the periodicals of the day, besides designs which were published in the *Art Journal* under the heading of " Original Designs for Manufacturers." These articles appeared occasionally and contained many excellent suggestions for manufacturers and carvers, amongst others the drawings of H. Fitzcock, J. Strudwick and W. Holmes. An illustration of one of these designs is given on page 381. They show that while there were some good designers in England as a general rule Art was at a very low ebb with regard to furniture.

In decorative woodwork straight lines and simple curves may be plain
and uninteresting but they are by no means so objectionable as the over-
ornamentation of the debased rococo style which obtained in this country
about the middle of the century. It is bad enough to find scrolls and
flowers, the shells and rockwork of mirror frames, sideboard backs, sofas

DESIGN FOR ONE OF THE WINGS OF A SIDEBOARD.
By W. Holmes. Exhibited at the "Society of Arts" in 1848, and published in the *Art Journal*, in 1849.

and chairs, thoroughly debased in style, even when skilfully carved, but
it is infinitely worse when, for the sake of economy, this elaborate and
laboured work is executed by inferior craftsmen.

In drawing room furniture the free use of composition was another
mark of decadence. We find large mirrors with gilt composition frames

in place of carving occupying the place of honour on the chimney-piece, or on the pier table, which was also itself of gilt composition; the ugly and ill-constructed chiffonier was also a favourite article of furniture. The carpets, too, were badly designed and loud and vulgar in colouring; the chairs, as the carved ornament in vogue rendered it necessary, with the wood across the grain, while the fire-screen in a carved rosewood frame frequently contained a caricature in needlework of a spaniel or a family group of the time, ugly enough to be in keeping with its surroundings.

The dining room was sombre and heavy. The pedestal sideboard, with a large mirror in the scrolled frame at the back, had come in, while the chairs, though usually solid and substantial, were ugly survivals of the earlier reproductions of the Greek patterns.

In the bedrooms we find dressing tables and washstands with scrolled legs showing faulty construction and the old four-poster giving way to the Arabian or French bedstead in mahogany. This was gradually replaced by the iron or brass bedstead which came in after the Exhibition of 1851 had shown people the advantages of the lightness and cleanliness of these materials.

In a word from the early part of the last century until the impetus given to Art by this great Exhibition had had time to take effect the general taste in furnishing houses was with few exceptions at about its worst.

In the earlier periods of better taste architects had designed wood-work and furniture to accord with the style of their buildings, but now they appear to have abandoned the control of interior decoration. This neglect seems to be another of the many signs of these degenerate days.

In other countries the rococo taste had also taken hold. France maintained a higher standard than England and such figure work as was introduced into her furniture was better executed though her joinery was inferior. In Italy old models of the Renaissance still served as examples for reproduction, but the ornament was more carelessly carved and appropriate decoration less considered. Ivory inlaying was largely practised in Milan and Venice; mosaics of marble were *specialités* of Rome and of Florence and were much used in the decoration of cabinets; Venice was busy manufacturing carved walnutwood furniture, in buffets, cabinets, lamp-holders and consoles which often had as supports negro page-boys elaborately painted and gilt, while cupids and foliage were the chief ornament of carved mirror frames.

Italian carving has always been free and spirited, the figures have never been wanting in grace and though by comparison with the best time of the Renaissance there is a great falling off, still the work executed in Italy during the nineteenth century is of considerable merit though the ornament is often overdone. In construction and joinery however the Italian work was and still is for the most part very inferior. Cabinets of great pretension and elaborate ornament, inlaid perhaps with ivory, lapis lazuli, or marbles, are so imperfectly made that the producer

VENETIAN STOOL OF CARVED WALNUTWOOD.
(*Victoria and Albert Museum.*)

appears to have thought only of decoration and not durability of his work.

In Antwerp, Brussels, Liège, and other Flemish Art centres, the School of Wood Carving which came in with the Renaissance appears to have been maintained with more or less excellence. With the increased quantity of the carved woodwork manufactured there was a proportion of ill-finished and over-ornamented work produced; and although, as has been before observed, the manufacture of cheap marqueterie in Amsterdam and other Dutch cities was bringing the name of Dutch furniture into ill-repute—still, so far as the writer's observations have gone, the Flemish wood-carver appears to have been at the time now under consideration ahead of his fellow craftsmen in Europe; and when, in the ensuing chapter, we shall notice some of the representative exhibits in the great International Competition of 1851 it will be seen that the Antwerp designer and carver was certainly in the foremost rank.

The illustrations selected to represent this period will convey more accurately to the reader the prevalent taste than mere words can do. It was undoubtedly a period of decadence in Art and design, and in the latter part there was a distinct decline in construction. It is a remarkable fact that while the end of the nineteenth century was famous for a very high standard of painting, miniatures, porcelain, silver, Sheffield plate and also of furniture, we find that the period under review is marked by a sad falling off in all these Arts.

Perhaps an explanation is to be found in the rapid fortunes made during the industrial revolution with its increased use of machinery; a largely increased demand for furniture arose but the taste of the new purchasers was less discriminating than formerly.

CABINET IN THE MEDIÆVAL STYLE.

Designed and Manufactured by Mr. Crace, London.

1851 Exhibition.

BOOKCASE IN CARVED WOOD.

Designed and Manufactured by Messrs. Jackson and Graham, London.

1851 Exhibition.

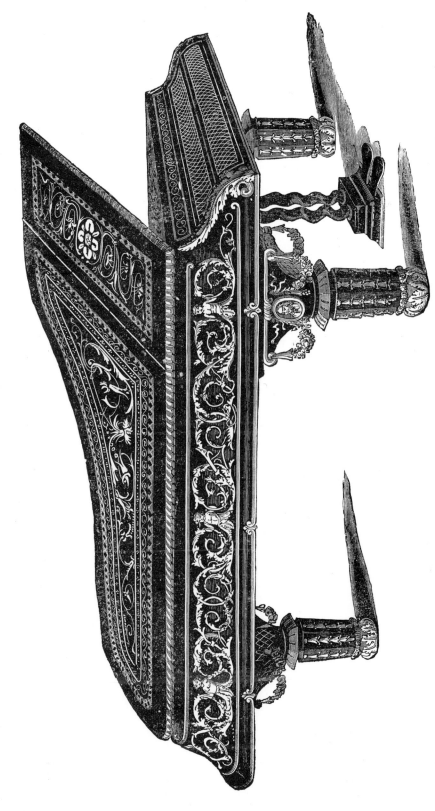

GRAND PIANOFORTE.

In Ebony inlaid, and enriched with Gold in relief.

Designed and Manufactured by Messrs Broadwood, London.   1851 Exhibition.

CHIMNEY - PIECE AND BOOKCASE COMBINED.

In Carved Walnut Wood with coloured marbles and doors of perforated brass.

Designed by Mr. T. A. Macquoid, Architect, and Manufactured by Messrs. Holland and Sons, London.
1851 Exhibition.

CHAPTER IX

From 1851 to the Present Time

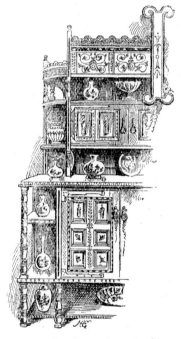

N the previous chapter some notice has been taken of the success of the National Exhibition in Paris of 1849, and about this time a general movement for holding an International Exhibition on a grand scale was started. Articles advocating such a step appeared in newspapers and periodicals of the time and after many delays a committee for the promotion of this object was formed. This resulted in the appointment of a Royal Commission and the Prince Consort as President of the Commission took a keen personal interest in every arrangement for this great enterprise. Indeed there can be no doubt that the success which crowned the work was in a great measure due to his patience and excellent business capacity. It is no part of our task to record all the details of an undertaking which at the time was a burning question of the day, but we must regard this Exhibition of 1851 as one of the landmarks in the history of furniture.

To Mr. (afterwards Sir) Joseph Paxton, then head gardener to the Duke of Devonshire, the general idea of the famous glass and iron building is due. An enterprising firm of contractors, Messrs. Fox and Henderson, were entrusted with the work ; a guarantee fund of some £230,000 was raised by public subscriptions ; and the great Exhibition was opened by Queen Victoria on the 1st of May, 1851.

The number of exhibitors was some 17,000, of whom over 3,000 received prize and council medals ; and the official catalogue, compiled by Mr. Scott Russell, the secretary, contains a great many particulars which are instructive reading when we compare the work of many of the firms of manufacturers whose exhibits are therein described with their work of the present day.

The *Art Journal* published a special volume entitled "The Art Journal Illustrated Catalogue," with woodcuts of the more important exhibits and by the courtesy of the proprietors a small selection is reproduced, which will give the reader an idea of the public taste in furniture in England and the chief Continental industrial centres at

LADY'S WORK TABLE AND SCREEN.
In Papier-maché.   1851 Exhibition, London.

that time. They have been selected as being fairly representative of the work of the period and not on account of their own intrinsic excellence.

As examples of technical skill such pieces as the Kenilworth sideboard and the ebony bedstead are worthy of high praise, but both are over-ornamented and the bedstead is impractical.

The manufacture of decorative articles of furniture of *papier-maché* was then very extensive, and the drawing-room of 1850 to 1860 was apparently incomplete without occasional chairs, a screen with painted panel, a work table, or some small cabinet or casket of this decorative but somewhat flimsy material.

SIDEBOARD.

In Carved Oak, with subjects taken from Sir Walter Scott's "Kenilworth."

Designed and Manufactured by Messrs. Cookes, Warwick.

1851 Exhibition, London.

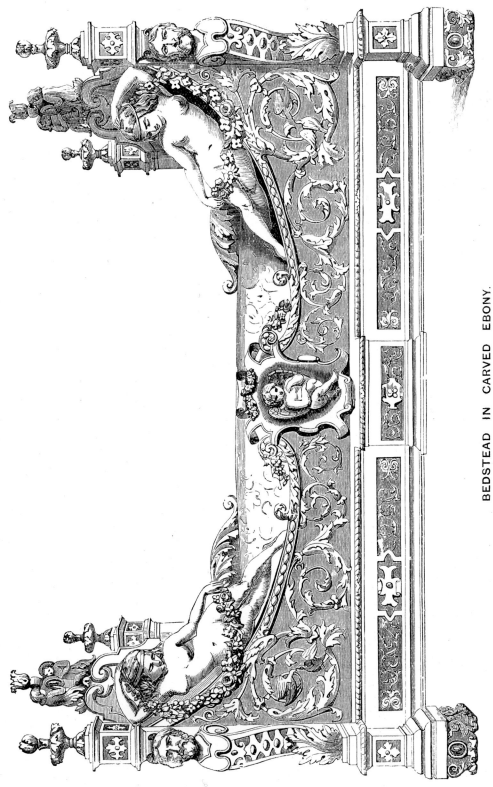

BEDSTEAD IN CARVED EBONY.

Renaissance Style.   Designed and Manufactured by M. Roulé, Antwerp.

1851 Exhibition.

The design and execution of mountings of cabinets in metal work, particularly of the highly chased and gilt bronzes for the enrichment of *meubles de luxe*, has always been and still is the *specialité* of the Parisian craftsman and almost the only English exhibits of such work were those of foreigners who had settled amongst us.

Among the latter was Monbro, a Frenchman, who established himself in Berners Street, London, and made furniture of an ornamental character in the style of his countrymen, reproducing the older designs of " Boulle " and marqueterie furniture. The present house of Mellier et Cie. are

TABLE.

In the Classic Style, inlaid with Ivory.   Manufactured for the King of Sardinia by M. G. Capello, Turin.
1851 Exhibition, London.

his successors, Mellier having been in his employ. The late Samson Wertheimer, father of Messrs. Charles and Asher Wertheimer, so well known in the Art world, was then in Greek Street, Soho, steadily making a reputation by the excellence of the metal mountings of his own design and workmanship, which he applied to caskets of French style. Furniture of a decorative character and of excellent quality was also made some sixty or seventy years ago by Town and Emanuel, of Bond Street, and many of this firm's " Old French " tables and cabinets were so carefully finished with regard to style and detail that with the " tone " which time has given them it is not always easy to distinguish them from the models from which they were taken. Toms was assistant to Town and Emanuel and afterwards purchased and carried on the business as "Toms and Luscombe," a firm well known as manufacturers of excellent and expensive "French" furniture, until their retirement from business.

CABINET.
An exact copy of the Windsor Castle Cabinet by Benemann.
Made by Webb, of Bond Street.

Webb, of Old Bond Street, succeeded by Annoot, and subsequently by Radley, Robson and Mackay, was a manufacturer of this class of furniture; he employed a considerable number of workmen and carried on a very successful business.

The illustration on opposite page is from a photograph of a replica of a famous cabinet by Benemann which is in the Windsor Castle collection: it was made by Webb to the order of Lord Hertford and is now in Lady Sackville's possession. Webb has managed to reproduce successfully the fine mountings of Gouthière which ornamented the original. The arms above the cornice are those of Savoy and France. The work of Benemann has been noticed in Chapter VI.

The name of Blake, too, is one that will be remembered by some of our older readers who were interested in marqueterie furniture of sixty

CABINET OF EBONY IN THE RENAISSANCE STYLE.
With Cornelians inserted.   Litchfield and Radclyffe.   1862 Exhibition.

years ago; an inlaid centre table which he made for the late Duke of Northumberland, from a design by Mr. C. P. Slocombe, is now in Syon House; he also made excellent copies of Louis XIV. furniture.

The next International Exhibition held in London was in the year 1862 and though its success was somewhat impaired by the death of the Prince Consort on 14th December, 1861, and also by the breaking-out of the Civil War in the United States of America, the exhibitors had increased from 17,000 in 1851 to some 29,000 in 1862, the foreign entries being 16,456, as against 6,566.

The cabinet of carved ebony with enrichments of cornelian and other richly coloured minerals (illustrated) was made by the firm in which the author's father was senior partner; it received a good deal of notice, and was purchased by William, third Earl of Craven, a well-known virtuoso of his time.

Exhibitions of a National and International character had also been held in many of the Continental capitals. There was in 1855 a successful one in Paris, which was followed by one still greater in 1867 and they have since then been of frequent occurrence in various countries.

There are three illustrations of English, French and Italian cabinets from the 1867 Exhibition which are representative.

Fourdinois' beautiful cabinet of ebony, with panels of carved Turkey boxwood, which is in the Bethnal Green Museum, was purchased by our Government for £1,200 from the Paris Exhibition of 1867, and from the same exhibition they secured Wright and Mansfield's fine example of satin-wood, enriched with Wedgwood plaques in the style of Robert Adam. The reproduction of an Italian design by Andrea Picchi, of Florence, represents modern Italian Renaissance.

The design by Bruce Talbert, exhibited in the Royal Academy in 1870, indicates a taste for modified Gothic, which had some vogue about this time in England.

The Ellesmere cabinet which is a Jacobean design was made by the Home Arts and Industries Association, founded in 1883 by Lady Marian Alford, a well-known connoisseur and Art patron.

The writer was appointed by the Royal Commission for International Exhibitions as special representative of Great Britain for judging the awards to exhibits of furniture and woodwork for the great Centenary International Exhibition of St. Louis, U.S., in 1904, and since then he has served in a similar capacity at the White City, 1909 (Anglo-French); Brussels, 1910; Rome and Turin, 1911; Ghent, 1913, so that he has had ample opportunities of examining the exhibits of the manufacturers of different countries.

One noticeable feature of modern design in furniture is the revival of marquetry. Like all mosaic work, to which branch of Industrial Art it properly belongs, this kind of decoration should be quite subordinate to the general design; but it developed into the production of all kinds of fantastic patterns in different veneers. Within the last forty years the reproductions of Jacobean oak, William and Mary and Queen Anne

CABINET IN SATIN-WOOD.

With Wedgwood plaques and inlay of various woods in the Adams style.

Designed and Manufactured by Messrs. Wright and Mansfield, London.   1867 Exhibition, Paris.

(Purchased by the Victoria and Albert Museum.)

CABINET OF EBONY WITH CARVINGS OF BOXWOOD.

Designed and Manufactured by M. Fourdinois, Paris.

1867 Exhibition, Paris.

(Purchased by Victoria and Albert Museum for £1,200.)

EBONY AND IVORY CABINET.

In the Style of Italian Renaissance by Andrea Picchi, Florence.

Exhibited Paris, 1867.

Note.—A marked similarity in this design to that of a seventeenth century cabinet, illustrated in the Italian section of Chapter III., will be observed.

walnut, also Chippendale, Adam and Sheraton designs in marqueterie furniture have been manufactured to an enormous extent. Some of these reproductions made by our best firms are good and sound, others are poor parodies of their original models. Partly on account of the difficulty in obtaining the richly marked and figured old mahogany and satin-wood of a hundred and fifty years ago which needed little or no inlay as ornament, a great deal more inlay has been given to these reproductions than ever appeared in the original work of the eighteenth century cabinet makers. Simplicity was sacrificed and veneers thus used and abused came to be a term of contempt, implying sham or superficial ornament. Dickens in one of his novels introduced the "Veneer" family, thus stamping the term more strongly on the popular imagination.

The method of producing marquetry to decorate furniture is very similar to the one explained in the description of "Boulle" furniture given in Chapter VI., except that instead of shell the marquetry cutter uses veneer for the groundwork of his design; sometimes, instead of using many different kinds of wood, when a polychromatic effect is required, holly-wood and sycamore are stained different colours, and the marquetry thus prepared, is glued on to the body of the furniture, and subsequently engraved and polished.

This kind of work is done to a great extent in England, but still more extensively and elaborately in France and Italy, where ivory and brass, marble, and other materials are used: this effect is either satisfactory or the reverse according as the work is well or ill-designed. It must be obvious that in the production of marquetry the processes are obtainable by machinery, which saves labour and cheapens productions of the commoner kinds; this has a tendency to result in superabundant ornament which is often inappropriate.

Perhaps it is allowable to add here that marquetry, or *marqueterie*, its French equivalent, is the more modern survival of "Tarsia" work, to which allusion has been made in previous chapters. Webster defines the word as "Work inlaid with pieces of wood, shells, ivory and the like," derived from the French word *marqueter*, to checker: it is distinguished from parquetry (which is derived from *parc*, an enclosure, of which it is a diminutive), and signifies a kind of joinery in geometrical patterns, generally used for flooring. When however the marquetry assumes geometrical patterns (frequently a number of cubes shaded in perspective), the design is often termed in Art catalogues a "parquetry" design.

In considering the design and manufacture of furniture of the present day as compared with that of former times there are two or three main

DESIGN FOR A DINING ROOM. Exhibited in the Royal Academy in 1870.

By Bruce J. Talbert.

(By permission of Mr. Batsford, Holborn.)

factors to be taken into account. Of these the most important is the enormously increased demand for some classes of furniture which formerly had but a limited sale. This enables machinery to be used to advantage in economising labour and therefore one finds in the so-called " Queen Anne " and " Jacobean " cabinet work of the well-furnished house of the present time rather too prominent evidence of the lathe and the steam plane. Mouldings are machined by the length, then cut into cornices, mitred round panels, or affixed to the edge of a plain slab of wood, giving it the effect of carving. The everlasting spindle, turned rapidly by the lathe, is introduced with wearisome redundance, to ornament the stretcher and the edge of a shelf; the busy fret or band-saw produces fanciful patterns which form a cheap enrichment when applied to a drawer-front, a panel or a frieze; and carving is produced by machinery, which in the seventeenth and eighteenth centuries was the careful and painstaking result of a practised craftsman's skill.

Again, as the manufacture of furniture is now chiefly carried on in large factories both in England and on the Continent the sub-division of labour causes the article to pass through different hands in successive stages and the wholesale manufacture of furniture by steam power has taken the place of the personal supervision by the master's eye. As a writer on the subject has well said, "the chisel and the knife are no longer in such cases controlled by the sensitive touch of the human hand." In connection with this we are reminded of Ruskin's precept that " the first condition of a work of Art is that it should be conceived and carried out by one person."

Instead of the carved ornament being the outcome of the artist's educated taste, which places on the article the stamp of individuality—instead of the furniture being, as it was in the seventeenth and eighteenth centuries in England, and some hundred years earlier in Italy and in France, the object of the craftsman's pride—it is now the result of the rapid multiplication of some pattern which has caught the popular fancy, and can be produced for a small price.

Public taste and the interest of the large furnishing firms who cater for it must share the responsibility for this unsatisfactory state of things and when decoration is pitted against simplicity, although the construction be ever so faulty, the more pretentious article will be selected. When a successful pattern has been produced, and arrangements and sub-contracts have been made for its repetition in large quantities, any considerable variation made in the details (even if it be the suppression of ornament) will cause an addition to the cost which only those who understand something of a manufacturer's business can appreciate.

Over forty years ago an Art movement sprung up called Æstheticism, which has been defined as the "Science of the Beautiful and the Philosophy of the Fine Arts" and aims at carrying a love of the beautiful into all the relations of life. The fantastical developments which accompanied the movement brought its devotees into much ridicule and the pages of *Punch* of that time will be found to happily travesty its more amusing and extravagant aspects. The great success of Gilbert and Sullivan's operetta, "Patience," produced in 1881, was also to some extent due to the humorous allusions to the extravagance of the "Æsthetes." There was also what may be termed a higher Æstheticism, which found a powerful advocate in Mr. Ruskin who has written much to give expression to his ideas and principles for rendering our surroundings more beautiful. The names of the late Lord Leighton and of Sir Alma Tadema are conspicuous amongst those who carried such principles into effect, and among others who were, more or less, associated with this movement may be named Rossetti, Burne-Jones, Holman Hunt and William Morris. As a writer on Æstheticism has observed:—"When the extravagances attending the movement have been purged away there may be still left an educating influence which will impress the lofty and undying principles of Art upon the minds of the people."

For a time, in spite of ridicule, this so-called Æstheticism was the vogue and considerably affected the design and decoration of furniture of the time. Woodwork was painted olive green; the panels of cabinets were painted in sombre colours with pictures of sad-looking and anæmic maidens, and there was an attempt at a "dim religious" effect in our rooms quite inappropriate to such a climate as that of England. The reaction however from the garish and ill-considered colourings of a previous decade or two left behind it much good, and with the catholicity of taste which marks the furniture of the present day; people see some merit in every style and are endeavouring to select that which is desirable without running to the extreme of eccentricity.

Perhaps the advantage thus gained is counterbalanced by the loss of our old "traditions," for amongst the wilderness of reproductions of French furniture, more or less frivolous—of Chippendale, as that master is generally understood—of what is termed "Jacobean" and "Queen Anne"—to say nothing of a quantity of so-called "antique furniture," it is difficult to identify the latter end of the nineteenth century or the present time with any particular style of furniture. By "tradition" we understand the old-fashioned manner of handing down from father to son, or from master to apprentice, for successive generations, the knowledge and skill requisite to produce a particular design or object of Art.

Tradition may be said to still survive in the country cartwright, who produces the farmer's wagon in accordance with custom and tradition, modifying the method of construction somewhat perhaps to meet altered conditions of circumstances and then ornamenting his work by no particular set design or rule, but partly from inherited aptitude and partly from playfulness or fancy. In the house-carpenter attached to some of our old English family estates there will also be found here and there surviving representatives of the traditional "joyner" of the seventeenth century; and in Eastern countries, particularly in Japan, we find the dexterous joiner or carver of to-day is a descendant of a long line of more or less excellent mechanics.

It must be obvious, too, that "Trade Unionism" of the present day cannot but be in many of its effects prejudicial to the Industrial Arts. A movement which aims at reducing men of different intelligence and ability to a common standard, and which controls the amount of work done and the price paid for it, must have a deleterious influence upon the Art products of our time, whatever its social or economical advantages may be.

Writers on Art and manufactures of varying eminence and opinion are unanimous in pointing out the serious drawbacks to progress which will exist so long as there is a demand for cheap and meretricious imitations of old furniture as opposed to more simply made articles designed in accordance with the purposes for which they are intended. Within the past few years a great many well-directed endeavours have been made in England to improve design in furniture and to revive something of the feeling of pride and ambition in his craft which in the old days of the Trade Guilds animated a Jacobean joiner. One of the best directed of these enterprises is that of the "Arts and Crafts Exhibition Society" of which Mr. Walter Crane, A.R.W.S., was president and which includes in its committee and supporters a great many influential names. As suggested on the "cover" of their Exhibition Catalogue designed by the President one chief aim of the Society is to link arm in arm "Design and Handicraft," by exhibiting only such articles as bear the names of individuals who respectively drew the design and carried it out: each craftsman has thus the credit and responsibility for his own part of the work instead of the whole appearing as the production of some firms.

In the catalogue published by this Society there are several short and useful essays in which furniture is treated generally and specifically by capable writers, amongst whom are Mr. Walter Crane, Mr. Edward Prior, Mr. Halsey Ricardo, Sir Reginald T. Blomfield, Professor W. R.

Letharby, Mr. J. H. Pollen, Mr. Stephen Webb, and Sir T. G. Jackson, R.A., the order of names being that in which the several essays are arranged. This small but valuable contribution to the subject of design and manufacture of furniture is full of interest and points out the defects of our present system. Amongst other regrets, one of the writers (Mr. Halsey Ricardo) complains that the "transient tenure that most of us

THE ELLESMERE CABINET.
In the Collection of the late Lady Marian Alford.

have in our dwellings and the absorbing nature of the struggle that most of us have to make to win the necessary provisions of life, prevent our encouraging the manufacture of well-wrought furniture. We mean to outgrow our houses—our lease expires after so many years, and then we shall want an entirely different class of furniture—consequently we purchase articles that have only sufficient life in them to last the brief period of our occupation and are content to abide by the want of appropriateness or beauty, in the clear intention of some day surrounding ourselves with objects that shall be joys to us for the remainder of our life."

The School of Art Woodcarving at South Kensington which was established some forty-five years ago at the City and Guilds Institute is also doing a useful and practical work. With a very moderate grant from the City Guilds and the use of free quarters, the School maintains itself and is the means of educating either free or at reduced terms a great many students who go out into the world the better prepared to compete with their foreign rivals. The Council, composed of artists and architects of note and others, not only give their moral support to the institution but bring some of their ornamental woodwork to the School for execution under their direction. The teaching staff, of which Mr. H. H. Grimwood is the principal, are practical carvers who can not only correct but can design and cut the patterns set for their pupils. After the first year of probation the professional students receive a fair proportion of the value of their work, which is assessed by the instructors.

It is by the maintenance of such technical schools, which with more or less success have been started by local authorities in different parts of England, that we can to some extent replace the advantages which the old system of apprenticeship gave to the learners of a craft.

About the early part of the nineteenth century the custom of employing architects to design the interior fittings and furniture to harmonise with their buildings appears to have been abandoned; this was probably due partly to some indifference to this subsidiary portion of their work, but also to the change of taste which led people to prefer the cheapness of painted or artificially grained pine-wood, with decorative effects produced by wall-papers, to the expensive but more solid wood-panelling, architectural mouldings, well-made panelled doors and chimney-pieces, which are found down to quite the end of the previous century, even in houses of moderate rentals. Furniture therefore became independent and "beginning to account herself an Art, transgressed her limits . . . and grew to the conceit that it could stand by itself, and as well as its betters went a way of its own."* The effect of this is to be seen in "interiors" of our own time which are handed over from the builder, as it were, in blank, to be filled up from the upholsterer's store, the curiosity shop and the auction room, while a large contribution from the conservatory or the nearest florist gives a finishing touch to a mixture which characterises the present taste for furnishing a boudoir or a drawing room.

* Essay by Mr. Edward S. Prior, "Of Furniture and the Room."

THE SALOON AT SANDRINGHAM HOUSE.

(From a Photo by Bedford Lemère and Co., by permission of H.M. King Edward VII.)

THE DRAWING ROOM AT SANDRINGHAM HOUSE.

(From a Photo by Bedford Lemére & Co., by permission of H.M. King Edward VII.)

There is of course in very many cases an individuality gained by the "omnium gatherum" of such a mode of furnishing. The cabinet which reminds its owner of a tour in Italy, the quaint stool from Tangiers and the embroidered piano cover from Spain are to those who are in the habit of travelling, pleasant souvenirs; as are also the presents from friends (when they have taste and judgment), the screens and flower-stands and the photographs, which are reminiscences of the forms and faces separated from us by distance or removed by death. The test of the whole question of such an arrangement of furniture in our living rooms is the amount of judgment and discretion displayed.

Two favourable examples of the present fashion, representing the interior of the Saloon and Drawing Room at Sandringham House, are reproduced. It was the intention of the writer to include a recent illustration from Sandringham, but he has been informed by Sir Dighton Probyn that there is no change of importance since the two photographs produced were published in the first edition of this book in 1892.

There is at the present time an ambition on the part of many well-to-do persons to imitate the effect produced in houses of old families where, for generations, valuable and memorable articles of decorative furniture have been accumulated, just as pictures, plate, and china have been preserved; and, failing the inheritance of such household gods, it is the practice to acquire, or as the modern term goes, "to collect," old furniture of different styles and periods until the room becomes incongruous and overcrowded, an evidence of the wealth rather than the taste of the owner. As it frequently happens that such collections are made very hastily, and in the brief intervals of a busy commercial or political life, the selections are not the best or most suitable; and where so much is required in a short space of time it becomes impossible to devote a sufficient sum of money to procure really valuable specimens; therefore reproductions of old patterns (with all the faults inseparable from such conditions) are substituted. The limited accommodation of houses built on ground which is too valuable to allow spacious halls and large apartments makes this want of discretion and judgment the more objectionable. There can be no doubt that want of care and restraint in the selection of furniture by the purchasing public affects its character both as to design and workmanship.

Among the designers of quite modern furniture the following names occur in recent exhibitions; some of these show originality and all seem to strive after suitability: Sir Edwin Lutyens, R.A., Professor Lethaby, Sir Albert Lorimer, and Messrs. Philip Webb, Gimson, W. A. S. Benson and Ambrose Heal, Junior. The "Trade" Journals too have contributed their influence by publishing drawings of work completed, suggestions for their readers to carry out and also by illustrated notices of the different exhibitions which take place from time to time.

The disadvantages which we have noticed as prejudicial to English design and workmanship and which check the production of really satisfactory furniture are also to be observed in other countries; and as the English and English-speaking people are probably the largest purchasers of foreign manufactures these disadvantages act and re-act on the furniture of different nations.

In France the cabinet maker has ever excelled in the production of ornamental furniture; and by constant reference to older specimens in the Museums and Palaces of his country he is far better acquainted with what may be called the traditions of his craft than his English brother. To him the styles of François Premier, of Henri Deux and the "three Louis" are "classic" and in the beautiful chasing and finishing of the mounts with which the French *bronziste* ornaments his *meubles de luxe*, it is almost impossible to surpass his best efforts provided the requisite price be paid; but these amounts are in many cases so considerable as hardly to be credible to those who have but little knowledge of the subject. As a simple instance the "copy" of the "Bureau du Louvre" (described in Chapter VI.) in the Hertford House collection cost the late Sir Richard Wallace a sum of £4,000. This fine piece was the work of Zwiener; other contemporary makers of reproductions of the greatest excellence were Beurdeley, Dasson, Sormani (for Vernis Martin), Roux and Fourdinois.

There is a very large section of the public both in England and on the Continent who cannot pay the high prices which must of necessity be charged for reproductions of a costly character; and there is therefore an enormous manufacturing trade carried on in France for the production of furniture which affects but does not attain to the merits of the better made and highly finished articles. Besides this extensive reproduction of the classic styles there has within the last few years been a new movement termed "L'Art Nouveau" which shows originality and eccentricity. This expression of the designer's desire to develop new ideas is to be found in every country where artistic furniture is manufactured. In every international exhibition and in magazines devoted to Art we see examples of departures from recognised styles, and as such they must be judged on individual merit.

In Holland and Belgium, as has already been pointed out, the manufacture of ornamental oak furniture on the lines of the Renaissance models still prevails and such furniture is largely imported into this country.

The illustration of a carved frame in an exaggerated rococo style of Chippendale with a Chinaman in a canopy, represents an important school of woodcarving which has been developed in Munich; and in the

CARVED FRAME, BY RADSPIELER, MUNICH.

"Künst Gewerberein" or "Workman's Exhibition" in that city the Bavarians have a very similiar arrangement to that of the Arts and Crafts Exhibition Society of this country, each article being labelled with the name of the designer and maker.

The German exhibits in the St. Louis Exhibition and in those more recently held at Brussels in 1910; Turin, 1911; and Ghent, 1913, displayed an æsthetic movement which reminded one of the extravagances of the extreme followers of our own æsthetic development already mentioned. It is possible that when this ultra-æstheticism has worn down there may result a better taste in German furniture and decoration.

Italian carved furniture of modern times has already been noticed; it compares unfavourably with the older Renaissance work which it attempts to reproduce, and with regard to other countries it may be said generally that the furniture most suitable for display is produced abroad, while none can excel English cabinet makers in the production of useful furniture and woodwork when it is the result of design and handicraft, unfettered by the detrimental but too popular condition that the article when finished shall appear to be more costly than it really is.

In conclusion it seems evident that with all the faults and short-comings of the present time there is no lack of men with ability to design and no want of well-trained patient craftsmen to produce furniture which would equal the finest examples of the Renaissance and Jacobean periods and our best eighteenth century work. With the improved means of inter-communication between England and her Colonies and with the chief industrial centres of Europe united for the purposes of commerce the whole civilised world is as it were one kingdom: merchants and manufacturers can select the best and most suitable materials, can obtain photographs or drawings of the most distant examples, or copies of the most expensive designs, while the public Art Libraries of London and Paris and other cities contain valuable works of reference, which are easily accessible to the student or to the workman. It is very pleasant to bear here testimony to the courtesy and assistance which the student or workman invariably receives from those who are in charge of our public reference libraries.

There needs however an important condition to be taken into account. Good work requiring educated thought to design and skilled labour to produce must be paid for at a very different rate to the furniture of machined mouldings, stamped ornament and other numerous and inexpensive substitutes for handwork which our present civilisation has enabled our manufacturers to produce and which finds favour with the multitude.

CHAPTER X

Colonial Furniture

Works of reference on Colonial Furniture—Virginia the first Colony—Thackeray quoted—Charleston and its development—First use of mahogany—The North-Eastern States—Gate-legged tables, bureaus, escritoires—Walnut-wood in general use—New York Furniture and Fittings—Some Inventories of the time—Mirrors made and imported—French influence—New Colonial Furniture—Conclusion.

THE term "Colonial furniture" appears to have been generally accepted as applying to that which was imported into or made in America. Such furniture dates from the early part of the seventeenth century and shows the combined influence of England, Holland and France. The two chief works of reference on the subject are "The Furniture of our Forefathers," by Esther Singleton and Russell Sturgis, and "Colonial Furniture in America," by Luke Vincent Lockwood; both are published in America and are fully illustrated, reproducing numerous inventories, extracts from wills and other documents in which various articles of furniture are specified.

In this short chapter an attempt will be made only to give some notes on the different types of Colonial furniture, while the reader is referred to the two works mentioned for fuller information. By the courtesy of the publishers a few illustrations are reproduced, and the information given by the authors has been laid under contribution.

The average Englishman is apt to consider that the purchase of old furniture by Americans is a fashion of recent years, but he does not realise that the importation of European furniture dates from the first settlement of the English and Dutch emigrants, and that many fine old pieces have been carefully preserved in American homes.

VIRGINIA

Virginia was the first English Colony, founded in 1607. Among the early settlers were families of gentle birth and considerable means who took with them some of their household belongings. Some of these men became prosperous planters, built themselves houses, the designs of which were to a considerable extent influenced by the Anglo-classic style of Inigo Jones and Christopher Wren, prevalent in England during that period, but with limitations and modifications dictated by climatic and other conditions. They were generally constructed of brick and wood, stone being rarely used, and white painted wooden columns, pilasters, cornices and panelling were prevalent features in interior decoration. The furniture consisted of the carved oak buffets, court cupboards, tables, benches, chests and chairs of the kinds described in the chapters of this book dealing with early Jacobean furniture, supplemented no doubt by locally manufactured details.

In the earlier history of Virginia values were calculated in pounds of tobacco instead of in sterling, and there are inventories in existence in which we find such items as "a carved oaken buffet, 2,000 lbs.," the value of a pound of tobacco about this time varied from 3d. to 5d.

We find in the inventories and wills of the time evidence of the attachment to favourite articles of furniture by some of these well-to-do settlers, and the old Elizabethan and Jacobean four-post bedstead figures frequently in these documents. But we also find such entries as "a Virginia-made table" which shows that some of the imported furniture was copied by native craftsmen; and there is mention of some of the native woods such as American oak, maple, sycamore and in one case of "a cabinet veneered with thorn acacia."

Leather chairs are mentioned, and from illustrations available of furniture of about the middle of the seventeenth century some of these were not unlike the chairs which we now recognise as Cromwellian, while others were of the type which are known to us as seventeenth century Spanish and were probably brought from Spain. "Turkey-work" chairs are also mentioned, the term of course referring to the covering material.

Thackeray in "The Virginians" gives us a picture of the Esmond family with their aristocratic connections and attachment to the old family traditions which had obtained in England. In Colonel Esmond's "Castlewood," named after his patrimonial home in the old country, Thackeray conveys to his readers the picture of a comfortably furnished Colonial residence during the early years of the Hanoverian succession in England. Mentioning some economies rendered necessary by legal difficulties about

CABINET OF OAK.

The outer doors are veneered on the face with hexagonal pieces of " Thorn Acacia " wood.

The drawers are veneered with walnut with an edging of sycamore.

CLOSE OF THE SEVENTEENTH CENTURY.

From " The Furniture of our Forefathers " (E. Singleton), by permission of author and publishers
(Doubleday and Page, N.Y.)

a legacy, we read:—"The fine buildings were stopped which the Colonel had commenced at Castlewood, who had freighted ships from New York with Dutch bricks, and imported at great charge, mantelpieces, carved cornicework, sashes and glass, carpets and costly upholstery from home."

Miss Singleton gives some particulars of the contents of Mount Vernon, Virginia, for a time the residence of George Washington and quotes letters of his dated in 1753 ordering furniture from London for his use: in some of these letters he refers to chairs with the seats painted in different colours to accord with the wall papers, a decorative treatment of furniture which may have been either a local fashion or a matter of personal taste. He also complains that some of the chairs which he had made locally were not strong enough for hard wear. In 1761 he ordered from a Mr. Plinius, of Audley Street, Grosvenor Square, London, a harpsichord.

CHARLESTON

Charleston, or as it was at first called Charles Town, seems to have developed quickly as a district of great prosperity and a good deal of furniture appears to have been manufactured there. In Miss Singleton's book there is an illustration of a tall (grandfather) clock bearing a date 1717, the case made of San Domingo mahogany with the clockmaker's name, William Lee, of Charles Town, and this date taken together with the record in an inventory dated 1708 of some mahogany furniture, proves that this wood was used in America some years before it came into general use in England, and we have records of the importation of San Domingo mahogany in logs and planks in the early years of the century.

About this time there appeared numerous advertisements in the American newspapers of recently arrived London tradesmen, skilled cabinet makers, joiners, carvers, upholsterers and clockmakers, who were prepared to import or manufacture furniture of the latest London fashions. Some of these mention that they will make up the customers' "own stuffe." These imported workmen are stated to have received very high wages for making furniture copied from English designs or models.

With regard to the manufacture of clock cases in America, we may quote from the "Boston News Letter," of April 16th, 1716, an advertisement which runs:—"Lately from London a parcel of very fine clocks— they go a week and repeat the hour when pulled—in Japan cases or wallnut." This would show that these clocks were a novelty: the term "Japan" no doubt refers to the lacquered decoration of the case which was at this time the fashion in England.

NORTH-EASTERN STATES

In the North-Eastern States there appears to have developed during the latter half of the seventeenth century a considerable manufacture of furniture which more or less followed Dutch and English designs, but with methods of decoration peculiar to America. The native craftsman was unable to copy the elaborately carved figure-work of the imported furniture, and therefore contented himself with decoration by means of surface carving or painting, while on some examples he had recourse to the split turned ornament applied to the surface which is recognised as

CARVED OAK CHEST.

With typical ornament in low relief.   DATE 1690–1710.

*From "Colonial Furniture in America" (Luke Vincent Lockwood).   Copyright, 1913-21 by Charles Scribner and Sons.
By permission of author and publisher.*

typical of Stuart times in England. Furniture in these Northern States appears to have been of a simpler character than that which the richer and more prosperous planters affected in the Southern States. Their craftsmen seem to have specialised in chests judging from the numerous illustrations of these articles which are given in the works of reference already noticed.

These were at first of simple box-like character made in various native woods such as walnut, different kinds of American oak, cedar, beech, maple or pine, in some cases painted black to imitate ebony. An

East Indian wood named rosetta which had for a long time been used by
Spanish and Indian craftsmen was also favoured for the panels of some of
these American-made chests; it is of a brilliant red colour with black
graining.　The various kinds of American oak, among others swamp oak
and white oak, were also used, and while the English oak chests were

HIGH CHEST.
With scroll top and carved rising sun ornament.　DATE ABOUT 1730.

*From " Colonial Furniture in America" (Luke Vincent Lockwood).　Copyright, 1913-21 by Charles Scribner and Sons
By permission of author and publishers.*

treated with stain and polish the American showed the better taste in
leaving the wood its natural colour.　The favourite floral designs on these
chests, both in carved and also in painted work, appear to have been the
tulip blossom conventionalised and the Connecticut sunflower.

GILT MIRROR AND MAHOGANY DRESSING TABLE.

Owned by Mrs. Wainwright, Hartford, Conn.   DATE 1710-20.

From " The Furniture of our Forefathers " (E. Singleton), by permission of author and publishers
(Doubleday and Page, N.Y.)

In some of the Northern Dutch towns such as Alkmaar the painting of furniture was in use early in the seventeenth century and it is quite probable that this may have been carried to America by Dutch settlers.

The simple form of chest developed later and was made to contain one or two drawers, then came chests of drawers, chests on chests such as we call "tall-boys" in England and "high-boys" which were chests of drawers standing on frames generally with six legs, four in front and two at the back. These "high-boys" frequently had the front of the middle drawer ornamented with a carved design, such as a rising sun or a shell, and the latter ornament was also carved on the knees of the legs of chairs and tables. The gate-legged table also seems to have been

DRESSING TABLE.

The earliest form of Dressing Table known to American Collectors.   DATE 1680-1700.

From "Colonial Furniture in America" (Luke Vincent Lockwood).   Copyright, 1913-21 by Charles Scribner and Sons.
By permission of author and publishers.

fashionable about this time. They were sometimes extravagantly called "hundred legged" tables and were made with such a number of legs as rendered them very inconvenient. Dressing tables with toilet boxes and mirrors, tall clocks, desks and chairs with the claw-and-ball feet were also made in considerable quantities about this time and later as the eighteenth century advanced.

About 1720 we find notices of tea tables and the "buro table with drawers" or bureau appears to have come into use in the New England States, and some years later we find in inventories the mention of "screetores" or escritoires, also chime clocks in cases with carved capitals as part of the decoration,

MAHOGANY SECRETARY AND BOOKCASE.

With original brasses. In the house of Mr. Charles R. Waters, Salem, Mass.

From " The Furniture of our Forefathers " (E. Singleton) by permission of author and publishers
(Doubleday and Page, N.Y.)

Walnut-wood in solid form for chairs and legs of tables, but especially in veneers for level surfaces of cabinets and table tops, came into general fashion about the latter part of the seventeenth century in England, to a great extent replacing oak, and this use of walnut was freely adopted by American cabinet makers of whose work there are many excellent examples which often show ornamental details peculiar to native workmanship. The brass mounts, forming the handles and keyhole plates, were similar to those in fashion in the old country, that is a flat shield with handle hanging from two small staples or else a drop handle.

The Jacobean day-bed is a familiar article to collectors and a characteristic example is illustrated in Chapter IV. When the American craftsman reproduced this day-bed or " couch " as it is termed in the American books, he varied the design of the legs, and we have illustrations, some details of which show that he sought inspiration from Italian, Flemish and Spanish designs.

In considering the furniture of these North-Eastern States New York requires special mention. Originally a Dutch Settlement it was founded early in the seventeenth century and known as New Amsterdam, and we have a record that in 1625 the Dutch Colonial authorities despatched a vessel with a few families and their household furniture to this young Colony. Holland was at this time a great sea power with an extensive trade to the East and West Indies, Spain, Portugal and Italy, and wealthy Dutch citizens possessed some of the best furniture in the world.

When this Colony came into English possession in 1664 and was re-named New York, it rapidly became an important sea-port and began to develop an extensive trade, and we find that furniture and other products designed for comfort and luxury were increasingly imported.

About 1725-30 there appears to have been a fashion in New York for panelled rooms, and as a relief from the plain panels buffets and cupboards were introduced as fittings; these had carved ornaments such as fluted pilasters with carved caps and carved enrichments in the panels of the doors.

Rush-seated chairs with backs of the ladder pattern and also some with banister rails were introduced about this time. Plymouth, Salem, Philadelphia and Connecticut, as well as New York, all seem to have been active in the production of furniture in the early part of the eighteenth century, these designs being similar to those of either Dutch or English manufacture.

Rosewood and "honey-coloured" satin-wood, cedar from Bermudas are mentioned towards the end of the seventeenth century, in addition to the native woods such as "American white oak," nut wood, wild cherry, curled maple and black walnut. Dutch marqueterie is also frequently mentioned.

As some further evidence of the interest in furniture which was taken in these Northern States during the seventeenth century, we may briefly refer to some of the correspondence and inventories of the period.

, Miss Singleton quotes the inventory taken in 1696 of the house of Sir William Phipps, the Governor of Salem, as containing a hall, my lady's room, hall chamber, white chamber, maid's chamber, chaplain's chamber and closet with a bed and a little chamber for a negro servant, kitchen and garret for servants; there is also mention of a coach, saddle horses and a yacht.

The same author quotes the various instructions sent by William Penn to his agent in London, James Harrison, respecting the kind of furniture which was required to be shipped from London to the new Colony of Pennsylvania which was founded in 1681. There is also an interesting correspondence between Benjamin Franklin (1706-90), who was in London in 1765, and his wife, who wrote to him about the furniture of their new house; she mentions card tables, chests of drawers, a harpsichord, some "old" black walnut chairs, also materials for curtains and other details which he was to obtain and send out.

Another inventory of the contents of the house of William Burnet, who was Governor of New York in 1729, mentions some seventy chairs and twelve tables made of walnut and mahogany, and as some of these are illustrated we see how exactly they correspond with the types of English furniture of the time. Curiously enough, in this inventory there is mention of an iron bedstead which was probably one of the first to be in use either in America or Europe.

Mirrors in various frames of carved and also of gilded wood appear to have been in considerable demand in the early part of the eighteenth century. Mr. Lockwood quotes an advertisement which appeared in "The Baltimore Directory," 1819, and was pasted on the back of a mirror of early Georgian character, as follows:—" Joseph Hillier informs his friends and the public that he has opened a Store Number 76 Market St Baltimore for the convenience of his Western Sothern customers wholesale and retail at the Philadelphia prices. All these looking glasses correspond to the English styles of the same time."

The " Boston News Letter" of 1819 also advertised "looking glasses of divers sorts and sizes lately imported from London to be sold at the glass shop in Queen Street."

As the eighteenth century advances and we have Thomas Chippendale and his contemporaries succeeding William Kent in England, we find that in America also there is the same change of style and to a considerable extent of material also, mahogany taking the place of walnut.

FRENCH INFLUENCE

It is difficult to trace the earliest influence of French design upon Colonial furniture but it is probable that this may have had its origin in Huguenot immigration. We know that religious persecutions in France had caused many industrious people to leave that country, and when the wholesale scattering was caused by the revocation of the Edict of Nantes in 1685 no doubt many Huguenots found their way to America as well as to England and Holland, and they would carry with them their various trades and industries. During the reigns of Louis XV. and his successors, French furniture to a limited extent was imported by some of the wealthier Americans.

At the end of the eighteenth century this influence of French design was probably stimulated by the purchase of an estate in Maine for Marie Antoinette who intended to take refuge in the United States, and a quantity of French furniture was sent from Paris. This influence was not confined to the New England States and in Miss Singleton's book there are many illustrations of carved and gilt and also white painted suites of furniture upholstered in Aubusson and Beauvais tapestries. These are generally in the Louis XV. and Louis XVI. styles. This furniture was not only imported but also manufactured in America and when French tapestry was not available was upholstered with silk and velvet which came to be more generally used by the wealthier classes of America.

After the Declaration of Independence and the interchange of Ambassadors by the sending of Benjamin Franklin to Paris and of Lafayette to Washington, social and commercial intercourse between the two countries would be encouraged, and we know that Lafayette was popular with Washington Society and that French furniture and fashions were adopted. There is an example of this in one of Miss Singleton's illustrations of an interior of George Washington's house, Mount Vernon, in Virginia, where the Louis XVI. style is affected.

The furniture which came into fashion in France after the Empire was established, made of richly figured mahogany mounted with gilt bronze ornaments of the period, was to a considerable extent adopted by America and as we shall notice in some remarks upon " New Colonial " furniture this style in a simpler form has recently been reproduced in great quantities.

WASHINGTON'S BEDROOM, MOUNT VERNON, VA.

From " The Furniture of our Forefathers " (E. Singleton), by permission of author and publishers (Doubleday and Page, N.Y.)

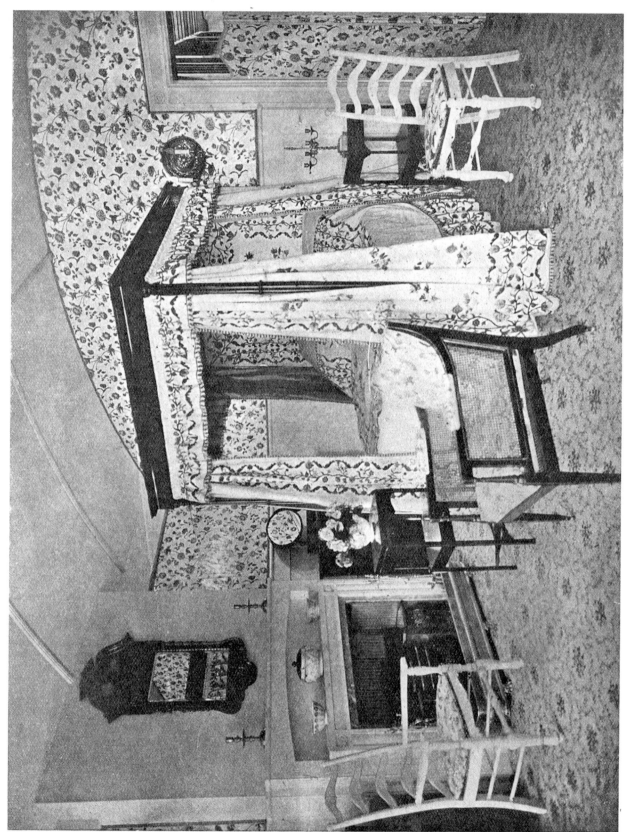

BEDROOM.

Furnished in the New Colonial style by Waring and Gillow.

THE NEW COLONIAL FURNITURE

When the writer visited the United States some few years ago there was a great deal of modern furniture made of mahogany varying in quality from richly marked kinds to the cheaper and softer woods, generally of the design which we call "First Empire," only lacking the gilt metal mounts which ornament the old French Empire furniture. This was turned out in great quantities in the manufacturing district known as "Grand Rapids," Michigan, and seemed to be in considerable demand. It was described as Colonial or New Colonial to distinguish it from the seventeenth and eighteenth century furniture which is to be found in different Museums, some of the public buildings and in private houses. Among these historical documents in furniture are George Washington's chairs, Jefferson's desk, the chair in which he signed the Declaration of Independence and many others of National and local interest.

In the Centenary Exhibition of St. Louis, 1904, there was a special exhibition of this old Colonial furniture with contributions by the descendants of seventeenth and eighteenth century families, inheritors of this highly prized furniture.

Several of these exhibits were of American manufacture, but copied more or less faithfully from English originals which had been brought out or imported later by their forefather immigrants.

About fourteen or fifteen years ago Messrs. Waring and Gillow, in London, made a speciality of what they termed "New Colonial" furniture. This was really a free adaptation of our late eighteenth century designs, selecting those of simple and less ornate character. It was generally enamelled white or ivory colour and was especially suitable for bedrooms and morning rooms.

*   *   *   *   *

CONCLUSION

A point has now been reached at which our task must be brought to its natural conclusion; for although many collectors and others interested in the subject have invited the writer's attention to numerous descriptions and examples from an examination of which much information could without doubt be obtained, the limits of a single volume of moderate dimensions forbid the attempt to add to a story which it is feared may perhaps have already overtaxed the reader's patience.

As has already been suggested in the preface this book is not intended to be a guide to "*collecting*" or "*furnishing*"; nevertheless it is possible that in the course of recording some of the changes which have taken place in designs and fashions and of bringing into notice here and there the opinions of those who have thought and written upon the subject, some indirect assistance may have been given in both these directions. If this should be the case and if an increased interest has been thereby excited in the surroundings of the Home or in some of the Art collections which form part of our National property, the writer's aim and object will have been attained and his humble efforts amply rewarded.

PAINTED SILK PANEL OF EIGHTEENTH CENTURY ENGLISH POLE SCREEN.
(*Victoria and Albert Museum*).

Appendix

THE following List of the Names of some Artists and Manufacturers of past times in alphabetical order will be useful for reference. The Author is indebted to Mr. J. Hungerford Pollen for his list in "Ancient and Modern Furniture" (published in 1874) and also to Lady Dilke for particulars of some of the French *ébenistes* given in "French Decoration and Furniture in the Eighteenth Century" (published in 1901). The names of existing firms are not included, partly on account of the large number who might fairly claim a place amongst the makers of furniture of the present time and partly because any selection of names by a contemporary would appear to be invidious and arbitrary.

Names of Artists or Manufacturers.	Country and time in which they worked.		Remarks and References.
A			
Adam, J. (and R.) . .	England	1728-1792	Chapter vii.
Agnolo, B. d' . . .	Italy	1460-1563	Architect who designed much intarsia work, also carved church work.
Agnolo, D. d' . . .	,,	16th century	Son of above.
Agnolo J. d' . . .	,,	,, ,,	Ditto.
Ambrogio, G. . .	,,	17th ,,	
Annoot, — . . .	England	19th ,,	Chapter ix., p. 394 (French style).
Ards, W. . . .	Flanders	15th ,,	Executed carvings in the roof of Hotel de Ville, Malines.
Armand, Jean . .	France	18th ,,	Marquetry.
Asinelis, A. . . .	Italy	16th ,,	
Aubiche, Jacques d' .	France	18th ,,	Faubourg Ste. Antoine.
B			
Bachelier, — . . .	France	16th century	
Baerze, J. de . .	Flanders	14th ,,	Carved figure work, preserved in Museum of Dijon.
Baker, — . . .	England	18th ,,	Flower painter.
Balthazar, Lieutand .	France	,, ,,	
Barili, A. . . .	Italy	16th ,,	Carved woodwork for Cathedral of Siena.
Barili, G. (Florence) .	,,	,, ,,	Carved doors in the Vatican.
Barili, S. . . .	,,	,, ,,	Carved work for Cathedral of Siena.

Names of Artists or Manufacturers.	Country and time in which they worked.		Remarks and References.
Barry, Sir Charles (architect)	England	19th century	Chapter viii., woodwork of Houses of Parliament.
Baumgartner, U. . .	Germany	17th ,,	Made the celebrated Pomeranian Art Cabinet in Berlin Museum.
Beaugreant, G. de . .	Flanders	16th ,,	One of the designers of the chimney-piece at Bruges, see p. 87.
Beck, S. . . .	Germany	,, ,,	
Belli, A. A. . . .	Italy	,, ,,	
Belli, G. . . .	,,	,, ,,	
Benemann, G. . .	France	18th ,,	"Maitre ébeniste" in 1785, worked at Fontainebleau. Richly mounted furniture (Marie Antoinette), p. 267.
Bennett, Saml. .	England	17th ,,	See p. 182.
Berain, J. . .	France	1636-1711	Chapter vi., designed for Boulle.
Bergamo, D. da . .	Italy	1490-1550	Intarsia work in Church of S. Dominic in Bologno.
Bergamo, S. da . .	,,	16th century	Brother and assistant.
Bernardo, — . . .	,,	,, ,,	
Berruguete, — .	Spain	1480-1561	Chapter iii. (Spanish section), pupil of M. Angelo.
Bertolina, B. J. .	Italy	16th century	
Beurdelet, — . . .	,,	19th ,,	Made excellent reproductions of fine old French furniture.
Beyaert, J. . .	Flanders	15th ,,	Carvings in roof of Salle de Marriage, Hotel de Ville, Louvain.
Binson, Andrieu de .	France	18th ,,	Furniture and carriage decorator, worked in 1736.
Blake, S. . . .	England	19th ,,	Marqueterie furniture (French style), p. 395.
Blondel, L. . .	Flanders	1495-1560	Designed the chimney-piece at Bruges, see p. 87.
Boffrand, Germain .	France	18th century	Chapter vi., Architect of Hotel Soubise and Hotel Toulouse.
Bolgié, G. . .	Italy	,, ,,	
Bonzanigo, G. M. . .	,,	,, ,,	Carver of mirror frames, very minute work, frequently in box wood.
Borello, F. . .	,,	16th ,,	
Borgona, F. de . .	Spain	,, ,,	
Botto, B. . . .	Italy	,, ,,	Famous wood carver.
Botto, G. B. . .	,,	,, ,,	
Botto, P. . . .	,,	,, ,,	
Botto, S. A. . .	,,	,, ,,	
Boulle, A. C. (generally spelt "Boule")	France	1642-1732	Chapter vi. Born 1619, premier *ébeniste* to Louis XIII.
Bourdin, M. . .	,,	16th century	Chapter iii., p. 77.

Names of Artists or Manufacturers.	Country and time in which they worked.		Remarks and References.
Brandri, — . . .	France	17th century	An Italian, worked with Goletti at "Pietra Dura" under Colbert.
Brescia, R. da . .	Italy	16th ,,	
Bross, — de . . .	France	17th ,,	
Bruggeman, H. . .	Germany	15th ,,	Carver.
Bruhl, A. . . .	Flanders	16th and 17th centuries	Carved stalls of San Giorgio Maggiore in Venice.
Brunelleschi, F. . .	Italy	1377-1446	. .
Brustolone, A. . .	,,	1670-1732	
Buontalenti, B. T. .	,,	16th century	
Burb, — . . .	France	18th ,,	Said to have worked for Mde. de Pompadour (Vernis Martin style).

C

Names of Artists or Manufacturers.	Country and time in which they worked.		Remarks and References.
Caffieri, Jacques .	France	18th century	Chapter vi. (worked with Riese-
Caffieri, Ph., son of the above . .	,,	,, ,,	ner) famous mounters.
Campbell and Sons .	England	,, ,,	Chapter vii., p. 345.
Canabas, Joseph . .	France	,, ,,	Made mechanical tables, Rue du fg. St. Antoine.
Canavo, J. de . .	Italy	16th ,,	
Cano, A. . . .	Spain	17th ,,	
Canozii, C. . .	Italy	16th ,,	Executed intarsia work in S. Marco, Venice.
Canozii, G. M. . .	,,	,, ,,	Carvers of church decorative
Canozii, L. . . .	,,	,, ,,	work.
Capitsoldi, — . .	England	18th ,,	Louis Seize style of furniture.
Capo di Ferro, Brothers .	Italy	16th ,,	
Carlin, E. . . .	France	18th ,,	Stamped on table in Jones Collection.
Carlin, Martin . .	,,	,, ,,	Chapter vi., ebony with porce-lain plaques, lac, and "Pietra Dura," pp. 259–262.
Carlone, J. . . .	Italy	,, ,,	
Carnicero, A. . .	Spain	1693-1756	Sculptor, carved in convent of Valladolid.
Carter, — (architect) .	England	18th century	Chapter vii.
Castelli, Q. . .	Italy	16th ,,	
Cauner, — . . .	France	18th ,,	Chapter vii. (frames in Louis XV. style.)
Cauvet, G. P. . .	,,	1731-1788	
Ceracci, G. . .	England	18th century	Italian, modelled for R. Adam.
Cervelliera, B. del .	Italy	,, ,,	
Chambers, Sir W. .	England	1726-1796	Chapter vii., introduced Chinese style in furniture.
Chippendale, I. . .	,,	18th century	Chapter vii., frame carver, father of the celebrated Thomas Chippendale.
Chippendale, T. . .	,,	,, ,,	Chapter vii.

Names of Artists or Manufacturers.	Country and time in which they worked.		Remarks and References.
Cipriani, G. B. . .	England	18th century	Chapter vii., employed by Chambers and others to paint furniture.
Claude, Charles S. . .	France	,, ,,	Faubourg Ste. Antoine, 1752, good plain work with metal mounts.
Claude, Lebesque . .	,,	,, ,,	Worked in Paris, 1771.
Cleyn, F. R. . . .	England	17th ,,	Chapter iv., worked for Charles II.
Coech, P. . . .	Flanders	16th ,,	Chapter iii., p. 86,
Coit, —	England	18th ,,	Chaser of metal mounts.
Collett, A. . . .	,,	,, ,,	Chapter vii., carver.
Collins, William . .	,, early	19th ,,	Signature on Empire suite of furniture in Admiralty House, Whitehall. Chap. viii., p. 361.
Collinson and Lock .	,,	,, ,,	Succeeded Jackson and Graham absorbed by Waring and Gillow, p. 377.
Collmann, L. W. . .	,,	,, ,,	Designed furniture for London Clubs, p. 377.
Columbani, — . .	,,	18th ,,	Designed mirror frames and chimney-pieces for woodwork and stucco, somewhat in the Adam style.
Copeland, — . . .	,,	,, ,,	See Lock and Copeland.
Cosson, J. L. . . .	France	,, ,,	Stamped on the table in Jones Collection.
Cotte, Robert de . .	,,	,, ,,	Chapter vi., Architect who decorated the Hotels de Toulouse and Soubise.
Cotton, C. . . .	England	,, ,,	
Couet, L. Jacques . .	France	,, ,,	Rue de Bussy in 1774.
Crace, John . . .	England	19th ,,	Designer of good furniture, p. 348.
Cramer, M. G. . .	France	18th ,,	Stamped on marqueterie furniture, Louis XVI. style.
Cressent, Charles . .	,,	,, ,,	Chapter vi., p. 223, the Regency period. Wallace and Jones Collections.

D

Darly, Mathias . . (See Edwards and Darly)	England	18th century	Chapter vii., p. 347, designer, published books of drawings 1765, 1770, 1776.
Dasson, Henri . .	France	19th ,,	Made excellent reproductions of fine old French furniture.
David, — (see Röntgen)	,,	18th ,,	Chapter vi., famous for marqueterie.
Davy, R. . . .	England	1750-1794	Wood carving, Chapter vii.

Names of Artists or Manufacturers.	Country and time in which they worked.	Remarks and References.
De la Fosse . . .	France 18th century	Chapter vi., p. 267.
Dello Delli . . .	Italy 14th and 15th centuries	
Deloose, — . . .	France 18th century	Stamped on table in Jones Collection.
Delorme, — . . .	France 18th century	Stamped on table in Bethnal Green Museum (Mainwaring Collection).
Denizot, — . . .	,, ,, ,,	
Dolen, — van . .	Flanders ,, ,,	Carvings in Church of S. Gudule, Brussels.
Donatello, — . . .	Italy 1380-1466	
Dorsient, A. C.; C. Oc. .	Flanders 16th century	Signed on carved door in Victoria and Albert Museum, dated 1580.
Dowbiggin, — .	England 18th and 19th centuries	Chapter vii. and viii. (Gillow's apprentice).
Dubois, I. . . .	France 18th century	Chapter vi., famous mounter of style de Régence, p. 263.
Ducereau, A. . . .	,, 1515-1518	
Dugar, E. . . .	Italy 16th century	
Dugourc, — . . .	France late 18th ,,	Designed for Benemann, Swerdfeger, and others.
Duplessis, — . . .	,, ,, ,,	Famous mounter of furniture.
Du Quefnoy, F. H. and J.	Flanders 17th ,,	
E		
Edwards and Darly .	England 18th century	Published designs inferior to those of Mathias Darly, 1770, 1773.
Ellaume, Jean C. .	France ,, ,,	Worked in Paris, 1754.
Elliott, Charles . .	England ,, ,,	Chapter vii., p. 345.
Etienne, Avril .	France	Lived at the Rue Charenton in 1774, good plain work with metal mounts.
F		
Faydherbe, L. (artist and architect)	Flanders 1627-1694	Chapter iii, p. 88.
Feucheré, — (mounter) .	France 18th century	Chapter vi.
Filipo, D. di . .	Italy 16th ,,	
Fitzcook, H. . . .	England 19th ,,	Chapter viii., designed for manufacturers.
Flaxman, John, R.A. .	,, and Italy 18th ,,	Chapter vii., designed for Josiah Wedgwood.
Flörein, J. . . .	Flanders 15th ,,	
Floris, C. . . .	Netherlands 16th ,,	Chapter iii, p. 86.
Flötner, P. . . .	Germany ,, ,,	Designs for furniture in the Berlin Museum.

Names of Artists or Manufacturers.	Country and time in which they worked.		Remarks and References.
Forestier, — . . .	France	18th ,,	Mounter of mahogany furniture.
Foulet, — . . .	,,	,, ,,	Chapter vi., p. 263, stamped on marqueterie panel.
Fourdinois, — . .	,,	19th ,,	Chapters viii. and ix., exhibited 1851, 1867.
France, — . . .	England	18th ,,	Chapter vii., pp. 343–4.

G

Gabler, M. . . .	Germany	17th century	
Gaine, — . . .	France	18th ,,	
Gallé, — . . .	Holland	17th ,,	Ebony, with metal and hard pebbles.
Galletti, G. . . .	Italy	18th ,,	
Gallieux, — (mounter) .	France	,, ,,	Stamped on tables in Jones Collection.
Garnier, P. . . .	,,	,, ,,	Stamped on table, and on marquetry encoignures in the Duke of Westminster's Collection.
Gaudreaux, — . .	,,	,, ,,	Heavily mounted and rather over-decorated furniture, p. 270.
Genfer, M. . . .	Germany	17th ,,	
Gervasius, — . .	England	,, ,,	
Gettich, P. . . .	Germany	,, ,,	
Geuser, M. . . .	,,	,, ,,	
Gheel, F. van . .	Flanders	18th ,,	
Gibb, James . .	England early	18th ,,	Chapter iv., published book of designs, woodwork, chimney-pieces, etc.
Gibbons, Grinling . .	England	17th ,,	Chapter iv., worked for Charles II.
Gillet, Louis . .	France	18th ,,	Worked in Paris, 1776.
Gillow, R. . . .	England	18th and 19th centuries	Chapters vii., viii., ix.
Giovanni, Fra . .	Italy	16th century	
Glosencamp, H. . .	Flanders	,, ,,	Chapter iii. (Bruges chimney-piece), p. 87.
Goletti, — . . .	France	17th ,,	"Pietra Dura," worked under Colbert.
Goujon, J. . . .	,,	16th ,,	Sculptor, designed much furniture.
Gouthière, P. . . .	,,	18th ,,	Chapter vi., born 1740, worked with Riesener, famous mounter.

H

Habermann, — . .	France	18th century	Rococo or Pompadour style.
Habert, — . . .	Italy	16th to 17th ,,	Stamped on examples in Hamilton Palace Collection.
Haeghen, — van der .	Flanders	18th ,,	

Names of Artists or Manufacturers.	Country and time in which they worked.	Remarks and References.
Haig and Chippendale .	England late 18th century	Chapter vii.
Heckinger, J. . .	Germany 17th ,,	
Hedoin, J. B. .	France 18th ,,	
Heinhofer, Ph. . .	,, 16th and 17th centuries	Designed the celebrated Pomerian Art Cabinet in Berlin Museum.
Helmont, — van . .	Flanders 18th century	Carved pulpits in St. John Baptist, Cologne.
Heppelwhite, A., and Co.	England ,, ,,	Chapter vii.
Heppelwhite, George .	,, late ,, ,,	Chapter vii.
Hernandez, G. . .	Spain 1586-1646	
Herring, — . . .	England 19th century	Chapter viii.
Hervieux, — . . .	France 18th ,,	Chapter vi., famous mounter (Bureau du Roi).
Holbein, Hans . .	England early 16th ,,	Chapter iii. (English section).
Holmes, W. . .	England 19th ,,	Chapter viii. (designer).
Holthausen, H. J. .	France 18th ,,	Stamped on table in Bethnal Green Museum (Mainwaring Collection).
Hool, J. B. van .	Flanders ,, ,,	
Hope, T. (architect) .	England early 19th ,,	Chapter viii., classical style.
Huet, — . . .	France 18th ,,	
Huygens, — (lacquer) .	,, and Holland 17th ,,	Chapter vi., introduced the making of lacquer in Holland.
Hyman, F. . .	England 18th ,,	
I		
Ince, W. . .	England 18th century	Chapter vii., contemporary with Chippendale.
Ince and Mayhew . .	,, ,, ,,	
J		
Jackson and Graham .	England 19th century	Chapters viii. and ix., exhibited 1851.
Jacob, Georges . .	France 18th ,,	Fine table at Fontainebleau, signed by him, period Louis XVI.
Jacob, Georges (son) .	,, 19th ,,	Chapter viii.
Jansen, G. . . .	,, 18th ,,	Stamped on table in Jones Collection.
John of Padua . .	,, 15th ,,	Chapter iii., employed by Henry VIII.
John of St. Omer (Frenchman)	,, 13th ,,	Court painter and house decorator to Henry III.
Johnson, T. . . .	,, 18th ,,	Chapter vii., published book of designs for mirror frames and pier tables similar to Chippendale's rococo period.

Names of Artists or Manufacturers.	Country and time in which they worked.		Remarks and References.
Johnson and Norman .	England	19th century	Successor to Seddons, p. 368.
Johnson Garrett . .	,,	17th ,,	p. 181.
Jones, Inigo (architect) .	,,	1572-1652	Chapter iv.
Jones, W. . . .	,,	18th century	Published book of designs on furniture, 1739, entitled " Gentlemen or Builders' Companion."
Joubert, — . . .	France	18th century	Designed Louis XVI. furniture.
Juni, J. D. . . .	Spain	16th and 17th centuries	
K			
Kampen, Lambert van .	Germany	16th century	Carved the Chapter House panels in Münster, Westfalen.
Kauffmann, A. (artist) .	England	18th ,,	Chapter vii. (painted furniture).
Kent, William (architect)	,,	1684-1748	Designed furniture, woodwork enrichments, chimney-pieces, etc., pp. 278-9.
Kiskner, U. . . .	Germany	17th ,,	
Kraft, J. C. (architect) .	England	18th ,,	Chapter vii.
Kuenlin, J. . . .	Germany	17th ,,	
L			
La Croix, Robert Victor	France	18th century	His initials stamped on a commode in the Victoria and Albert Museum, p. 249.
Ladetto, F. . . .	Italy	,, ,,	
Lalonde, — . . .	France	,, ,,	Furniture with mechanical contrivances (Louis XVI.)
Lardant, Jacques . .	,,	16th ,,	Chapter iii.
Lathille, Pierre . .	,,	18th ,,	Worked in Paris, 1737.
Lawreans, —. . .	England	17th ,,	Pupil of G. Gibbons (chapter iv.)
Lebrun, Charles (artist) .	France	,, ,,	Chapter vi., designed for Boulle.
Lecreux, N. A. J. . .	Flanders	1757-1836	Carved pulpits.
Le Gaigneur, Louis .	England	19th century	French immigrant, made furniture in style of Boulle, a table in the Wallace Collection, see pp. 371-3.
Leleu, J. F. . . .	France	18th ,,	Chapter vi., stamped on specimen in Jones Collection. Worked for Madame du Barri, p. 262.
Le Moyne . . .	,,	1645-1718	
Leopardi, A. . . .	Italy	1450-1525	
Le Pautre, J. . .	France	1617-1682	

Names of Artists or Manufacturers.	Country and time in which they worked.	Remarks and References.
Le Roux, J. B. . .	France 18th century	Chimney-pieces and room decorations. Worked in 1777.
Letellier, J. P. . .	,, ,, ,,	Stamped on mahogany, Louis XVI. chairs, Massey Mainwaring Collection. Sold Christies, April, 1907.
Levasseur, — . .	,, ,, ,,	Chapter vi.
Lieutland, — . . .	,, ,, ,,	Stamped on specimens in collection " National Mobilier," Paris.
Linnell, J. . . .	England ,, ,,	Furniture in Chippendale style.
Lock, Matthias, also Lock and Copeland	,, 18th ,,	Chapter vii., carver and gilder, published " Book of Pier Frames " and of " Original Designs," similar to Chippendale's rococo period of design.
Loir, A. . . .	France 1630-1713	
L'Orme, Ph. de . .	,, 16th century	
Lunigia, A. da . .	Italy ,, ,,	
M		
Macé, J. . . .	France 17th century	" Menuisier en ébéne," was lodged in the Louvre to work, in 1644.
Claud, Isaac, Louis (?) sons of above Macé		
Macret, — . . .	,, 18th ,,	Stamped on a commode of black lacquer, Massey Mainwaring Collection. Sold Christies, April, 1907.
Maffeis, P. di . .	Italy 15th ,,	
Magaritome, — . .	,, 1236-1313	
Maggiolino, — . .	,, 18th century	A Milanese cabinet maker (marquetry chests of drawers), contemporary with Riesener.
Maigret, — . . .	France late 18th, early 19th century	Signature on an upright secretaire (Empire) exhibited Burlington Fine Arts Club, 1918.
Maigster, O. . .	Italy 16th century	
Majano, B. da . .	,, 15th ,,	Coffer maker to Matthias Corvinus, King of Hungary.
Majano, G. da . .	,, 1432-1490	
Manwaring, Robert .	England 18th century	Chair maker (chapter vii., p. 317).
Marot, D. . . .	France 1650-1695	Said to have influenced Chippendale's rococo period.

Names of Artists or Manufacturers.	Country and time in which they worked.		Remarks and References.
Marot, G. . . .	France	17th century	
Marot, J. . . .	,,	1625-1679	
Martin, R. . . .	,,	1706-1765	Chapter vi., introducing Vernis-Martin.
Martincourt, Jean . .	,,	18th century	Chapter vi., bronze mounter.
Mayhew, — . . .	England	,, ,,	Chapter vii., contemporary with Chippendale.
Meissonnier, J. A. . .	France	1693-1750	Introduced broken shell-shaped curves and the more rococo style of Louis XIV. to XV.
Mendeler, G. . . .	Germany	17th century	
Meslee, R. . . .	France	late 18th, early 19th century	Signature on an upright secretaire exhibited Burlington Fine Arts Club, 1918.
Meulen, R. van der .	Flanders	1645-1717	Carved chimney-pieces (G. Gibbons' style).
Miglionné, Ferdinand Filoppo de	France	17th century	Invited to France by Colbert.
Miles and Edwards .	England	19th ,.	Chapter viii., p. 368.
Minore, G. . . .	Italy	15th ,,	
Modena, P. da . .	,,	,, ,,	Chair of S. Francesco in Trevisco in 1486.
Moenart, M. . .	Flanders	17th ,,	Carved the stalls in St. James', Bruges.
Monbro, — . . .	England	19th ,,	Chapter ix., p. 393.
Mondon, François Adrien	France	18th ,,	Stamped on a Louis XV. commode at Mutton's restaurant, Brighton.
Montepulciano, G. da .	Italy	16th ,,	
Morand, de Pont de Vaux	France		Stamped on a clock case at Versailles, with date 1706.
Morant, — . . .	England	19th ,,	Chapter viii., p. 368.
Moser, L. . . .	Germany	15th ,,	
Müller, D. . . .	,,	17th ,,	
Müller, J. . . .	,,	,, ,,	

N

Newrone, G. C. . .	Italy	16th century	
Nilson, — . . .	France	18th ,,	Chapter vii., carver.
Nys, L. de . . .	Flanders	,, ,,	Carved confessionals, work dated 1768.
Nys, P. de . . .	,,	,, ,,	

O

Oeben, Jean Francis	France	18th century	Chapter vi., stamped on secretaire in Jones Collection. In 1751 *ébenistes* were bound to stamp their work. This Oeben died in 1765.

Names of Artists or Manufacturers.	Country and time in which they worked.	Remarks and References.
Oeben, Simon (probably son of the foregoing)	France 18th century	Called the "inventor" of cylinder secretaires.
Oost, P. van . . .	Flanders 14th ,,	
Oppen, Oorde Jean .	Holland and 18th ,, France	
Oudry, Jean Baptiste .	France 18th ,,	Director of the Gobelins Tapestry Works and designer of tapestry for furniture, chapter vi. and Appendix.
P		
Pacher, M. . . .	Germany 15th century	
Padova, Z. da . .	Italy 16th ,,	
Pafrat, Jean . . .	France 18th ,,	On tables in Jones Collection, see chapter vi., p. 263.
Panturmo, J. di . .	Italy 1492-1556	
Papworth, John . .	England 19th century	Architect and ornamentalist, p. 361.
Pardo, G. . . .	Spain 16th ,,	
Pareta, G. di . . .	Italy ,, ,,	
Passe, C. de . . .	France ,, ,,	Chapter iii.
Passe, C. de, the younger	,, ,, ,,	Chapter iii.
Percier and Fontaine (architects)	,, 18th and 19th centuries	Chapter viii., pp. 357-8, Empire furniture.
Pergolesi, Michael Angelo (artist)	England 18th century	Chapter vii., employed by Robert Adam.
Peridiez, P. . . .	France ,, ,,	Stamped on a Louis XVI. marqueterie cabinet in the Massey Mainwaring Collection. Sold Christies, April, 1907.
Perreal, J. . . .	,, 15th ,,	
Petit, Gilles . . .	,, 18th ,,	See chapter vi. } p. 267.
Petit, Jean Marie .	,, ,, ,,	See chapter vi. }
Pettit (otherwise Petit), Nicholas	,, ,, ,,	Stamped on specimens in Jones Collection and in Bethnal Green Museum, " 1761."
Philippon, A. . . .	,, 16th ,,	
Picau, — . . .	,, 18th ,,	Chapter vii., carver of frames (Louis XV. style).
Picq, J. . . .	Flanders 17th ,,	
Piffetti, A. P. . .	Italy 1700-1777	Furnished Royal Palace of Tusin (Boulle style).
Pigalle, — . . .	England 18th century	French sculptor.
Pillon, G. . . .	France late 16th ,,	Chapter iii.
Pineau, Nicholas .	Russia 18th ,,	Famous wood carver (architectural ornaments).
Pinodo, — . . .	Spain ,, ,,	Signature on painted cabinet in Bethnal Green Museum.
Pioniez, — . . .	France ,, ,,	Stamped on secretaire in Jones Collection.

Names of Artists or Manufacturers.	Country and time in which they worked.		Remarks and References.
Piranesi, Jean Baptiste .	England	late 18th century	Designer of furniture, see pp. 287-8.
Plumier, P. D. . .	Flanders	1688-1721	
Poitou, Phillipe . .	France	18th century	" Ebeniste de France."
Porfirio, B. di . .	Italy	16th ,,	
Prignot, — . .	England	19th ,,	Designed for Jackson and Graham.
Puget, — . .	France	18th ,.	Furniture and ship decorator.
Q			
Quellin, A. . . .	Flanders	1609-1668	
Quellin, A., the younger .	,,	1625-1700	
Quellin, E. . . .	,,	17th century	
R			
Raephorst, B. van .	Flanders	15th century	Carver of Church reredos in 1740.
Ramello, F. . .	Italy	16th ,,	
Ranson, — . .	France	18th ,,	
Rasch, A. . .	Flanders	15th ,,	Chapter iii. Chimney-piece in Palais de Justice, Bruges.
Revitt, N. (architect) .	England	18th ,,	Chapter vi.
Richardson, George .	,,	,, ,,	Chapter vii. Published several books of designs of rooms, chimney-pieces, ceilings, etc., 1792, 1795, 1798.
Richter, C. . .	France	,, ,,	Stamped on cabinet in the Jones Collection.
Riesener, — . .	,,	,, ,,	Born 1730. Chapter vi., *ébeniste* to Marie Antoinette, came from Gladbeck, near Cologne. Died in 1806.
Robin, — . .	,,	,, ,,	Stamped on tall clock, Louis XVI., in the Jones Collection, Victoria and Albert Museum.
Röntgen, D. (see also David)	,,	,, ,,	Chapter vi., contemporary with Riesener. Was living in 1780.
Rogers, H. . .	England	19th ,,	Carved in boxwood, Chapter viii., p. 380.
Rohan, J. de . .	,,	16th ,,	" Maitre Menuisiers" of Lyons, 1548.
Rohan, J. de . .	,,	,, ,,	
Rosch, J. . .	Germany	15th ,,	
Rossi, P. de . .	Italy	15th and 16th centuries	Lady artist of Bologna, carved minute work on peach stones.
Rovezzano, B. da . .	England	16th century	Employed by Cardinal Wolsey.
Ruckera, Th. . .	Augsburg	,, ,,	Chapter iii. (German section), steel chair, Longford Castle.

Names of Artists or Manufacturers	Country and time in which they worked.		Remarks and References.
S			
Saint-Germain . .	France	18th century	
Saint Yues, Antoine de .	,,	,, ,,	
Salambier, — . .	,,	18th and 19th centuries	Designed room decorations, mirror frames, etc.
Sangher, J. de . .	Flanders	17th century	
Saunier, Claude Charles .	France	18th ,,	Chapter vi., p. 263, *ébeniste*.
Schelden, P. van der .	Flanders	16th ,,	
Schwanhard, H. . .	Germany	17th ,,	Invented the " Wavy " mouldings used in Dutch and German furniture.
Schwerdfeger . . .	France		Chapter vi., *ébeniste*.
Seddon, Thomas . .	England	19th ,,	Chapter viii., contemporary with early Gillow.
Seddon, Thomas & George (sons of above)	,,	,, ,,	Chapter viii., furnished Windsor Castle.
Serlius, S. . . .	France	16th ,,	
Servellino, G. del . .	Italy	15th ,,	
Shackleton, — . .	England early 19th ,,		Chapter viii., partner with Seddon.
Shearer, Thomas . .	England	18th ,,	Chapter vii.
Sheraton, Thomas . .	,,	,, ,,	Chapter vii.
Simpson, Daniel . .	,,	,, ,,	Chippendale style, see p. 313.
Slocombe, C. P. . .	,,	19th ,,	Chapter ix., designer.
Smet, R. de . .	Flanders	16th ,,	Chapter iii. (Bruges chimneypiece).
Smith, G. . . .	England early 19th ,,		Chapter viii. (published book of designs), pp. 369-71.
Snell, — . . .	,,	,, ,,	
Somer, Jacques . .	France	18th ,,	
Sormani, — . . .	,,	19th ,,	Made excellent reproductions of the old Vernis Martin cabinets.
Stewart, Jas. (architect) .	England	,, ,,	Chapter vii.
Stobre, Laurent . .	France	17th ,,	
Stockel, Joseph . .	,,	18th ,,	Worked at Fontainebleau.
Stoss, V. . . .	Germany	1438-1533	
Street, Sir G., R.A. .	England	19th century	The New Law Courts (mediæval woodwork).
Swan, Abraham (architect)	,,	18th ,,	Chapter vii.
Swerdfeger, F. . .	France	,, ,,	Made the jewel cabinet of Marie Antoinette, now in the " Garde Meuble," Chapter vi.
Sympson, — . .	England	17th ,,	Made the bookcase for Pepys, p. 181.
Syrlin, J. . . .	Germany	15th ,,	
Syrlin, J., the younger .	,,	15th and 16th centuries	Chapter iii. (choir stalls, Ulm Cathedral, 1462-1474).

Names of Artists or Manufacturers.	Country and time in which they worked.		Remarks and References.
T			
Taillebert, U. . .	Flanders	16th century	
Talbert, B. J. (architect)	England	19th ,,	Chapter ix. Designed furniture in Gothic style.
Tasso, D. . . .	Italy 15th&16thcentr's. ⎫		Known as wood carvers in Florence. Worked from M. Angelo's designs.
Tasso, G. . . .	,, ,, ,, ,, ⎬		
Tasso, G. B. . . .	,, ,, ,, ,, ⎭		
Tasso, M. D. . . .	Italy	15th century	
Tatham, C. H. (architect)	England	18th ,,	Designed interior decorations, etc., for the Duke of York.
Taurini, R. . . .	Italy	16th ,,	Pupil of A. Durer (stalls of Milan Cathedral).
Thomas, — (architect) .	England	18th ,,	Chapter vii. Designed furniture in Adams style.
Thomire, P. Ph. (mounter)	France	1751-1843	Museum of " Mobilier National," Paris. Chapter vi. best work confounded with that of Gouthière.
Tolfo, G. . . .	Italy	16th century	
Toms and Luscombe .	England	19th ,,	Chapter ix., pp. 393-4 (French style).
Topino, G. . . .	France	18th ,,	On examples in Jones Collection.
Toro, — . . .	,,	,, ,,	Style of Boulle (made for Palace of Versailles).
Torrigiano, — . .	England	1472-1522	Designed shrine of Henry VII. (Westminster Abbey).
Toto, — . . .	,,	1331-1351	
Town and Emanuel .	,,	19th century	Chapter ix., pp. 393-4 (French style).
Travers, R. . . .	France	18th ,,	Worked in Paris, 1774.
Trevigi, G. da .	England	1503-1544	Court painter and decorator to Henry VIII.
Triard, J. B. . .	France	18th century	
Tuart, — . . .	,,	,, ,,	Lacquer work.
U			
Uccello, P. . . .	Italy	1396-1479	
Ugliengo, C. . . .	,,	18th century	
V			
Vasson, — . . .	France	18th century	A Mounter, or *Bronziste*.
Venasca, G. P. . .	Italy	,, ,,	
Verberckt, Jacques .	France	,, ,,	Carver of ornamental interior (the Queen's apartment, Versailles).
Verberckt, Nicholas .	,,	,, ,,	Carved ornament at Versailles.

Names of Artists or Manufacturers.	Country and time in which they worked.		Remarks and References
Verbruggen, P. . .	Flanders	17th century	Chapter iii.⎫ Carved church ornamental work.
Verbruggen, P., the younger	,,	1660-1724	Chapter iii.⎬ Pulpit of Jesuits' College, Antwerp.
Verhaegen, Th. . .	,,	18th century	Carved work in several Mechlin churches.
Vincenzo, Fra . .	Italy		Worked at Verona (intarsia).
Vion, — . . .	France	,, ,,	A Mounter, or *Bronziste*.
Voyers, — . . .	England	,, ,,	Louis Seize style of furniture.
Vriesse, V. de . .	France	17th ,,	Chapter iii.
W			
Waldron, — . .	England	18th century	Originally carver, afterwards actor.
Walker, H. . . .	,,	16th ,,	
Wallis, N. . . .	,, late	18th ,,	Published book of ornament in Greek taste, also the "Modern Joyner," 1772.
Watson, — . . .	,,	17th and 18th centuries	Chapter iv., pupil of G. Gibbons.
Webb, — . . .	England	19th century	Chapter ix., pp. 394-5.
Wedgwood, Josiah .	,,	18th ,,	Chapter vii., introduced his plaques for furniture.
Weinkopf, W. . .	Germany	16th ,,	Worked in Nuremberg, temp. A. Durer.
Weisweiler, Adam .	France	18th ,,	Chapter vi., p. 267, cabinet in Wallace Collection.
Wertheimer, S. . .	England	19th ,,	Chapter ix., p. 393.
Wilkinson, — . .	,,	,, ,,	Chapter viii.
Willemfens, L. . .	Flanders	1635-1702	
William the Florentine .	England	13th century	Court painter and house decorator to Henry III.
Wilton, J. . . .	,,	18th ,,	Employed by Sir W. Chambers.
Winant, — . . .	France	,, ,,	Chapter vi. Mounter.
Wren, Sir C. . .	England	16th to 17th centuries	Chapter iv.
Wright and Mansfield .	,,	19th century	Adams style of furniture.
Z			
Zabello, F. . . .	Italy	16th century	Stalls in Cathedral of Bergamo.
Zorn, G. . . .	Germany	17th ,,	
Zwiener, — . . .	France	19th ,,	Made excellent reproductions of the older French furniture (Boulle, etc., etc.)

NOTE.—The Monogram "M E," branded on some of the old eighteenth century French cabinets, stands for "Menuisier Ebeniste," and generally accompanies the name or initials of the maker.

WOODS

The following different kinds of wood are used in the manufacture of Furniture.

For the Best Furniture.

Amboyna.	Maple.	Sweet Cedar.
Black Ebony.	Oak (various kinds).	Tulip Wood.
Brazil Wood.	Rosewood.	Walnut.
Coromandel.	Satin Wood.	Olive.
Mahogany.	Sandal Wood.	Zebra Wood.
	Sweet Chestnut.	

For Common Furniture and Interior Fittings.

Pines.	Birch.	Walnut.
Deals.	Cedars.	Mahogany.
Beech.	Cherry Tree.	Ash.

also some selections of Honduras mahogany when finely marked, and different varieties of the eucalyptus.

The most expensive of these are used in veneers; and in the more ornamental and polychromatic marquetry, holly, horse chestnut, sycamore, pear tree and plum tree are used, being woods easily stained.

Amongst some of the rarer and more beautifully marked woods, used in small quantities, are the following :—

Mustaiba.	Peruvian.	Rosetta.
Palmyra.	Pheasant Wood.	Snakewood.
Partridge Wood.	Purple Wood.	Yacca Wood.
	Princes Wood.	

TEAK is an extremely strong East India wood: there is also an African teak (Sierra Leone), called African oak.

SHISHAM or BLACKWOOD (Dalbergia Sps) is a heavy close-grained wood, dark brown in colour, resembling ebony when polished, and is much used for furniture in India.

SANDAL WOOD, TEAK, MANGO WOOD.—Sir George Birdwood, in " Indian Arts," gives a complete list of these Indian woods, with their botanical names and other valuable information.

For a more complete list of the different woods used by cabinet makers, the reader is referred to Mr. J. Hungerford Pollen's " Introduction to the South Kensington Collection "; to many of these he has been able, after much research, to give their botanical names, a task rendered somewhat difficult owing to the popular name of the wood being derived from some peculiar marking or colouring, but giving no clue to its botanical status. Amongst these are tulip wood, rose wood, king wood, pheasant wood, partridge wood, and snake wood. It is worthy of remark that, whereas in England the terms "king wood" and "tulip wood" represent the former, a wood of rich dark reddish-brown colour, or "purple madder," and the latter one of a yellowish-red, prettily-streaked, in France these terms have exactly the reverse equivalents. These were very favourite veneers in the best French marqueterie furniture described in Chapter VI., and are frequently found, the one as bordering to relieve the panel or drawer front of the other.

In the Museum at Kew Gardens, and also in the Colonial Galleries of the Imperial Institute, are excellent collections of many rare woods well worth examination.

Some particulars of the different woods mentioned in the Bible, from which examples of Ancient Furniture were manufactnred, and to which reference has been made in Chapter I.

These notes were supplied by the late Dr. Edward Clapton, whose collection of specimens of these scarce woods was of great interest.

SHITTIM WOOD is the wood of the Shittah tree, or Acacia Seyal. This spiny tree especially abounded in the peninsula of Sinai and around the Dead Sea, but was also found in various parts of Syria, Arabia, and Africa. In the present day the shittah trees are very few and small, but in the time of Moses there were forests of them, and of a size sufficient to form long and wide planks. It is, as Jerome says, "a very strong wood of incredible lightness and beauty," and, he adds, "it is not subject to decay." This corresponds to the translation of the Hebrew term for shittim wood in the Septuagint, which is "incorruptible wood." Though light, it is hard, strong, and durable. As a proof of this, the Ark, and other furniture of the Tabernacle, which were made of shittim wood, must have lasted for a period of some 500 years before all traces of them were lost. Dean Stanley remarks that the plural word shittim was given to the wood of the shittah tree from the tangled thickets into which the stems of the trees expand.

ALMUG.—The wood of the Pterocarpus Santalinus, a large tree of the order "Leguminosœ." The wood is very hard, has a reddish colour, and takes a fine polish. It is a native of India and Ceylon, whence it was in Solomon's time conveyed to Ophir, on the east coast of Africa, and from Ophir to Palestine ; "and the navy also of Hiram, that brought gold from Ophir, brought in great plenty of almug trees, and the king made of the almug trees pillars for the house of the Lord, and for the king's house, harps also and psalteries for singers." 1 *Kings* x. 11, 12. Almug is not the same as Algum, which grew on Lebanon with the cedar and fir. 2 *Chron.* ii. 8.

THYINE WOOD.—The wood of the Thuja Articulata, now named Callitris Quadrivalvis, a tree of the cypress sub-order of coniferæ, from 20 to 30 feet high. It is a native of Algiers and the Atlas range of North Africa. The wood is dark coloured, hard, and fragrant, taking a fine polish ; it yields an odoriferous resin called Sanderach, which was much used by the Romans for incense in the worship of their gods. Thyine takes its name from "to burn incense." It was much prized by the ancient Greeks and Romans, not only because it was considered sacred, but also on account of the beauty of the wood for various ornamental purposes. Pliny speaks of the mania of his countrymen for ornaments made of this wood, and tells us that when Roman ladies were upbraided by their husbands for their extravagance in pearls, they retorted upon them for their excessive fondness for tables made of thyine wood. So great a rage was there for ornamental cabinet work in ancient Rome that Cicero had a table made of it that cost £9,000. Ornaments made of this wood can be seen in the Museum at Kew, presented by the late Jerome Napoleon. The ceiling and floor of the celebrated Mosque of Cordova are of thyine wood, and it is also referred to in the Bible.

TAPESTRY USED FOR FRENCH FURNITURE

GOBELINS, BEAUVAIS, AND AUBUSSON TAPESTRY.—The famous factory of Gobelins originated in the establishment of some dye works in the Faubourg St. Marcel of Paris, by two brothers, Gilles and Jean Gobelin, who had introduced from Venice the art of dyeing scarlet; they also produced some other excellent colours, and this enterprise—at first considered foolish, and acquiring the name of *Folie Gobelin*—afterwards became most successful. This was in the reign of François I.; they subsequently added a tapestry factory to their dye works. Either in 1662 or in 1667, as different authorities state, Colbert, who had succeeded Cardinal Mazarin as Chief Adviser and Minister of Louis XIV., purchased the factory from the Gobelin family, and reorganised the establishment as the Royal Upholstery Works, employing the artists Lebrun, Berain, Simon Vouet, and others, to furnish subjects for the cartoons, the former artist being appointed Director of the Works. Since 1697 the manufacture of tapestry only has been carried on, and the product of these celebrated looms has become known as Gobelins tapestry. Previous to this time, however, namely, 1669, Colbert ordered the manufacture at Gobelins of what is termed the "low warp" tapestry suitable for furniture—a branch of manufacture which had been transferred to the State works of Beauvais, where the special mode of making tapestry, suitable for the covering of chairs and sofas, has since been carried on, the looms of Gobelins being more generally employed to produce larger panels for hangings. The designs for suites of furniture with which we are most familar are those of Jean Baptiste Oudry, the best known of whose designs are Les Amusements Champêlu, Les Comédiens de Molière, Les Metamorphoses, and Les Fables de Fontaine. The Koypels also made designs and the signature "Audran, 1753," occurs upon a set of furniture tapestries with subject from "Don Quixote." The fine texture, the brilliant colourings of the famous tapestry, are world famous; and enormous sums are commanded by some of the older panels, the tints of which are softened by age, while the condition remains good. Besides the tapestry for furniture, sometimes made at Gobelins, and more generally at Beauvais, a great deal has been produced by the looms at Aubusson, a factory said to have been originated by the immigration of some Flemish workmen into La March during the fourteenth century. Owing, however, to the difficulty in obtaining good patterns and the quality of wool required, their tapestry did not acquire a very high reputation. Colbert granted these manufactories a Charter in 1669, and also gave them protection against foreign rivals; and the looms of Aubusson became busy and their proprietors prosperous. The productions of Gobelins and Beauvais being monopolised by the Court, the works of Aubusson had to provide for the more general requirements of the people, and, therefore, though good of its kind, and occasionally excellent, this tapestry has never attained the reputation of its more famous contemporaries. To those who would learn more of Tapestry, its history, methods of production, and many instructive details, the little South Kensington handbook, "Tapestry," is highly commended; it was written for the Science and Art Department by M. Alfred de Champeaux, and translated by Mrs. R. F. Sketchley. Lady Dilke's "French Furniture and Decorations in the. Eighteenth Century," gives voluminous details of the vicissitudes of these great tapestry works, with particulars of the different directors and designers from time to time in their history.

THE PROCESSES OF GILDING AND POLISHING

WOOD GILDING.—The processes of applying gold to wood and to metal are entirely different. In the former the gold, which has been supplied to the gilder in extremely thin layers, generally placed between the leaves of a little paper book to prevent them sticking together, is transferred therefrom to the surface to be gilt, by a dexterous movement of a flat gilder's camel's hair brush, or "tip," as it is termed, the wood having been previously prepared by successive coatings of whitening and thin glue, a thicker body of preparations being required for those parts which are to be burnished. A great deal depends upon the care and time bestowed on the preparation of the work, sometimes as many as ten coatings being given to the wood, and these are successively rubbed down with pumice stone and glass paper, care being taken not to lose the sharpness of carved ornaments. This application of gold leaf is termed mechanical gilding, and is used for gilt furniture, picture frames, or other decorations. Within the last twenty-five or thirty years or so the gold has been applied to the more richly carved furniture in a powder. This preparation of gold is very expensive, costing about £7 the ounce, and is only used for the more costly chairs and couches, etc., generally of old French make, which require re-gilding.

METAL GILDING.—The process of gilding metal which was practised by the mounters of the fine old French furniture described in Chapter VI., consisted in applying to the "ormolu" a mixture of gold and mercury; the latter was evaporated by heat, and the gold remained firmly adhered to the metal mount, and was afterwards coloured as desired, a slightly greenish tinge being effected by such masters as Caffieri, Gouthière and others. This kind of gilding requires a considerable quantity of the precious metal to be used, and is therefore very costly, but is rich in effect, and, under favourable conditions, permanent. It is, however, very injurious to the workers, on account of the fumes of the mercury poisoning the system ; and it has generally been abandoned in favour of the much quicker and far cheaper process of electro-gilding, by which an effect can be produced by an infinitesimal coating of gold. The water gilding process is still used to a moderate extent by the makers of the more expensive reproductions of old furniture. There is a very cheap and effective process of lacquering which sometimes is termed "gilding," used to give ormolu mounts the colour of gold ; this is done by applying a solution of shellac and spirits of wine to the metal when heated, and, as with water-gilding, the volatile spirit evaporates and leaves a thin coating of the shellac, which may also be treated so as to have very much the appearance of gold, to the inexperienced eye. It should be mentioned that where mounts are gilt, it is usual to make the metal of which they are composed more like the colour of gold than ordinary brass would be ; this is done by the admixture of a considerable amount of copper, the amalgam being generally termed "or-molu."

POLISHING.—The older method of polishing woodwork consisted in the application of a mixture of turpentine and beeswax to the surface ; this would be repeated again and again, and then well rubbed down with a hard brush, when a very durable polish was obtained. For flat surfaces, and particularly for the tops of dining tables which were formerly uncovered to show the wood, oil polishing was the fashion; this was effected by rubbing the table-top with a heavy weight backwards and forwards, using oil as a lubricant. Good housewives used to polish up their dining tables very frequently. Oil polishing had the great advantage, too, of producing a surface which hot plates did not easily mark. The cost, time, and trouble, however, caused these older processes to be abandoned in favour of " French " polishing, which is the application on a prepared surface of shellac dissolved in methylated spirit, and often other ingredients to give poor-looking wood a richer colour. The polish is quicker, and therefore cheaper, than the old-fashioned method. It has come into general adoption since the Great Exhibition of 1851.

THE PIANOFORTE

The Pianoforte is such an important article in the furniture of the present time, that a few notes about its development from a decorative point of view, may be acceptable. In " Musical Instruments," one of the South Kensington handbooks, Carl Engel traces the Pianoforte from the " Clavicembalo," which he tells us, " was in fact, nothing but a Cembalo or Dulcimer, with a keyboard attached to it." Our present Grand Piano was, however, more immediately a development of the Harpsichord* and Spinet, which had succeeded the Virginal of the sixteenth century. These were made of oblong shape and supported on stands, which were simply supports for the instruments and did not form a part of it as do the legs of a

* The Harpsichord made for Frederick the Great, by Burkardt-Tschudi, whose son-in-law was the first John Broadwood, was in the style of German Renaissance.

modern "Grand." In an original play bill, which is still preserved at Messrs. Broadwood's, there is an announcement that at the Theatre Royal, Covent Garden, on the 16th of May, 1767, at the end of Act I. (of the Beggars' Opera), "Miss Brickler will sing a favourite song from 'Judith,' accompanied by Mr. Dibden, on *a new Instrument, called Pianoforte.*"

There is an illustration in Chapter VI. of a Harpsichord which is in the Victoria and Albert Museum, and in the same collection are others, varying in types as instruments, and of different decorations. The one which belonged to Handel is a good specimen of the decoration bestowed on these instruments. Others of about the middle of the eighteenth century, were covered with a coating of lacquer, like some of the furniture referred to in Chapter VI., the parts of the cases to be so decorated having been sent to China, and returned when coated with the preparation, the secret of which was then only known to the Chinese, but afterwards imitated in Europe. Some of the lacquered cases are very beautiful, and those which were elaborately painted in the Vernis Martin style are finished with the care of cabinet pictures or miniatures. They have, as a rule, the fine subject painting, or landscape, inside the lid of the case, as in the illustration on p. 274, while the outside of the case is decorated with arabesques of gold on a dark coloured ground. Such an instrument was sold at the sale of Lord Lonsdale's furniture, a few years ago, for some three hundred pounds.

The rectangular shape appears to have been partially abandoned for the "Wing form," of which the modern "Grand" is a development, about the time of Queen Anne, and was, in some cases, adapted to the Harpsichord of the time. The earlier pianofortes were rectangular in form, with the idea of preventing the unequal appearance produced by the bent treble side of the Grand, and the writer once had in his possession such an instrument, without pedals, which bore the inscription :—"By Royal Patent. Longman and Broderip, Musical Instrument Makers, 13 Haymarket, and 26 Cheapside, London." Collard and Collard are the successors of this firm, and still retain the same premises in Cheapside. The oldest Broadwood *piano*, which the present firm owns, bears the name of "Schudi and Broadwood," with date 1780. It is square and without pedals.

Towards the end of the last century pianos were made to harmonise with the Adam, Heppelwhite, and Sheraton furniture of the day, and some were elaborately inlaid with small plaques of Wedgwood's jasper ware.

There are also instruments in existence, and designs, which show that as the style of furniture changed during the time of the French Revolution, and subsequently to the Classic Greek, the Piano followed a new fashion. There is in St. James's Palace the instrument made by Broadwood for the Princess Charlotte, who died early in the nineteenth century. This is square in form, and is veneered with a single sheet of ivory, the elephant's tusk having been first softened by acid, and then cut circular fashion.

In France, the older Harpsichord and the later Pianoforte have followed the different styles which have affected the decorative furniture of that country, and the same remark applies to the more limited productions of such instruments in other countries.

During the period of bad taste which prevailed in England in the first half of the nineteenth century, those who purchased pianos were content to have either the instrument in the most ordinary and commonplace case of mahogany, walnut, or the rosewood which about 1840 came into great favour, or else the cases were designed in an extravagant fashion, and covered with a super-abundance of ornament, quite out of keeping with the use of a musical instrument.

Latterly there has been amongst leading manufacturers, especially those of our own country, a marked improvement, and the cases are made of rare and carefully chosen woods, and the style adapted, in many instances, to the furniture of the room. Sir Alma Tadema designed cases in the Byzantine style. Sir E. Burne-Jones painted one with an elaborate design of figures and scrolls; another with a shower of roses right across the sounding board, and he also revived the old-fashioned trestle support, formerly used for harpsichords. Mr. Waterhouse, R.A., Mr. John Birnie Philip, who executed the podium of the Albert Memorial, Sir T. G. Jackson, R.A., and others, have also designed piano cases for friends and clients.

In the "Inventions" Exhibition, some years since, there was a very good opportunity of noticing the advance in design of the Pianoforte. In nearly every instance the old-fashioned fretwork front had been abandoned for a painting or a marquetry panel. Some were enamelled white, and relieved by gilding; others had a kind of gesso-work decoration, and the different fashionable styles of furniture were reproduced with various modifications. Amongst others, Kirkman exhibited a grand and an upright made from designs by Colonel Edis, and Hopkinson a boudoir grand and some small cottage pianos in satin-wood and marquetry, and also in satin-wood painted in the old English style, and having silk panels in front with copies of Bartolozzi prints. The designs were in the latter case made by the Author. Broadwood and other English firms also produced special designs.

Since this Exhibition, if there has not been improvement, there has been endless variety, and the piano case is now designed and decorated to please the taste of the most fastidious or the most eccentric.

INDEX

NOTE.—The Names of several Designers and Makers, omitted from the Index, will be found in the list in the Appendix, with references

Truslove and Bray, Ltd., Printers, West Norwood, London, S.E. 27.

WORKS BY THE SAME AUTHOR

Antiques, Genuine and Spurious

An Art Expert's Recollections and Cautions

Containing 78 Illustrations reproducing specimens of Porcelain, Furniture, Lacquer, Enamel, Bronzes of different periods.

With Coloured Frontispiece.

Medium 8vo.　　　*277 pages.*　　　*25s. net.*

LONDON: G. BELL & SONS, LTD.

How to Collect Old Furniture

With 40 Plates and numerous other Illustrations.

Third Edition.　　　Post 8vo, 8s. 6d. *net.*

" The book is, without question, the most interesting and informing guide that the modern fashion for antique furniture has produced."—*Pall Mall Gazette.*

LONDON: G. BELL & SONS, LTD.

Third Edition, enlarged and carefully revised.

Royal 8vo, cloth, gilt top. 30s. *net.*

Pottery and Porcelain

A Guide to Collectors.

Containing 200 Illustrations of Specimens of various Factories, Plates coloured in facsimile of the Specimens represented, and Marks and Monograms of all the important Makers.

With Coloured Frontispiece.

LONDON: TRUSLOVE & HANSON, LTD.